TO WIN HEARTS AND MINDS:

VIETNAM TO IRAQ

Printed in USA 2018

Cover illustration and design by Al Esper 2018
Editing by Rita Reali
Formatting by Debby Johnson http://nacauldron.com/

ISBN Paperback: 9780692148419
ISBN ebook: 9780692149782

All rights reserved

CONTENTS

	Acknowledgements	Page 1
	Prologue	Page 3
1	Early Influences	Page 6
2	The Academic Years	Page 25
3	The Path to Vietnam	Page 46
4	Vietnam	Page 66
5	Marriage and Search for a Career	Page 90
6	Dual Careers and a Commission	Page 105
7	First Command and Key Promotion	Page 126
8	Desert Shield/Desert Storm	Page 135
9	Mogadishu, Somalia	Page 151
10	A Time of Transition	Page 185
11	Bosnia Herzegovina	Page 199

12	The Politics of Peacekeeping	Page 212
13	Battalion Command	Page 239
14	Operation Enduring Freedom/Iraqi Freedom	Page 264
15	The Baghdad Brigade	Page 288
16	The Road to Retirement	Page 328
	Epilogue	Page 344
	Bibliography	Page 353

ACKNOWLEDGMENTS

First, I am thankful to my bride, Nancy, for her help in the initial editing and for her love, forgiveness, encouragement, and understanding. Her patience with me while this memoir came together has been saintly. During my deployments, she held down the home front and successfully handled every challenge as a single parent. She put her own dream of a musical career on hold to keep our family together and provide our children with a loving and stable home. She is the heart of our family.

I can never repay the sacrifices my mother, Margaret Orsino Mitchell, made as a single parent most of her life. She operated her own business for decades and still managed to provide my brothers, my sister, and me with the love and support we needed to become productive citizens and responsible, caring adults. I can only hope she is looking down from heaven with pride.

My maternal grandparents, John and Rose Orsino, left a legacy of a strong work ethic. Their vision and generosity in financing my college education opened opportunities for me that changed the course of my life.

Other family members were role models and provided me with valuable guidance and assistance: Frank Condella, my great-uncle who served in the Army Air Corps during World War II, was a strong male role model in the absence of my own father; my great aunt, Shirley Condella, who, with my great uncle set the example for an enduring, loving marriage; my great uncle, Pat Condella, who used his contacts to notify the National Labor Relations Board after I was unfairly dismissed from a furniture factory.

Several people provided me opportunities that otherwise would not have been available: Richard Salisbury, US Air Force

(Ret.) gave me my first opportunity as a federal employee at the VA Medical Center in Syracuse; Col. Carl Liberatore, US Army (Ret.) provided guidance and mentoring, and made it possible for me to receive a direct commission in the Civil Affairs Branch of the Army Reserve, paving the way for my eventual rise through the ranks; the Honorable Howard G. Munson and the Honorable Neal P. McCurn, U.S. District Judges, who gave me the opportunity to serve with the U.S. Courts despite the negative stereotype placed on Vietnam veterans; the Honorable Edward M. Conan, U.S. Magistrate Judge, known as a constitutional scholar who, through his rulings in court, taught me much about fairness and equality in my early years with the court; the Honorable Daniel Scanlon and the Honorable George H. Lowe, U.S. Magistrate Judges, with whom I served most of my years as a courtroom deputy clerk, where I learned much about patience and forgiveness; Lawrence K. Baerman, Clerk of Court for the Northern District of New York, who remained a friend and kept faith in me when my job performance suffered; Michael Langan, Esq., a senior law clerk at the U.S. District Court, friend and author, who assisted me with the initial editing, did a final read-through, and provided his writing experience as I plodded through this work; professors Eileen Schell and Ivy Kleinbart of Syracuse University, who established and mentored the Syracuse Veterans' Writing Group, where I was inspired to write and had my first published work in the group's anthology, *The Weight of My Armor*. My thanks go to Rita Reali, who did the final editing, and Al Esper, who designed the cover.

Finally, I am grateful to the many soldiers I served with through the years, my coworkers, and former classmates, who enriched my life in countless ways.

PROLOGUE

As our convoy crossed the berm into Iraq, our vision was limited by the sand kicked up by the vehicles ahead of us. My driver negotiated our Humvee through the clouds of dust while I thought back to my first deployment and the years of events that led me here. At age 56, I was heading to another war zone, a place I never imagined life would take me.

I enlisted in the U.S. Army after finishing college in 1968. I was convinced that, if I waited until I was drafted, I would be mismatched with a specialty unrelated to my interests and education. At the recruiting office, I chose the occupational title of counterintelligence special agent because of my fascination with the popular James Bond movies. I dreamed of the adventure and intrigue associated with being a secret agent.

After completing counterintelligence training, I was immersed in a yearlong Vietnamese-language course, then assigned to a counterintelligence detachment at Long Binh, the largest Army base in Vietnam. I spent most of my tour in civilian clothes with access to all the conveniences the base had to offer. I was what combat troops called an "REMF" (rear echelon motherfucker).

In April 2003, during our incursion into Iraq, I could no longer be called that. Modern warfare and increased guerilla-type operations blurred the meaning of "rear area" as it was used in a combat zone. Anyone within the combat zone could be–and in fact had been–subjected to enemy fire. The modern-day REMFs were geographically distanced from the combat zone or imminent-danger zone.

As our 22-vehicle convoy made its way toward Baghdad, carrying some 60 soldiers outfitted in full combat gear, I rode at the center in a radio-equipped Humvee to communicate with the lead and rear vehicles. Although our route was considered secure, we generally traveled in an open-column formation, with 80 to100 meters between vehicles, to create more dispersion and minimize ourselves as targets in case of an ambush. On unpaved roads it also permitted better reaction time between vehicles, with dust being kicked up by the vehicles' tires. A maintenance truck with a tow bar brought up the rear, in case of a breakdown.

Our mission would be to conduct civil-military operations in Baghdad after the "shock and awe" attack launched by the United States with the goal of defeating the Iraqi army and removing the regime of Saddam Hussein. I was assigned chief of the government team, whose goal was to help establish a democratically elected government and assist civil authorities in reconstituting the schools, the courts and public-safety institutions. Before we could accomplish any of those goals, we had to win the hearts and minds of the Iraqi people and their new leaders. We had to convince them we were liberators, not occupiers.

This memoir tracks my military and civilian careers, woven around my life story and the history-making events in which I took part. We can't always control our environment or the circumstances in which we find ourselves; but they often control the decisions we make. In my experience, I've learned timing and location can make all the difference.

Part of my motivation for penning this memoir was the realization my military service was unusual–because my career with the courts often complemented my military duties, a situation not typical of military service. I also wanted to make it clear that, like everyone, I had challenges to overcome. Some were self-imposed, and they stacked the odds against my rising through the ranks and enjoying two successful careers. I owe much of my career success to my devoted wife, Nancy, the love of my children, my faith in God, and the friends and mentors who cared enough to give me a second chance.

This memoir would not be complete if I left out the importance of music in my life as a coping device and a means of self-expression. I started piano lessons at age seven and have continued to play. I often accompanied Nancy, an excellent singer, when we performed in public. Through the years I found some songs expressed my emotions better than I could do verbally, especially songs written about love and war, two facets of my life that produced the strongest emotions.

This work reflects my memory of events and the written notes I took. When necessary I reference other sources to recall facts that have faded from my memory and to add background and depth to certain events. The people mentioned herein are real; descriptions or observations about them are solely my own. Opinions expressed about the military operations in which I participated are mine alone and do not represent the official policies of the United States government, the State Department, the Department of Defense, or the United States Army. Finally, any errors or omissions are mine and were not intentional or made with malice toward anyone.

Chapter 1
Early Influences (1946-1960)

Several things about my childhood suggested I was destined for military service. I was born at Soldiers and Sailors Memorial Hospital in Penn Yan, New York. I eventually became aware of my father's service during World War II, and that of several uncles. Growing up during the 1950s, I joined the Cub Scouts, Boy Scouts, and played Little League baseball, all of which involved some degree of order and discipline. I enjoyed building plastic models of war planes, ships, and tanks. My typical toys included cap guns, an air rifle, cowboy gear, and toy soldiers. We recited the Pledge of Allegiance every day in school. I was old enough to be aware of the Korean War, although I didn't understand it, and patriotism was visible everywhere. American flags flew outside homes and businesses every day, parades celebrated patriotic holidays, and veterans were honored for their service.

I grew up in a quiet, picturesque village nestled in a valley within the Finger Lakes Region of Upstate New York. Some of the best wines in the country are produced there; the sun-bathed hills that rise from the lake and the temperate climate make the Finger Lakes Region ideal for growing grapes.

My hometown of Penn Yan sits at the tip of the eastern branch of Keuka Lake, which is shaped like the letter Y. It's often called the most beautiful of the 11 Finger Lakes (Canadice, Canandaigua, Cayuga, Conesus, Hemlock, Honeoye, Keuka, Otisco, Owasco, Seneca, and Skaneateles Lakes), which were formed as glaciers receded at the end of the Ice Age. The name "Keuka" derives from an Indian word meaning "crooked." The area was originally inhabited by the Seneca and Cayuga Indians, who used the lake for transport.

Around 1957, my maternal grandparents, John and Rose Orsino, purchased a summer cottage on Keuka Lake. For years, every summer my mother's family–including aunts, uncles, cousins–and friends enjoyed gathering at the cottage at Indian Pines. We ate huge Italian meals prepared by my grandmother, after which we waited an hour, then enjoyed swimming, diving off the dock, boating, and sunbathing. Occasionally we were treated to ice-cream cones from the drive-thru window at nearby Seneca Farms.

Family Influences

During my first seven years I lived with my younger brothers, Dale and Gene, with our parents, Antonio "Tony" and Margaret (Orsino) Gigliotti, in a house owned by my maternal grandparents.

My mother was an only child. After high school, she attended the Rochester School of Cosmetology and became a licensed cosmetologist/beautician. She owned and operated a beauty salon for several decades, originally established by my grandmother.

Grandpa Orsino worked as a track supervisor with the New York Central Railroad, which later merged with the Pennsylvania Railroad to become the Penn Central. Born in 1902, he was too young to serve in World War I and too old to serve during World War II. He suffered a stroke within a year after he retired and died at age 69, the day before I was married. In addition to her training as a hairdresser, Grandma Orsino worked as a camp cook for the railroad, at a basket factory, and finally as a seamstress for a clothing manufacturer in Penn Yan. She died in 1990 at age 84, having suffered a stroke several years earlier.

When my brothers and I were young, our great grandmother, Marguerita (Albanese) Orsino, whom we called

"Big Ma," would care for us while our parents worked. She and our great grandfather, Frank Orsino, emigrated from the Abruzzi Region in central Italy around 1900. He passed away before I was born, and our beloved Big Ma passed away in 1953.

My father was the fifth of eight children born to Antonio and Saveria (Bonacci) Gigliotti, who emigrated from the Calabria Region in southern Italy around 1900. He never went beyond eighth grade and enlisted in the U.S. Army prior to the start of World War II. He served as an artilleryman during the war, in both the Pacific and European theaters. After the war, he returned home to Geneva, New York, where he married my mother on October 15, 1945. He found work on the railroad in Geneva and was later employed with a dry-cleaning company in Penn Yan. Grandpa Gigliotti was a police officer for many years in Geneva, New York, and retired at the rank of sergeant. Grandma Gigliotti was a homemaker.

Our lives seemed typical of the times until my father disappeared when I was seven. My mother had him arrested after a physical confrontation about his drinking. As I walked by their bedroom one evening, I heard her call out to me to telephone the police. I looked into the room and saw my parents locked in a physical struggle. I told her I didn't know how to call the police. Eventually she made the call and had my father arrested and put in jail. What happened next is unclear but, when he was released, he suddenly left Penn Yan, eventually changing his name to avoid having to pay child support. No one on my mother's side of the family knew where he was for more than 30 years. His parents and siblings protected his whereabouts and my mother's family broke off communication with most of them.

Within two years after he disappeared, my mother obtained an annulment from the Catholic Church and in 1960 married Clarence Mitchell, the manager of the local movie theater. He was transferred that summer and we moved to Ohio. That fall he legally adopted my brothers and me. I was old enough to decide whether to change my name to Mitchell. Initially I resisted changing my name, but my mother and grandparents convinced me it would be better for us to all have the same last name. I never felt comfortable with Clarence as a father figure. We were told never to mention we were adopted, but I would tell my new friends I came from an Italian family on my mother's side. I felt more attached to my missing father than my stepfather.

In 1961, during my sophomore year in high school, we were blessed with the birth of our sister, Rosemary. I embraced my role as big brother and often cared for her after school if Mom was busy in the beauty shop. In 1964, after I graduated from high school, her marriage to Clarence Mitchell ended in divorce, because of his physical abuse.

As the years went by, I went to college, joined the Army, married, and had children of my own. I opened to friends about my Italian background and revealed I was adopted. Curiosity about my biological father led me to research his name in the mid '70s, while I was employed in the medical administration section at the VA Medical Center in Syracuse. I discovered he contracted malaria while in the Pacific Theater during World War II. That further spurred my curiosity and gave me a new perspective about him.

It took until the spring of 1990 for me to make a concerted effort to learn more about him. I was in my mid 40s and felt a need to obtain closure with him. I contacted my aunt Sue, the widow of my father's older brother, Louis. She was still on speaking terms with my mother and had attended my wedding. I felt she would be sympathetic when I asked for information about my father. She kindly invited my family and me to dinner at her home in Geneva. What I didn't know was she also invited my father's youngest brother, Gino.

I knew from my mother that Gino lived in the Finger Lakes Region and worked for the government as a security officer. To say I was surprised when he showed up at Aunt Sue's place would be an understatement. I was nervous about meeting an uncle I had not seen since childhood, but he seemed friendly and genuinely interested in knowing about me. We had a long, pleasant conversation during dinner. He asked if I was curious about my father, to which I answered yes without hesitation. Gino said my father eventually settled in Auburn, Washington, and had remarried. I was given his contact information with some anxiety on Gino's part, because he told me Tony might "kill" him for revealing his whereabouts, but Gino said I had a right to know where my father was.

Sometime later, Dale and Gene told me Gino visited them in Penn Yan and asked if they wanted to know about their father. At the time Dale was an investigator for the Yates County Sheriff and Gene was an officer with the Penn Yan Police Department. They both declined. Maybe as the oldest I felt a closer connection to our estranged father and was more interested to know about him, but he was dead to my brothers. They said Gino told them it was time he got the information off his chest and made peace with himself. I was impressed he at least made the effort.

Closure with My Father

A few weeks after I met Uncle Gino, a job announcement was posted at my place of work at the U.S. District Court in Syracuse. The position was at the district court in Seattle. I checked a map and found it was only a half-hour drive from where my estranged father lived. That was a stroke of fate I couldn't ignore. I applied for the job and was invited for an interview. When I told my wife about it, Nancy encouraged me to go for the chance to meet my father. I flew there at my own expense but had no intention of accepting a position at the court if offered. The interview went badly, but I didn't care; my only purpose for being there was to contact my estranged father.

After the interview, I returned to my hotel room and, full of nervous anticipation, called the phone number Gino had given me. His voice on the phone was unmistakable.

"This is your oldest son, Terry," I told him.

His first words were, "What is your usual occupation?"

I thought it was a strange question, but I told him I was a deputy clerk with the U.S. District Court and an officer in the Army Reserve. I explained I wanted to meet with him and talk about the reasons he left. To my surprise, he agreed, and gave me directions to a shopping mall in Auburn, Washington. My guess is Gino warned I might contact him.

I was possibly the last of his sons to see him; soon after he left, he appeared while we were with our grandparents in Geneva, where they still owned a house. He asked to see me, and my grandparents agreed. In retrospect, it was a risky decision on their part, given his unpredictable behavior. He took me to a nearby ice cream shop, where he treated me with a dish of ice cream and explained why he left. His comments have become blurred and made little sense to me at the time.

I drove my rental car to Auburn, parked at the strip mall and waited outside, in front of a store. A few minutes later he arrived in a pickup truck and drove by slowly, checking me out. I recognized him right away, even after more than 35 years. I approached his vehicle as he got out. He looked at me and remarked I could have played football. I was 5'8" tall and weighed 165 pounds, so his football comment amused me, but I took it as a compliment. I mentioned I played a little in high school. My mother always said I had many of his features, notably a prominent nose, but she pointed out I was taller, and better looking. He was only 5'6" tall and weighed around 145 pounds. His hair was gray and thinning, but he still had most of it at age 70.

After a brief conversation, he invited me to follow him back to his house. It was a pleasant-looking, two-story, white, wood-frame house in what appeared to be a quiet, middle-class neighborhood. He showed me a pit he dug in the yard to change the oil on his truck. He also pointed out a makeshift barbell he made of concrete-filled cans attached to each side of a steel rod. The inside of the house appeared clean and neatly arranged.

He introduced me to his wife, Jeanne, who welcomed me cordially. She prepared us a light lunch and left my father and me to talk. He said he met Jeanne while working in Las Vegas at a dry cleaner's and proudly told me he once pressed Frank Sinatra's suit. They eventually married and moved to Washington State, where he found work as a bridge-construction worker until he retired five years earlier. He also had three sons by his second marriage, Anthony, Michael, and Thomas.

As we talked, I recalled some of my childhood memories of him. I mentioned how he used to flex his biceps at the dinner table and let my brothers and me feel how hard they were, so we would eat our meal and get strong like him. He used to call Dale and me Poncho and Cisco, after the television series, *The Cisco Kid*.

After lunch, we went into the living room to continue our conversation. I asked him at length about his disappearance. He was forthright and candid, and expressed remorse about leaving his family, but said he felt he had no choice.

He believed my mother's parents would "ruin" him if he stayed, because of the way he was treated. He told me he had to ride in the trunk of my grandfather's car when he and other coworkers carpooled to and from Geneva to work for the railroad, about 20 miles from Penn Yan, because, "I was the smallest," which apparently had deeply offended him.

I asked about the physical altercation between him and my mother I witnessed, and he replied it occurred because he was defending himself from her. I thought it was plausible, because she was taller and outweighed him by about 40 pounds.

At the end of our meeting I had a better understanding of his disappearance. I didn't forgive him for deserting us but wondered whether the malaria (or possibly post-traumatic stress) had something to do with his drinking. He'd related a story of walking on a muddy road somewhere in Europe during the war when he suddenly stepped on a partially buried dead German soldier. He also mentioned his Italian background got him detailed to translate for Italian POWs, something he expressed misgivings about, and apparently it caused him some stress.

He asked about Dale and Gene and said he received occasional news about us through his family, especially from Gino. He knew my mother had remarried but seemed surprised when I told him she was divorced.

Our visit lasted about three hours. We parted on friendly terms, and as I left he repeated his remorse about leaving but truly believed our mother's parents, John and Rose Orsino, would take care of us. We agreed to keep in touch. He asked if I still played the piano and told me he was proud I was an Army officer but cautioned me not to volunteer for anything.

We corresponded occasionally for about 10 years and talked on the phone a couple of times. In his letters he wrote about the trials of growing up in a large family and the frequent arguing. He said it was the reason he joined the Army in August

1940, to get away. He often ended his letters by calling me his "number one son."

At his request I sent him a tape recording of me playing one of his favorite songs on the piano, *Home on the Range*. I remembered he liked to wear sweatshirts, so one year I sent him a card and an Army sweatshirt for Father's Day. It was the only time I ever mailed a Father's Day card.

Shortly after my trip, I told my mother about my meeting with him. She acted surprised, but probably more shocked I had violated a long-standing family prohibition against contact with him. However, it raised her curiosity enough to fly out to Washington to see him. In her notes about the trip, she wrote that during their meeting he complimented her on her looks, to which she commented, "his hormones were still working." She wrote they had a cordial meeting and both agreed they'd made mistakes in their marriage long ago.

In an ironic ending, my mother passed away on his birthday, April 24, 2000; he died three days later. She was 75 and he was 81. She was buried at St. Michael's Cemetery in Penn Yan under the name Margaret Orsino Mitchell. He was buried at Tahoma National Veterans' Cemetery in Kent, Washington, under the name Tony Marino, the name he used to avoid child support from his first marriage. He remained somewhat of an enigma, but I took satisfaction in acquiring a sense of closure before he died.

I regret having made no effort to contact Uncle Gino again after our dinner meeting at Aunt Sue's place in 1990. In 2009, I attended his funeral in Clyde, New York. It also gave me the opportunity to get reacquainted with four of my Gigliotti cousins: Jeanette Schultz (Uncle Guy's daughter), Patty DeMetro (Aunt Mary's daughter), Lorraine Cacci (Uncle Louis' daughter), and Karen Ford (Uncle Gino's daughter).

A New Home with Our Grandparents

Sometime after my father disappeared, my mother moved us all in with her parents. Our grandparents soon purchased a large house on Elm Street in Penn Yan, from the estate of a doctor. It was large enough for all of us, with enough space for Mom's beauty salon. There were five bedrooms, two and a half baths, and a full basement with a second kitchen. I had my own bedroom; Dale and Gene shared a room. The basement had plenty of room for my brothers and me to play.

Upstairs, a set of sliding glass doors separated the formal living room from the family room. The main floor had two staircases–an open oak staircase in the front living room, and an enclosed wooden staircase at the back of the house, behind the main kitchen. The back staircase had an electric stair lift, which became a favorite plaything for my brothers and me when no one was looking. A large porch graced the entire front of the house, with another, smaller porch on the second floor. The third level contained a full-size attic crammed full of old furniture and miscellaneous junk. The most interesting thing was an old flintlock musket my brothers and I examined – but it was too heavy for us to have much fun with it.

There was a separate four-car garage in back of the house. In one of the stalls was an old horse-drawn buggy that dated from the 19th century. The entire house was a playground of sorts for us boys, with all its interesting rooms and features. Our grandmother swore she would live there until she died; but soon after I finished college, she sold the house to a bank.

Musical Influences

My first recollection of an interest in music occurred around age seven, while watching *The Liberace Show*, which aired each week from 1952 to 1969. Liberace was an accomplished pianist and popular entertainer. His show was broadcast in black and white during the early years. His set was adorned with only a lighted candelabrum atop a shiny black grand piano. Liberace seemed to have a constant smile on his face and his fingers appeared to glide effortlessly across the keys.

As my mother and I watched his show one evening, I was awestruck by his talent and showmanship. I turned to my mother and said, "I want to do that!" She may have sensed an unusual enthusiasm in my voice and thought the piano might spark a passion in my usually sluggish behavior. She was so concerned about me that she once took me to the doctor, who recommended I take Geritol to boost my energy level. She may have thought piano lessons would also distract me from any emotional trauma I might have suffered after my father left. A few weeks later she purchased a repossessed piano on an installment plan and enrolled me in private piano lessons. After a few lessons, I felt overwhelmed by the amount of practice necessary. I had to practice 30 minutes a day except on Sunday. My mother set an egg timer to make sure I practiced the full 30 minutes. If I knew beforehand reading music involved math, I might never have asked to play the piano. I had to count quarter notes, eighth notes, and recognize time signatures. I pleaded with my mother to let me quit, but she insisted I continue my lessons; I'm forever grateful she did.

My first piano teacher was Mrs. Ethel Price. She had gray hair and wore glasses, and her house felt dark and foreboding. She was a stern taskmaster and I must have tested her patience many times because the basics of music theory did not come easy to me. Years later, as an adult, I met with her to say thank you and proudly tell her I continued to play the piano. She seemed pleased and, always the teacher, told me to keep practicing. After

I became more proficient on the piano, I gained an appreciation for her strict instruction and my mother's persistence. Mrs. Price never suggested I quit, although there were times that recommendation would have been music to my ears (pun intended).

By the time I reached high school, I had taken piano lessons for about six years and thought by then I could convince my mother to let me quit. She told me when I learned how to play *Stardust*, by Mitchell Parish, I could discontinue lessons. During the next four years, I tried unsuccessfully to play it for her, but it wasn't until my senior year when she said it was finally good enough. *Stardust* remains part of my repertoire and I'm haunted by my mother's critical ear each time I play it.

During 10 years of piano lessons I participated in recitals and occasional talent shows. I was classically trained and took an interest in the French composer, Claude Debussy. I liked the slow, flowing style of *Reverie*, which became my last recital piece. As I entered my teen years I asked my teacher to help me learn some of the hit songs that came out in the '60s. She rarely accommodated me, so I would use money from my paper route to buy popular sheet music and learn the songs on my own time.

The skills I acquired during piano lessons would later transfer to the military in terms of discipline and attention to detail required. As a senior officer in the Army, I came across the following quote by Johann Sebastian Bach in a military publication. I interpreted it as a tongue-in-cheek metaphor about military leadership: "There's nothing remarkable about playing the piano. All one has to do is hit the right keys at the right time and the instrument plays itself."

Military Influences

My first recollection of an interest in military service began as a boy in the 1950s. As a child of the Greatest Generation, patriotism permeated every aspect of American society. When I was old enough to realize my father served during World War II, I became interested in studying it. He had brought home a Nazi helmet, a web belt, and a .45-caliber semi-automatic handgun with holster. He never explained how he acquired them, but they made great playthings. The Nazi helmet was painted white, perhaps to demilitarize it. The pistol was kept in a shed in the backyard. As I remember, it was not locked up–but it was never loaded. Dale and I eventually discovered it and played with it in the backyard. We took turns wearing the helmet and pistol when we played soldier.

When Dale was about six, he strapped the holster and pistol to his waist and took a stroll down the sidewalk. A police officer spotted him near our home and, probably more amused than shocked, confronted Dale and brought him home. No charges were brought against him for carrying a weapon in public.

Dale and I were the closest in age and were highly competitive. Whatever one liked, the other preferred the opposite. I liked the Yankees, Dale liked the Dodgers. I liked Chevys, he liked Fords. He joined the Marines, I joined the Army. If he got in a fight with Gene, I'd come to Gene's rescue; that's the way it was between us.

Somehow Dale and I developed an interest in the Civil War and often played war games. We fought many make-believe battles with toy Civil War soldiers in our early teens. Dale favored the Confederates; I preferred the Union. Our play often led to heated arguments, which sometimes turned physical. We had naïve notions about war in our youth, but years later we confronted its reality–Dale more so than I.

While I was in elementary school, my mother gave me a book titled, *The Story of General Custer*, by Margaret Leighton. It was a children's *Weekly Reader* selection about George Armstrong Custer who, at 23 years of age, became the youngest person ever promoted to general. I never understood why she chose it for me, but it served as my introduction to a historical military figure. Much of the book focused on Custer's childhood and his ambition to become a soldier like his father, which I identified with. It was the first time I read about a real person instead of the fictional animal characters depicted in the Little Golden Books.

Custer was a Civil War hero and an experienced Indian fighter who became one of my childhood heroes, along with Mickey Mantle and Yogi Berra of the New York Yankees. The story of Custer's death at the Battle of the Little Big Horn in 1876 made an indelible impression on me. My perception of him as a heroic figure diminished as I read more about him. I learned he was self-serving and driven by a relentless pursuit of glory, but I admired his audacity, loyalty, and sense of duty, all common traits in the military.

Movies about World War II were poignant reminders of the sacrifices made by my parents' generation. The first war movie I remember was *The Fighting Sullivans*, released in 1944. When it was broadcast on television in the mid-1950s, Mom thought the movie was so important she let the three of us stay up late to watch it. It depicted the true story of five brothers in the Sullivan family from Waterloo, Iowa, who enlisted in the Navy and requested to serve together on the same ship. On November 13, 1942, their ship, the U.S.S. *Juneau*, was torpedoed and sunk by a Japanese submarine, killing all five brothers.

Our mother pointed out the strong bond among the brothers, how they took care of each other and stayed together until the end. She hoped as we got older we would remain close and watch out for each other. When Dale and I volunteered for military service, she was supportive. Dale enlisted in the Marines soon after he finished high school and went into law enforcement after he was discharged. I enlisted in the Army after college. Gene, my youngest brother, never enlisted but went into law enforcement and eventually became chief of police in Penn Yan. Our mother, who came of age during WWII, believed military service was a good way to instill discipline in us, especially because we lacked the presence of a father for most of our childhood. I believe she thought it would build character. It's no coincidence we all eventually pursued long careers in public service.

When I was old enough, my mother signed me up for Cub Scouts, followed by the Boy Scouts. I liked the regimentation, the uniform, and especially the camping trips. I became a patrol leader in the Boy Scouts and rose to the rank of First Class Scout before I lost interest. However, the Boy Scouts served as an important part of my childhood and early teens, because it provided me some outdoor skills and an appreciation for nature. Those childhood experiences would become the foundation for my future decisions.

Margaret Orsino, Circa 1944

Antonio Gigliotti, Circa 1944

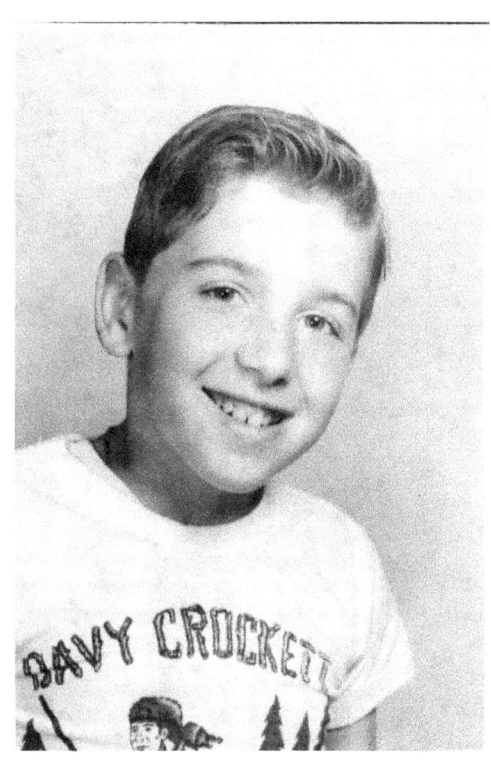

Me, Age 10

John and Rose Orsino, 1948

Chapter 2
The Academic Years (1960-1968)

The summer before I started high school, shortly after my mother remarried, my future stepfather was transferred from Penn Yan to manage a movie theater in Fostoria, Ohio. In northwest Ohio, Fostoria was known for the glassware that bore the town's name. For many years Fostoria was a manufacturing hub because several railroad tracks crisscrossed the town. The area's economy declined as the trucking industry became the primary mode of transporting commercial goods.

Mom moved us out to Fostoria in August 1960, a few months after her marriage to Clarence Mitchell. He had gone on ahead, to begin his new job and to rent a house. I had graduated from St. Michael's in June and said I wanted to continue in a Catholic school. My brothers and I were enrolled in St. Wendelin schools. I was a freshman at the high school, and Dale and Gene were in seventh and fifth grades respectively at the elementary school.

St. Wendelin High School was a small Catholic school with a mixed faculty of lay and religious teachers. The Sisters of Notre Dame taught most classes. During high school, I became involved in the French Club, CYO, altar servers, madrigal choir, concert band, and dance band. I also continued piano lessons in Fostoria with a new teacher.

The French Club became one of my favorite activities, as most of its members were girls, but I also enjoyed learning about French culture. I learned enough vocabulary during French class to compose a short song I titled *Mon Cherie*. It had a standard chord progression and was mentioned in the school news section of the local paper.

During my sophomore year, I joined the football team. At 5'7" and a scrawny 125 pounds, I wasn't built for football, but I decided to go out for the team after a little flattery overcame any good sense I might have had at age 14. During a game of sandlot football late the previous summer, one of the kids remarked I was a pretty good player and said I should join the football team. Naturally, I thought he must be right.

During position tryouts the coaches noticed I had some speed, so I was listed as an offensive and defensive back. In the 1960s, everyone played both offense and defense in high school.

The head coach, Ken Herman, was a former all-state scholastic football player and, like my piano teachers, a strict taskmaster. If you didn't attend practice, learn the plays and show some skill, you didn't play; but no one was cut from the team if they showed effort and had passing grades. Because it was a small school, there weren't many students to choose from for the only two sports, football and basketball. One of the assistant coaches, Chuck Bryant, had played football in college. He was much younger than Coach Herman, with a chiseled jaw and brush cut to complement his muscular frame. The varsity consisted of several experienced players; and my sophomore classmates on the team had an extra year of experience from the junior-varsity team, so I sat on the bench my first year.

During junior year, I played sparingly. When I got in a game, it was only for one or two plays, because I didn't spend much time studying the play book. I had no concept about the learning curve I needed to overcome to become proficient at the game–just as I was clueless about the amount of math involved in piano playing. I wasn't as athletic as the kid let me believe during that pick-up football game, but I liked the status of being on the football team. Girls seemed to dig football players.

My mother was skeptical about me joining the football team, but she let me do it – maybe because of the discipline and physical conditioning it involved. Although I was the eldest of her three sons, it was apparent by our teens I was going to be the smallest. To my mother's credit, she always kept us involved in something, whether it was the Boy Scouts, music lessons, target shooting, or even dance lessons. At one point, against our will, she enrolled Dale and me in dance lessons. As I remember it, she said it was to help us overcome our shyness with girls. When the dance instructor asked each of us our reason for taking lessons, I blurted out that my football coach sent me to improve my coordination and footwork. I doubt she bought it, but it helped me cope with the embarrassment of learning to dance.

Our mother's foresight eventually improved my confidence on the dance floor–but only enough to ask a girl to dance the fast dances during the school sock hops. It still took me most of the night to get up the courage to ask for a slow dance. I considered it a success if I got one slow dance in before the night ended.

Dance lessons didn't help make me a better football player; but if nothing else, I was persistent. I attended every practice and hoped for a chance to play; except for the one time I had the audacity to tell the coach I had to leave practice to do my paper route. He looked at me, amazed, and said to go ahead, and don't bother coming back.

I really didn't think he meant it and came to the next practice anyway.

I guess Coach Herman was so surprised I had the nerve to return, he let me stay on the team. I never asked to leave during practice again. I had to give up something, so it was the paper route.

To stay on the team, I even turned down the music instructor's invitation to join the school marching band (I played the tuba in the concert band). I wanted to be an athlete, not a musician. I could have performed each week with the marching band in front of an audience, but I chose to put on pads, a helmet, and a uniform just to feel like an athlete. I hit the blocking sled during practice, ran sprints, and endured violent hits by bigger teammates during scrimmages to be part of the team.

Because I played so seldom, events that might be routine for regular players became significant for me. We had an offensive/defensive end named Wade Oberle who stood 6'8" tall and weighed more than 200 pounds. During one scrimmage play I had a backfield blocking assignment when Wade charged in from his defensive-end position and hit me so hard I was lifted off my feet and knocked flat on my ass. I didn't realize how badly he hit me until years later a doctor asked me when I'd broken my nose. During another scrimmage play I was playing defensive back when Steve Kinn, our starting fullback, broke through the defensive line and came charging toward me. I was the only player between him and an open field. Steve was a power runner and had picked up a head of steam by the time he reached me. I tried to tackle him head on around the legs, but he ran right over me. I was dazed but rolled over and looked up as he stumbled and fell down a few yards past me. I must have tripped him up enough to make him lose his balance.

After the play Coach Herman looked at me, amused, and said, "Way to hang in there."

As if the punishment I took during practice wasn't enough, afterward the first-string players boarded the bus first and would pull at our leg hairs as the rest of us ran a gauntlet to the seats in the back.

I received a small amount of celebrity before my senior year as we prepared for the start of the season. The team was at school to get fitted for pads and uniforms prior to the start of summer practices. I happened to be in the equipment room to get fitted when a reporter came in and wanted a picture to include in his pre-season report about local high-school football. Coach Herman was asked to pose with me while I was fitted for shoulder pads. I thought the coach might ask one of his starters to pose for the picture, but he let me stay. I stood there, shirtless, hands on my hips, while the coach laced up my shoulder pads. The reporter reminded me to stand up straight as the coach laced up the strings. I sucked in my stomach, which only served to emphasize my rib cage.

I anxiously awaited the newspaper to see my picture when it was published. When it appeared, my initial excitement turned to embarrassment as I looked closer and saw how skinny I looked. Maybe the coach let me pose to mislead our opponents into thinking we had a scrawny team that year.

No opponent would be misled by my photo in the paper. During the last three seasons, the St. Wendelin Mohawks captured two conference championships with undefeated seasons. Despite the loss of nine starters, we were picked to have another outstanding season in 1963. We had 17 returning lettermen, excluding yours truly, but many of us received our first letters the previous season. We had fewer experienced players than before.

By my senior year, I weighed 145 pounds. According to the team roster, I only outweighed four other players–and they were all sophomores. In my final season on the team, I continued to spend most of my time on the bench, sometimes not even getting to suit up for the game. I became very depressed prior to one game when, despite one of my best offensive performances during a practice scrimmage, I didn't make the squad that dressed for the game. It was the only time I seriously thought about quitting; but if I learned one thing from my mother, it was to never quit, whether it was piano lessons or dance lessons – and I certainly wasn't going to quit football, which I enjoyed more for the status than for love of the game.

A couple guys quit when they didn't get the playing time they thought they should, but I stayed on, if for no other reason than personal pride. Besides, I was useful as a scrimmage player and a live blocking dummy for the starters.

Occasionally I was awarded with some playing time during a game. Once I made a tackle in the defensive backfield shortly after I replaced fellow senior Jim Marchion. I was excited, not only because I made the tackle but because I was going to hear my name announced over the loudspeaker for the first time. Instead, the announcer called Marchion's name. When I came off the field everyone razzed me about it. Rodney Dangerfield had nothing on me.

We finished my senior season with a respectable record of six wins and three losses. However, the bar for St. Wendelin football had been set so high by the previous class of seniors, the season was a disappointment by comparison. During the athletic awards handed out after the season, I sat in the bleachers and listened as the most-valuable player, all-conference players, and varsity-letter recipients were announced. I didn't expect a letter because I didn't play much, but I was interested to see who received recognition. Then I heard my name called to receive a varsity letter. I could hear some students in the bleachers whisper as I walked down to receive what some called a "charity" letter.

As Coach Herman presented it to me, he said, "Congratulations, you stuck it out."

I beamed with pride as I returned to the bleachers. I was a football letterman! And after all the aches and bruises I suffered the past three years, I felt I'd earned it.

High-school football helped build my confidence and my character, and I learned hard work and perseverance were necessary to succeed. Unfortunately, I didn't translate that to my courses in school, where my grades were mediocre at best. But my physical and mental toughness would benefit me later in life. More importantly, football taught me the importance of teamwork. Everyone needed to know his position and how it related to other positions on the team.

After football season ended, I turned my attention to music. As a senior, I was the first-chair sousaphone player in the concert band and the pianist for the school dance band, The Swingin' Saints. Our repertoire consisted of dance tunes from the 1940s and '50s; our director was Timothy McGee, the school music teacher.

A Mantra Is Born

On November 22, 1963, as I practiced the sousaphone on stage in the school auditorium, the loudspeaker broke in with an announcement that President Kennedy had been assassinated. Classes were cancelled the rest of the day. When I arrived home, I watched the news unfold on television. President Kennedy's assassination was a tragedy of such magnitude that, for the first time in my life, I felt our country's security was in jeopardy. Three years earlier, I had been an impressionable teenager when President Kennedy gave his inaugural address and said, "Ask not what your country can do for you, ask what you can do for your country." Like many people of my generation, it became a mantra that led me to a career in public service. Soon after President Kennedy's assassination I read his book, *Profiles in Courage*, a compilation of stories about people throughout history who spoke up about what they believed was right, even though it wasn't popular.

In the aftermath of President Kennedy's death, I composed a piano piece I named *Utopia*. In a way, it helped me deal with the assassination by putting my feelings into music. I showed it to Mr. McGee, who suggested some changes and added a bridge to it, then surprised me by arranging it for the high-school dance band. When we performed it at a school dance, for the first time I felt validated as a musician and a piano player. The piano would eventually change my life.

Off to College

During my junior year in high school, my maternal grandparents visited us in Ohio and gave me the greatest single opportunity of my life: a chance to attend college tuition free. All I had to pay for was books and personal expenses. Neither of my grandparents had gone beyond the eighth grade, but they were a visionary couple who believed in the importance of a college education. This was a time when most high-school graduates joined the work force, enlisted in the armed forces, or went to a trade school. At St. Wendelin I knew several of my classmates were college bound and I realized that would prepare me for a better future. The excellent academic environment and the discipline enforced by the nuns at St. Wendelin were intended to prepare us for college. I'd only had average grades in high school, except for an anomaly in sophomore year when I made the honor roll. In my favor was a broad background, including foreign languages, music, and sports. I applied to Bowling Green State University in Bowling Green, Ohio, because it was the closest university to Fostoria, just 30 miles away, and my chances of getting accepted were greatest at a state university.

I was excited to get accepted for admission to the freshman class in September 1964. I would be the first in my family to attend college; but lack of confidence about my academic abilities tempered my excitement. Bowling Green was a mid-size state university, in a small manufacturing city in northwest Ohio, noted for its business and education programs. There was a Heinz plant next to the campus which became a convenient resource for business majors to complete projects assigned by our professors. Some of Bowling Green's most famous alumni included actor/comedian Tim Conway, actress Eva Marie Saint, and future NBA Hall of Famer Nate Thurmond.

Shortly after my high-school graduation in June 1964, and after her divorce from Clarence Mitchell, my mother moved us back to Penn Yan to live with her parents. Contrary to the emptiness I felt when my biological father abandoned us, I felt relieved our abusive stepfather was out of our lives.

My mother and I returned to Ohio later that summer to attend freshman orientation. The summer before classes started, Grandma Orsino introduced me to Dan Chacchia, after she learned through friends in Geneva he would also be attending Bowling Green. Dan lived just 20 miles from Penn Yan, and I later learned he played saxophone in a local rock band. It seemed a natural fit for us to be roommates. We both came from Italian-American families and had musical backgrounds. Coincidentally, I learned from an old newspaper clipping of my mother's that when we were six years old, Dan and I attended a birthday party at my uncle Louis and aunt Sue Gigliotti's home in Geneva for my cousin Louis. Dan's parents were Louis' godparents.

Like many college freshmen, I was unsure of my career goals. I told my counselor I wanted to major in business, music, or French. I mentioned French because it had been one of my favorite subjects in high school and I enjoyed the French culture and its music. I said business because my grandparents envisioned me employed with a large corporation like Kodak or Xerox, both based in Rochester. And I said music because I enjoyed dance band and the popularity I gained playing the piano in high school. The counselor wisely suggested I enroll in a liberal-arts program my first year, to get a feel for different subjects before deciding on a major.

After classes began in September I inquired at the music department about majoring in music as a pianist. It was then I received a dose of reality about my musical ability. One of the professors said if I hadn't performed at Carnegie Hall by the time I was 18, I was unlikely to have a career as a pianist. She sympathetically advised me to take a course in music theory to get a taste of what was required to major in music, which I did in my second semester. I got a C, which I interpreted as a personal failure after 10 years of piano lessons. It also involved more effort than I ever anticipated it would, so I never took another formal music course. I had average grades during my first year of college but poor study habits, and my newfound social life, would catch up to me during sophomore year.

<u>The Rock Band</u>

Although I wouldn't make a living playing piano, I found playing by ear came fairly easy to me. Chord progressions for some of the popular rock songs of the 1960s were pretty standard and it was only a matter of picking out the melody with my right hand and matching it with the chords.

During freshman year, Dan and I met some other musicians in the dormitory and we began to hold regular jam sessions. Eventually we had a lead guitarist, a bass player, and a drummer. Dan played the sax and I either used a piano or rented an electric keyboard. After several jam sessions we decided we were good enough to play in public, so we put the word out to get gigs on campus. Dressed in coats and ties, we called ourselves The Impromptus, because we came together rather spontaneously. Our coats and ties were influenced by groups like The Four Seasons and The Beatles. We obtained gigs at a couple of fraternity houses on campus and at the Newman Center, just off campus.

I also arranged a gig in Fostoria through contacts I had from high school. I rented an electric keyboard from a music store in Bowling Green for $10 and paid for it with my share of the money from our performance. We managed to borrow a van and drove to Fostoria.

As we entered town, we arrived at a teen center that was converted from a former movie theater. The name of our band was lit up on the marquee and we were elated at the sight of it. It felt like we were rock stars. We entertained a crowd of about 100 teens with our repertoire of rock 'n' roll songs. My featured vocal was *House of the Rising Sun*. That gig turned out to be the high-water mark of our band. We played a few more gigs that school year and even changed our name to The Renegades, to make us sound more badass. The band ended after a series of challenges. Our lead guitarist dropped out of school. We never expanded our repertoire, and transportation outside campus was difficult. We dissolved the band, but I continued to play the piano, mostly for my own entertainment, whenever I had the chance. I continued to learn new music and improve my skills but concentrated too much on music and not enough on my courses.

The Sophomore Jinx

Sophomore year, I became more involved with socializing on campus and my grades started to suffer. I went to dances, dated, pledged a fraternity, and spent many evenings at the local hangouts in town. College life was great, but I lacked the maturity to manage my time properly. My new social life and lack of attention to my course work combined to put me on academic probation after the first semester of sophomore year.

Poor grades also ruined my chance to become an officer through ROTC. My interest in the military led me to enroll in the Army ROTC program freshman year. I was issued a uniform to wear during class, and I reprised my role as a sousaphone player in the ROTC field band. Although I maintained a C average in ROTC, I was dropped from the program after sophomore year because my overall grade-point average was too low.

Music resulted in the unintended consequence of contributing to my academic problems. Sophomore year I was assigned to eat at the dining hall in the girls' dormitory closest to where I lived at the Newman Center. Several times a week, I would sit at the spinet piano outside the dining hall after dinner, just to relax and entertain myself ... at least initially. Soon, as many as 20 coeds gathered to listen. They'd encourage me to play more, and I gladly obliged. It may have been the first time I realized I could win hearts and minds. Before I realized it, more than an hour had passed. As one group of coeds left, another group would flock around the piano. Sometimes Dan joined me and sang a soulful version of the Animals' *Bring it on Home to Me*, while I played. I often sat at the piano until no one was left in the dining hall.

I was so emotionally high from all the female attention, I had little energy left to study. I met several girls at those sessions and dated a couple of them, but I should have taken a cue from a sign some girl posted in a stairway that read, "Anyone want to date the piano player?" I thought, *Is no one interested, or do I seem desperate?*

These sessions at the piano continued for the remainder of sophomore year. Because of the probation, I had to maintain a C average during the next two semesters or I would be dismissed from the university. My grandparents paid my tuition and took pride in having the first member of the family attend college. Grandpa Orsino proudly told his friends in Penn Yan his grandson was in college. I dreaded the thought of failing them.

The Girl Friend

I began the first semester of my junior year with a sense of impending doom. I knew I needed to pay more attention to my courses and less to my social life, but did I have enough self-discipline to do it? During sophomore year I dated one girl fairly often, and she became aware of my academic problems. Karen was a year behind me in college but years ahead in maturity. I don't recall how we met but she was bright, outgoing, and flirtatious. It was a case of opposites attract. She was also tremendously goal oriented and maintained a perfect 4.0 average as an education major.

During my critical junior year, Karen helped redirect my focus and suggested having study dates rather than going out socially. She essentially managed my study time and gradually my grades improved. We enrolled in a psychology course together and each earned a B, which boosted my confidence, as well as my GPA. My grade-point average after the first semester rose to a mediocre–but still acceptable–2.01. I was elated and felt ready to resume a more active social life during second semester. I started to hang out more with my roommates and went to the local bars. I felt liberated, but Karen was determined to get me refocused and away from the influence of my roommates – who enjoyed having a good time, but who had much better study habits.

My roommates and I lived at the Newman Center in adjoining rooms with a shared bathroom. A large poster of Sophia Loren decorated the wall of one room. Each room had bunkbeds and two study tables. We were close, at first only because we lived together, but eventually we became friends. They nicknamed me Mitchelli, to make me feel more Italian. Our gang included Dan Chacchia, Dick Aquila and Jim Meighan (the token Irishman), both from the Buffalo area, Tom Manoni, whom we met at Bowling Green, and Bob Alge (the token German), my classmate at St. Wendelin. Dan, Dick, Jim, and I carpooled to Bowling Green from New York State in Dan's car for our last two years of college. Many weekends we would play a pick-up game of tackle football on a lawn across the street. After the game, we'd go back to our adjoining rooms for a cold beer. Jim and I joined the newly created gymnastics club during junior year and were featured in an issue of the campus newspaper, *The BG News*. The five of us had great times together.

During the winter of our junior year, I dutifully walked across campus through the snow virtually every night to meet with Karen to study. My roommates chided me and said Karen had a chain around my neck, but I needed the structure and discipline she provided for studying. Their observations eventually proved true, but they weren't immediately apparent because I was infatuated with her. She admired my talent on the piano, but it was secondary to her interest in my academic success. My grades continued to improve, largely because of her help ... but the fear of disappointing my mother and my grandparents was a huge motivator.

At the end of my junior year, I returned to Penn Yan for the summer and waited for my grades. If my average dropped below 2.0, I would be ineligible to return to college in the fall, which meant I would lose my student deferment and be subject to the draft – but it would hurt me more to disappoint my grandparents. When my grades arrived, I was full of anticipation. They read: Management, B; Math, C; Labor Economics, C, Business Finance, C, Introduction to Contracts, B. My grade point average was 2.07, good enough to return for my senior year.

With a sigh of relief, I gave the good news to my mother and my grandparents and telephoned Karen. She was excited to hear I passed and we made plans to visit each other.

I flew out to visit her in Glen Ellyn, Illinois, a quiet suburb, 23 miles west of Chicago. Widowed at an early age, her father had remarried. I had met Karen's father and stepmother during a visit they made to campus. They were quite kind and invited me out to dinner with them. On my visit to her home, Karen played to my Italian roots and spent the good part of one day making lasagna. She was meticulous about everything she did and the lasagna was done to perfection. She knew my interest in music and got us tickets to see Neil Diamond at a nightclub in Chicago. We enjoyed a memorable, romantic weekend together. Things were getting serious.

Later that summer, I invited her to visit my family in Penn Yan. I introduced her to my mother and grandparents and took her to the family cottage on Keuka Lake. Sweet and personable, she became an instant hit with my mother. They even corresponded with each other after Karen returned to Illinois. We talked about our future together as if we would get married someday but I remained non-committal. When classes began in the fall, I was motivated to improve my grades and graduate the following June. I felt more self-assured and tried to distance myself from Karen's rigid study program, which created a rift between us. We decided to date other people, but she still inquired about my studies when we were together. Our relationship became strained when I started dating another girl. Whenever we did see each other, and our conversation would lag, she would ask what I was thinking.

I usually said, "Nothing," because I didn't always want Karen to know what I was thinking ... and sometimes I honestly wasn't thinking about anything at all.

As time went on, I realized my roommates were right: Karen exerted more control over me than I wanted to admit. She had helped me through a difficult time in college and instilled in me the self-discipline I needed, but her tendency to be didactic and controlling eventually pulled us apart. Life was taking us in separate directions. The day I graduated we had an emotional parting. Karen was in tears and it put me at a loss for words. She had another year of college ahead of her and my life was about to change dramatically.

Vietnam on the Horizon

In 1968, with news of Vietnam and other events in America, it seemed the country was on the verge of revolution. On January 31, 1968, the North Vietnamese launched the Tet Offensive, which reached all the way to the U.S. Embassy in Saigon. The Tet Offensive was particularly disturbing because just two months earlier, Gen. Westmoreland, the commander of U.S. forces in Vietnam, had spearheaded a public-relations drive for the Johnson administration to bolster the decline in public support. In a speech before the National Press Club, he said a point in the war had been reached "where the end comes into view."

The American public was shocked when the North Vietnamese demonstrated the ability to mount such a large offensive. Our armed forces inflicted heavy casualties on the North Vietnamese and subdued the offensive, but the public-relations victory went to Hanoi. In March 1968, as opposition to the war increased and his approval rating plummeted, President Johnson announced he would not seek re-election. Also, in March, the massacre of South Vietnamese civilians by American troops at My Lai provided more fuel for the anti-Vietnam protests.

In addition to the grim news from Vietnam, two shocking events occurred in the spring of 1968. In April, Rev. Martin Luther King, Jr., the civil rights leader, was assassinated as he stood on the balcony of his hotel room in Memphis. And on June 5, just days before I graduated from college, Robert F. Kennedy, a Democratic presidential candidate, and younger brother of President John F. Kennedy, was assassinated at a campaign rally in Los Angeles.

During my final weeks of college, I witnessed a protest to the "conflict" in Vietnam on the Bowling Green campus. I was inside a classroom building and some noise caused me to look out a window. I noticed several white wooden crosses on the lawn planted by student demonstrators to represent American dead in Vietnam. A couple dozen students sat on the lawn as someone addressed them. I watched in disbelief as several other students suddenly arrived at the makeshift demonstration, pulled the crosses out of the ground and broke them. The demonstrators dispersed and at that point I realized how much our involvement in Vietnam had polarized people.

I was about to lose my draft deferment after graduation and wondered how Vietnam would affect me. I didn't realize it at the time, but just as World War II had defined my parents' generation, Vietnam would define mine.

TERRY MITCHELL
Halfback

Letterman Photo 1963

St. Wendelin Dance Band 1963-64

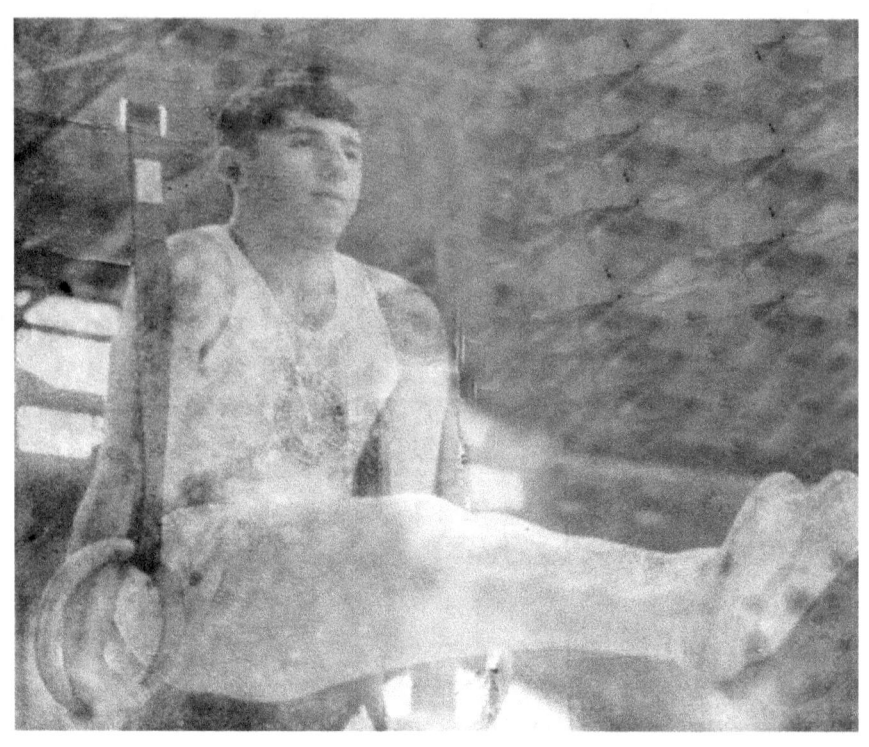

BGSU Gymnastics Club 1967

Jim Meighan, Dick Aquila, Me, Dan Chacchia at BGSU

Chapter 3
The Path to Vietnam (1969-1971)

When my student deferment ended, the draft loomed. I had no job prospects in Penn Yan and didn't want to gamble on my chances with the draft, so the summer after graduation I enlisted in the Army. I reasoned it was better to be proactive and choose a specialty I wanted than to be assigned something the Army chose, which might not be based on my interests or my education. I'd heard too many stories about draftees being mismatched with a military specialty.

I made an appointment with an Army recruiter in Syracuse and was given a list of career fields to scan. My eyes fixed on "counterintelligence special agent." I immediately knew it was the job I wanted. The James Bond movies of the '60s fascinated me because they contained lots of action, adventure, drama, sex, and some great music.

When I asked the recruiter about the position, he said it was a sensitive position that required a high-level security clearance. Undeterred, I took the Armed Forces Qualification Test and the physical exam for entrance into the armed forces. In addition, to qualify for admission into the counterintelligence specialty field, I had to undergo a background check more extensive than the routine NAC (National Agency Check) performed for enlistees. The process required me to submit a full-length photograph to ensure I had ordinary features that would not attract attention, and I had to submit a writing sample. I also underwent a personal interview to determine my mental suitability for the position, which could involve dangerous covert operations.

I was given a tentative date to attend boot camp and awaited the results of my background investigation and a decision about my qualifications. I maintained a casual attitude about it, knowing I had an ordinary appearance, no criminal or seditious leanings, and I could write in complete sentences. Several weeks later, I was accepted for admission to the U.S. Army Intelligence School at Fort Holabird, Maryland, pending successful completion of basic training. I enlisted for six years on the delayed-entry program, which gave me six months to get my affairs in order.

Army Roots

The Army was the branch I was most familiar with because my father and several uncles served in it during World War II and, in college, I spent two years in the Army ROTC program.

I also had distant cousin on my mother's side, Jim Trepoy, who made the Army a career, and he made an indelible impression on me.

I met him during a visit with his family when I was 10. He was still in the Army when my grandparents took Dale and me to visit Washington, D.C., as a reward for our promotion to the next grade in school. Gene was considered too young to appreciate a trip to our nation's capital. Our grandparents made arrangements to stay with Jim's family during our visit. At the time Cousin Jim was a sergeant assigned to the Military District of Washington (MDW).

I was impressed by Cousin Jim's starched khaki uniform adorned with sergeant stripes, ribbons, and the shoulder patch that designated his unit of assignment. The embroidered oval patch had a red border. In the center was a red sword superimposed diagonally over a replica of the Washington Monument in white on a blue background. Twelve years later, I would wear the same shoulder patch while assigned to Fort Myer, Virginia.

I renewed my acquaintance with Jim periodically through the years. Nancy and I visited him and his family in Salina, Kansas, after we became engaged. In 2002, long after he retired, I resumed contact with him via email. At the time, he was making regular medical visits to McConnell Air Force Base near Wichita, Kansas, where our son Gregory was stationed.

Jim retired as a command sergeant major, the highest enlisted grade in the Army. During his long and distinguished career, he served in World War II, Korea, and Vietnam. His many decorations included the Bronze Star Medal for Valor and the Combat Infantry Badge. He was also an atomic veteran who witnessed above-ground tests of the atomic bomb in Nevada during the 1950s. He passed away in 2010 from cancer, a result of the radiation he absorbed from those tests many years ago. He was a hero to me and I was grateful to have known him as well as I did.

Florida Bound

While I waited to enter the Army, my high-school and college classmate Bob Alge visited me in Penn Yan. He invited me to share an apartment with him in Florida to save expenses. It didn't take much for him to convince me to spend the rest of my free time in Florida before entering the Army.

I first visited Florida with Bob, Dan, Tom, and an underclassman I only remember as Tony during spring break of senior year at Bowling Green. We stayed in Fort Lauderdale, the mecca for spring break during the 1960s. I basked in the daily sunshine on the beach, admired the palm trees and the whole spring-break experience. Everywhere we looked there were girls in bikinis–even in the bars across the street from the beach. It was a college guy's paradise!

Bob apparently liked Florida enough to pursue a teaching position there. He was a bright guy with an engaging personality and a great sense of humor. I'm certain he had no trouble keeping the attention of his students.

My mother and grandmother did not approve of my trip to Florida, but I felt it was something I needed to do before giving the next six years of my life to the Army. With no thought about how I would return to Penn Yan to report for my enlistment, I purchased a one-way airline ticket to Fort Lauderdale with money I saved from my summer job at the Penn Yan Department of Public Works.

Construction was booming in Florida in 1968, so I easily found work as a laborer at one of the several condo sites in the Fort Lauderdale/Pompano Beach area to help pay the rent. At night Bob and I frequented clubs and restaurants, met some girls, and generally led a carefree, bachelor life. My biggest concern was the union representatives who inspected the construction sites for non-union workers. Since I was only there temporarily, I had no desire to pay the union dues that would put a strain on my meager income. The carpenters I worked with were kind enough to alert me whenever a union rep arrived. A few times, I had to leave a job site in a hurry to avoid being caught. Fortunately, other construction sites were available nearby. The site foremen apparently had no problem hiring non-union workers because they always needed help and it was cheap labor.

By early December I was enjoying the warm weather and the Florida life so much I phoned my mother to tell her I planned to stay in Florida for the holidays but would return home in time for my reporting date in late January. She started to cry. I had never been away from home for Christmas and the sound of my mother in tears was too much to bear, so I reluctantly agreed to return home for Christmas. Bob had planned to go home to Ohio for the holidays, so we hitched a ride north with a couple of girls we'd met. They dropped us off at Purdue University in Indiana, where we both found rides. I managed to hitchhike from Indiana to Penn Yan in time for Christmas. During one ride, I was crunched up in the back seat of a Corvette. About 50 miles from home, I was picked up by someone from Penn Yan, who took me to my grandparents' front door.

Basic Training

I was scheduled to report at Fort Dix, New Jersey, for basic combat training on February 4, 1969, but first I had to report to the in-processing station at Syracuse. My mother offered to drive me and, as luck would have it, the morning we left Penn Yan, a snowstorm hit Central New York. We had driven about 50 miles toward Syracuse when the road conditions became so bad my mother stopped at a New York State Police station just west of Auburn for assistance. She explained to the trooper on duty that I had to report to Syracuse that day to enter the Army and asked if they could drive me the rest of the way. The road conditions were getting worse and she feared we might get stranded. The state trooper agreed to get me transported in the next car leaving for Syracuse, a distance of about 20 miles, and I arrived in time to begin my six-year enlistment.

I spent one night in Syracuse at a hotel contracted by the government, assigned with other recruits to austere-looking double-occupancy rooms with no television. The next day we were picked up by the recruiter in a van and driven to the military processing center on South Salina Street. We were lined up, told to stand at attention and raise our right hand to take the oath of enlistment: *"I will support and defend the Constitution of the*

United States against all enemies, foreign and domestic; that I will bear true faith and allegiance to the same; and that I will obey the orders of the President of the United States and the orders of the officers appointed over me, according to the regulations and the Uniform Code of Military Justice, so help me God." There were no photos taken, and no family members present. After reciting the oath, we received our orders to be hand carried to Fort Dix. Soon we were taken to the Syracuse Airport for an all-expenses-paid flight to New Jersey. At the Newark airport we were met by two soldiers who escorted us to a bus and drove us to Fort Dix.

It was cold and dark when we arrived, and the ground was covered with several inches of snow. We were greeted by a drill sergeant who ordered us off the bus into the cold, dry air and directed us to form up in lines for a roll call. Afterward we were herded into the mess hall for our first Army meal. We had only a short time to eat before being herded outside again.

We were each issued an entrenching tool and ordered to shovel snow in a large parking lot. The entrenching tool was a small, wooden-handled folding shovel intended for digging trenches and foxholes. Shoveling snow with it was like using a paper cup to empty a swimming pool. The drill sergeants must have been amused to see fresh recruits shoveling snow in the parking lot. I think we shoveled for 30 minutes before we were told to fall into formation to march back to our barracks for the night. The task seemed to be an exercise in futility, but it was used to teach obedience and teamwork: lessons that would be repeated many times during basic training.

Boot camp was a test of our physical endurance, mental toughness, and ability to follow instructions. The goal was to mold recruits into soldiers and prepare us for the challenges and hardships of military duty; but, perhaps more importantly, it taught us how to work together under adverse conditions.

Because of the many anti-war and draft protests on college campuses in the late '60s, there was a perception among the drill sergeants that college kids were troublemakers who might threaten the good order, discipline, and teamwork necessary in the Army. College graduates who enlisted for active duty were rare in the draft years, so when they saw my record, I was taken aside by Staff Sgt. Molina, an olive-skinned, barrel-chested guy who questioned my motivation to enlist, inquiring why I didn't go to officer-candidate school.

I explained I'd spent my first two years of college in the Army ROTC program but was dropped because of poor grades in my other courses, so I decided to enlist rather than be drafted. I was also asked about my participation in anti-war or draft protests on campus. I assured him I was never involved in such activities.

Staff Sgt. Molina seemed amused to learn I was an ROTC dropout, but he was satisfied I wasn't some hippie protester who would cause trouble in the ranks. I was eventually given a couple of leadership roles, first as a squad leader then as a platoon leader.

Our days in basic training were regimented and there was little time for recreation. We had one "free" weekend toward the middle of our cycle when we were allowed visitors but could not leave the post. That weekend my mother brought Dale to Fort Dix for a visit. He had joined the Marines while I was in college and returned from Vietnam a few weeks earlier. It was more than a year since I saw him, and I enjoyed the chance to visit with him. While in college I wrote him to say I wish I could have been there with him. Dale was a forward artillery observer and saw combat. He lost a close buddy there and was knocked down by an enemy bullet after landing by helicopter in a hot LZ (landing zone). Fortunately, the distance the bullet had traveled–combined with the thickness of his backpack and the metal mess kit inside–prevented him from getting wounded, or worse. He missed a Purple Heart Medal by inches.

Basic training involved a variety of instruction. It included classroom lectures on citizenship, military courtesy, rank structure, marksmanship, and a history of the United States Army. We were taught the Army way to make our beds, brush our teeth, and fold our clothes. We were issued everything we needed. If it wasn't issued to us we didn't need it. There was little privacy and none at all in the latrine. We had open-bay toilets and showers large enough to accommodate several recruits at a time.

Field training consisted of basic soldiering skills like first aid, weapons qualification, physical fitness, the bayonet, hand grenades, and land navigation. Land navigation would be the bane of my existence throughout my Army career. I thought I understood the principles, but rarely succeeded during practical exercise. We also underwent chemical-warfare training. We had to put on our chemical-protective mask in nine seconds, enter the gas chamber, and when the order was given we took off the mask long enough to recite our name, rank, and serial number while our eyes became irritated from the tear gas. We had to be able to communicate clearly under stress.

We received instruction on hand-to-hand combat, during which we practiced judo-type movements–a series of hand chops and leg kicks to fight off an opponent. I think we learned enough to make us more dangerous to ourselves than to the enemy. If it became necessary to fight hand to hand, the instinct to survive would surely take over and, in theory, those judo movements would become automatic. We underwent a night-infiltration exercise once. We crawled under strands of barbed wire dressed in full combat gear with our weapon cradled in the crook of our arms for about 20 yards while machine-gun fire buzzed above our heads. We joked among ourselves that the exercise was really a way for the drill instructors to get rid of the recruits they didn't like. The firing range and live hand-grenade toss added a touch of realism to our training.

At night in the barracks, we each took turns acting as fire guard. The fire guard's job was to stay awake for a four-hour shift, to make sure the coal-heated stove was kept hot, and to alert everyone in case of a fire. We were expected to memorize the General Orders and could be quizzed on them by a drill instructor at any time. There were three General Orders: 1. I will guard everything within the limits of my post and quit my post only when properly relieved. 2. I will obey my special orders and perform all my duties in a military manner. 3. I will report violations of my special orders, emergencies, and anything not covered in my instructions to the commander of the relief.

The winter of 1969-70 was so cold our bivouac exercise was cancelled. Several of us came down with upper-respiratory infections, and I missed a day or two of training. If we missed too much training, we would get left behind and recycled to another basic-training company to finish our training. To be recycled was like repeating a grade in school, and nobody wanted to suffer through it again. After a visit to the medical clinic, I was cleared to rejoin training after 24 hours' rest.

After reveille sounded early one morning in the dead of winter, we were marched to the medical clinic before breakfast to give blood. It was the first time I ever gave blood and I wasn't prepared for the shock to my body on an empty stomach. Afterward I got up from the cot, took a few steps and passed out. When I regained consciousness, I was given some water and told to sit down for a few minutes before I rejoined training.

Fitness training was one of my favorite activities, because it offered an outlet for stress and pent-up aggression. I scored high during the physical-fitness assessments and received one of our company's highest scores on the final fitness test, 464 out of a possible 500 points. Those who scored more than 400 stood at the front of the line for chow. As a slow eater, I enjoyed the extra time to eat.

One day at lunch I was so engrossed in my meal I didn't notice everyone else had already finished. Suddenly Staff Sgt. Paul Thomas, a black drill sergeant who I believed was the most abusive, yelled at me to get up. Either I didn't hear him, or I thought he yelled at someone else, so I continued to eat. When I didn't get up, Staff Sgt. Thomas lost what little patience he had. He came up from behind and pulled my chair out from under me, knocking me to the floor. As I lay on the floor, he told me to get up, then shoved me against the wall. He stared at me and asked who the hell I was to disobey an order, then dared me to hit him back. I stood there, dumbfounded, and stared back in disbelief. I came to my senses and decided it would be no contest if I threw a punch. We were about the same size, but I suspected he was much tougher, and by the look in his eyes he didn't need much of an excuse to beat me to a pulp.

Drill sergeants had few restrictions concerning the treatment of recruits in those days. I told Thomas I wasn't going to hit him, so he lectured me, with a litany of profanities, about obeying instructions and pointed out that by failing to finish my meal on time I held up training for the rest of the company. Then he told me go to outside to join the formation.

I obeyed the rules and acted like a model recruit from then on, but inside I harbored a growing animosity toward what I perceived to be the drill sergeants' constant harassment and abuse. I was a college graduate and found their methods draconian and demeaning. My attitude changed from a desire to be a model recruit to contempt for the drill sergeants. I felt we should be treated better and did what I could to mentor other recruits in my company, especially those who had a more difficult time and seemed targeted for harassment by the drill sergeants.

One day, I was at the head of my platoon on a road march with the rest of the company and began a chant to boost our morale. Marching chants, or Jody Calls, consisted of short, rhythmic phrases spoken in cadence: a kind of precursor to rap. Suddenly Staff Sgt. Molina halted the company and sarcastically asked who the "hero" was who started the Jody Call. I admitted responsibility and was called out of the formation. He told me no platoon was better than another and trainees were not to call out chants during a march unless instructed to do so by a drill sergeant. I was ordered to drop to the ground and do pushups, an exercise I became quite proficient at during basic training.

The Missing Bullet

My contempt for the drill sergeants and the basic-training process came to a head on the firing range. We were scheduled to fire the M14 rifle, which used 7.62 mm ammunition, in preparation for qualification. In 1969 the Army was in transition from the M14 to the new M16 rifles that used a 5.56 mm round. We were one of the last rotations to qualify with both weapons. Ammunition was strictly controlled, and all the spent brass cartridges were collected after each firing order to account for the ammunition expended. I decided to get a measure of revenge on the drill sergeants by concealing a live 7.62 mm round inside my uniform. After the exercise, we were lined up in formation while the drill sergeants counted the spent brass. When they finished, the company commander was advised it appeared one round had not been fired. He passed in front of each recruit and questioned us individually about the missing round. When he came to me I looked at him with my best poker face and denied any knowledge of it. The drill sergeants conducted a cursory search at the firing range while I secretly reveled in my deception. I gambled correctly that they wouldn't take the time to search all the pockets of every recruit, and it might be illegal to do so.

 Later that evening the company commander, 1st Lt. Edward Kenneally, stormed into our barracks. He was obviously drunk, which amplified his anger. We were lined up and he again asked all of us about the missing round. I continued to deny any knowledge of it and had not told any of my fellow trainees. Inexplicably, there was never a thorough search of our belongings. There was no further mention of the missing round and I managed to hide it for the remainder of basic training. They must have passed it off as a lost, spent cartridge. After I returned home, I separated the brass casing from the bullet and emptied out the powder to render the round inert. When I reflected on the whole incident, I realized it was a foolish prank and it could have resulted in a court martial with a less-than-honorable discharge. I had dodged my first bullet, so to speak.

 By the end of basic training I met all the requirements and endured the harassment and the regimentation I often resented. I graduated with our company as a private in the United States Army in April 1969. My mother made the trip to New Jersey for graduation and drove me home. Despite my feelings about basic training, I felt next to my graduation from college it was the biggest accomplishment of my life, simply because I "stuck it out", as my high school football coach once said.

 In 1969 many in our class of 240 recruits were destined for Vietnam. I don't know how many of us went, but years later I checked for all their names on the Vietnam Wall and learned one recruit, Albert Haslam, and our company first sergeant, Arcadio Torres, didn't make it home. They were killed in separate incidents during 1970, about a year after we completed basic training.

Advanced Individual Training

I had 30 days of leave before I reported to the U.S. Army Intelligence School at Fort Holabird in May 1969, for the counterintelligence-agent course. While on leave, I purchased my grandparents' 1962 Chevrolet sedan for $300 so I would have transportation at my new assignment.

On July 8, 1969, the first U.S. troop withdrawals from Vietnam were announced; on July 25, President Richard Nixon pronounced the Nixon Doctrine. Its premise was that the United States expected the South Vietnamese to eventually take care of their own defense, which started the Vietnamization of the war. It gave me hope of avoiding Vietnam.

While I waited for my course to begin, I was assigned to Casual Company, a unit designated for those waiting an assignment. Those in casual company performed work details each day until they received an assignment or when their class started. They included barracks cleanup, policing the grounds for cigarette butts, or KP (kitchen police) duty. During Memorial Day weekend we were detailed to place flags on veterans' graves at the Baltimore National Cemetery.

When the course finally started in June, we were taught about classified-document security, interview and interrogation techniques, and the recruitment and management of confidential sources. We also learned how to conduct background investigations. One of the more interesting phases of the course involved an exercise in surveillance and counter-surveillance measures.

Chasing Rabbits

The nearby city of Baltimore was used as the practice ground for a surveillance exercise. Instructors at the school acted as our "rabbits," or surveillance targets. People there must have thought it odd every couple of months when another group of short-haired young men wandered through the city and invariably had to ask for directions when their rabbit eluded them. I enjoyed the exercise because it gave me a practical example of the techniques involved in the counterintelligence field.

I found the entire course interesting and usually did well, but I had some difficulty with the interview and interrogation techniques. I needed extra help in that area because I wasn't aggressive enough. I was naturally laid back, with a non-confrontational personality that required some "adjustment" to be an interrogator. One of the contract actors at the school was assigned to spend extra time with me. It took some practice, but eventually my dark side emerged.

At one point during the special-agent course, we were given a language-aptitude test to determine our potential for foreign-language study. The exposure I had to spoken Italian by my grandparents and my mother, and the French courses I took in high school and college apparently gave me an aptitude for foreign languages. It also helped that Latin was a required course in high school.

While I was immersed in Army life, my past caught up to me in the form of a letter from Karen, forwarded to me from home. She wrote to let me know she was engaged to be married. After I wrestled with the meaning of her letter and did some soul searching, I decided not to respond. We were worlds apart and I had no desire to return to that world–especially in a long-distance relationship.

After completing the counterintelligence-agent course, I was sent to study Vietnamese at the Defense Language Institute (DLI) at Fort Myer, Virginia. Other graduates with foreign-language aptitudes were assigned to study Korean, German, Russian, or Arabic. DLI operated a course that met six days a week for one year in Crystal City, near Alexandria. It was taught by a Vietnamese native under contract with DLI. We were each issued a reel-to-reel tape recorder to get more immersed in the language.

In October 1969, as I drove to my next assignment, I had the radio on as the New York Mets won their first World Series, against the Baltimore Orioles. After the violence and protests of the previous year, it was another sign the world was not right. In the world I grew up in, the Yankees would have been in the World Series and would probably have won.

At Fort Myer I met Cyril Wyche, who was assigned to the Korean-language course; I called him Cy for short. We often hung out together after class and got to be friends in time. Cy was a tall, handsome, outgoing guy, who exuded self-confidence. He always found something to break up the boredom we experienced after a day of classroom instruction. We found work during our off-duty hours as jockeys for a car-rental company in Virginia. We washed cars and shuttled customers back and forth from Washington National Airport.

Thinking my 1962 Chevy needed to be pimped up, Cy convinced me to remove the hubcaps, paint the wheels black and replace the standard lug nuts with chrome ones. It gave the car a younger, customized appearance. It was equipped only with a standard six-cylinder engine and two-barrel carburetor, but at least it didn't look like something my grandparents would own.

We often visited Bob Priddy's, a restaurant and bar in Alexandria, where I took a part-time job playing piano. I was paid $20 a night and became a popular draw for a couple of weeks. My limited repertoire caused the owner to replace me with a small band, but the experience made me feel like my mother's investment in those piano lessons was justified.

My Future Bride

One evening in January 1970, Cy and I decided to check out the USO Club in D.C., for some relaxation, a chance to meet some girls, and to enjoy some free refreshments.

Nancy Riley volunteered at the USO as a hostess. Hostesses were typically young, single girls who served refreshments, socialized and danced with servicemen. They were encouraged to ask servicemen to dance–and could not turn down a request to dance. As Nancy told it, she had started to approach me for a dance when Cy jumped in and asked her to dance. I was always slow to get up the nerve to dance, so when they started dancing, I did what felt comfortable and sat at a piano at one end of the room. When the evening ended, as Cy and Nancy went to retrieve their coats, he asked if she would be there next Saturday night. She said yes and told Cy to "bring your friend."

Back at our barracks, Cy suggested we return to the USO the following Saturday because a girl he met wanted to meet me. I was intrigued and asked Cy if she was cute. He assured me she was. I knew Cy had good taste in women, so Saturday we went back to the USO and he introduced me to Nancy.

She was attractive, outgoing, and one of my first impressions was her pleasant-sounding voice, which I felt was an important trait in a woman. She seemed to have an upbeat outlook on life. It also helped that her short skirt revealed a nice set of legs. Nancy was from Holton, Kansas, a small city about 30 miles north of Topeka. As we became more acquainted I learned her mother ran a restaurant and her father was a truck driver hauling fuel to gasoline stations in the region.

After she graduated from high school, Nancy moved to Topeka to look for work. She was under 18 at the time and had difficulty getting hired, so she went to the Kansas Department of Labor in Topeka. She thought her interviewer was joking when he asked if she wanted to work for the U.S. government. He explained they had sent out a nationwide announcement for clerical workers. She received permission from her parents and accepted a position with the Navy Department in Washington, D.C.

It wasn't long before we discovered a shared interest in music. More accurately, I had an interest in music but Nancy was *passionate* about it. She won first place for her performance on the trumpet at a district-wide competition in high school, and she loved to sing. I wasn't surprised by her beautiful singing voice because even when she spoke it was as if she was singing the words.

There was an instant chemistry between us, and we dated for several months while I attended language school. I hadn't felt that interested in a girl since I dated Karen; but Nancy was different. She didn't pry into my thoughts or pester me with questions about what I was thinking all the time.

Nancy and I spent many weekends on double dates during the summer of 1970 with Cy and his girlfriend. We often traveled to Ocean City, Maryland, for a day at the beach. My relationship with Nancy became serious, but I reminded her I would be going to Vietnam and wasn't ready for a long-term relationship. We agreed to keep in touch but were free to date other people.

During May 1970, in the middle of my study of Vietnamese, a shooting occurred at Kent State University in Ohio, a conference rival of my alma mater, Bowling Green State

University. The Army National Guard, which had been called out to quell anti-war rioting on campus, killed four students and wounded nine others. The National Guard troops had used lethal force on unarmed civilians. I sympathized with both sides as a former college student and a member of the U.S. Army, but as I read more in depth about the incident, it became apparent neither side was without fault. Some students had been violent and destroyed campus property, including the Army ROTC building, in protest of the bombing in Cambodia. The National Guard troops, faced with a growing and increasingly hostile crowd when they arrived on campus, initially fired tear gas to disperse the crowd but then opened fire, probably as the result of a mistaken order someone shouted when they felt threatened. The President's Commission on Campus Unrest concluded the shooting by the National Guard was not justified. It was a tragic event that didn't have to happen.

I graduated from Vietnamese-language school on my 24th birthday in October 1970, with a secondary MOS (Military Occupational Specialty) as a Vietnamese linguist. I could only speak, listen, read, and write at a basic level, but I met the standards set by DLI. My mother, who was always there for support, drove to Virginia for my graduation.

I was soon given orders to report to Oakland Army Base, California, in November for assignment to Vietnam, but first I had 30 days of leave back home. The days passed quickly while I dated other girls, frequented the local bars, and lived aimlessly. I wouldn't need a car for the near future, so I sold it before I left for Oakland.

The day I left for Vietnam, I stopped in to say goodbye to my grandparents. Grandpa Orsino had suffered a stroke during my last year of college that left him partially paralyzed. He'd worked 40 years in a physically demanding job at the New York

Central and Penn Central railroads and barely had time to enjoy retirement before his stroke.

Before I left, he told me, "Be a good soldier."

Those were the most profound words he ever said to me. I thought back to the foolish stunt I pulled in basic training and realized I had not always been a good soldier. I was about to be sent to a combat zone and I needed to remember his instruction to me, if only to survive what lay ahead.

Onward to Vietnam

My time at Oakland Army Base seemed like an eternity while I waited for my name to appear on a flight manifest to Vietnam. We were essentially quarantined on base, so I had a lot of time to think about the danger and uncertainty that awaited me. Fortunately, a piano at the base helped me pass the time and divert my fears about Vietnam. The troops seemed to enjoy my music, but it was a far cry from entertaining coeds in college. In early December, my name finally appeared on a manifest and I prepared to deploy. I said a silent prayer that I would return home safely. Within a couple of days, I boarded a chartered commercial jet into the unknown, but perhaps better prepared than most troops because I had spent a year immersed in the Vietnamese language and culture.

Ft. Myer Talent Competition, 1970

Chapter 4
Vietnam (Dec 1970-Dec 1971)

I arrived in Vietnam on December 9, 1970, after a stopover at a base in Japan. During our approach to Tan Son Nut Airport in Saigon, the pilot announced the aircraft would remain on the runway with the engines on after we landed. We would disembark directly onto the runway so the aircraft could take off as soon as we safely cleared. The less time the plane remained on the ground, the less chance it would be exposed to rocket or mortar fire. It was dark when we got off and I wondered whether the timing was planned to cover our arrival.

After reporting in at the airport, we boarded a bus to the reception station at Long Binh, the largest U.S. base in Vietnam. Covering about 18 square miles, it was home to more than 100,000 troops at the height of its existence. When construction started in 1965, it was known as Camp Ranger, home to Headquarters, U.S. Army Vietnam (USARV). Long Binh was 16 miles north of Saigon (later renamed Ho Chi Minh City). Our bus had steel bars on the windows to prevent rocks or grenades from being thrown into it. As we drove through Saigon I stared out the window in a semi-trance, tired from the long trip from California. The lights from the shops along the narrow streets formed a kaleidoscope of colors as I thought about how my life was about to change. Suddenly I was startled by a thud against the window. Someone had thrown a piece of fruit at the bus. It was my first indication some people in South Vietnam didn't appreciate our presence.

When we arrived at Long Binh, we received assignments to our units. I was assigned to the 702nd Military Intelligence Detachment (MID) (Counterintelligence), a unit under the USARV Special Troops Detachment. When I arrived, it was under the overall command of Gen. Creighton Abrams, who replaced Gen. William Westmoreland. The MID was on Long Binh Post, so I wouldn't have to travel again to join my unit. When the Jeep arrived at our destination, I was introduced to the other agents and the detachment commander.

The mission of the 702nd MID was to support the operations of Headquarters and Headquarters Company, USARV, through the detection of treason, sedition, subversive activities, and disaffection, and "the prevention or neutralization of espionage and sabotage within or directed against Headquarters, USARV." The 702nd MID had an authorized strength of 17 personnel, 11 of whom were counterintelligence special agents. I was assigned as a replacement for a special agent who rotated back to the States. The detachment also had a mission to ensure Headquarters USARV and its subordinate units were provided with early warning of hostile enemy activity directed against Long Binh Post.

By December 1970, the mood of the people in the United States was clearly against the war. President Nixon had begun to withdraw troops as part of his Vietnamization Program. When I arrived, troop strength had fallen from a high of 536,100 in December 1968 to 335,800. The South Vietnamese government was encouraged to take more responsibility for fighting the war. When the Vietnamization effort was first announced, I hoped I would be spared from going. When I arrived, I hoped I wouldn't have to stay a whole year.

During my first week in country I was assigned as a perimeter guard inside our unit sector. I was issued the standard web gear (belt, suspenders, first-aid pouch, two ammo pouches, canteen), a steel helmet with liner, M16 rifle, and a basic load of 5.56-millimeter ammunition. It was a sobering reality check to know I was responsible for a portion of our perimeter and had to decide when and if to pull the trigger. I didn't know what the threat level was so I prepared for the worst. My pucker factor was high that night. Fortunately, the night passed quietly and the next morning I asked one of the guys to take a couple of "John Wayne" pictures of me to send home. It was one of the rare times I wore my battle rattle (slang term for combat gear).

In my capacity as a counterintelligence agent, I carried identification as a Department of the Army Civilian. It required me to wear either civilian clothes or olive-drab fatigues labeled "D.A.C" above the right breast pocket instead of "U.S. Army." The civilian cover helped me gain access to higher-ranking personnel and leveled the rank structure for me, which facilitated performance of my duties. I was still a soldier, however, and held the rank of corporal when I arrived in country. I was promoted to sergeant about halfway through my tour of duty.

I was soon involved in a daily routine of performing personnel security investigations on U.S. personnel. They were required when someone in the Army was considered for a position requiring a security clearance. I interviewed character references stationed at Long Binh and followed up with other leads at Long Binh if they revealed prejudiced information. I referred the investigation to the originating office if they were not based at Long Binh. My reports were mailed back to the United States. After a while the investigations became too routine for me and didn't involve the adventure or intrigue I imagined.

The fighting in Vietnam continued, even though it felt relatively peaceful from my vantage point. There were occasional reminders we were still confronted by an enemy. One quiet evening I stood outside our building and marveled at the warm January weather and the clear night sky. After a few minutes, the serenity was interrupted by the sound of rapid gunfire. I looked toward the noise and witnessed a Cobra attack helicopter light up the sky with tracer rounds from the cannon mounted on its nose. The rounds seemed directed at a ground target about a mile or so from where I stood. I wondered whether the Viet Cong had attempted to infiltrate our base. Anything or anyone on the ground must have been destroyed as those rounds rained down on their target.

When the opportunity presented itself, I volunteered to operate a confidential source network from another agent who completed his tour. My training as a Vietnamese linguist helped me get the assignment because it would require working with an intelligence detachment from the Army of the Republic of Vietnam (ARVN). They were purposely located next to our headquarters. I was warned the work might be dangerous, but I was eager for the chance to do some real counterintelligence work and leave the confines of Long Binh Post.

I was introduced to the ARVN soldiers and began working with them daily. They seemed to have a positive attitude and were a likeable group. We interviewed confidential sources in hamlets around Long Binh to gather information about enemy activity in the area, which more directly related to our unit's primary mission. Conducted in Vietnamese, the interviews usually yielded seemingly routine information, but it wasn't my job to evaluate whether it was actionable intelligence. Every interview generated a report to headquarters for evaluation. On occasion, we were able to obtain information about VC movement in the area.

I quickly discovered counterintelligence work in Vietnam wasn't like the movies. There were no tuxedos, no beautiful women, no high-tech weapons, and no vodka martinis. In fact, military intelligence was jokingly referred to by some as a contradiction of terms. Instead of a tuxedo, I usually wore shirt and slacks. Instead of vodka martinis, I drank beer. Instead of beautiful women, we had two homely Vietnamese housekeepers. The fabled Aston Martin coupe was a Jeep, and the magazine-fed Walther PPK semiautomatic pistol was a Smith & Wesson .38 revolver. However, I did have an impressive-looking badge and credentials, and I was presumed to have a "license to kill," if necessary.

My language ability improved because I spoke Vietnamese every day with my ARVN counterparts and the sources we interviewed. The ARVNs were capable soldiers and I felt safe with them as we moved around the area to meet with our sources. While working with the ARVN agents, I became very acquainted with Lt. Nguyen Huu Khanh. We became friends and he invited me to his wedding, scheduled for July 20, 1971, in Saigon.

The day before the wedding we received a report that the building across the street from where the reception was to be held was bombed, which gave me second thoughts. Lt. Khanh assured me the area was safe, and after my supervisor gave me permission, I figured the odds were against another incident in the same place.

I attended the wedding in civilian clothes, met his family, mingled with other guests and sampled the Vietnamese food. It was exactly the kind of immersion I prepared for when I studied the Vietnamese language and culture. I sometimes wondered what happened to Lt. Khanh and his bride after I left and after the United States completed its withdrawal. Were they able to escape Vietnam or did they melt into the population? Was he sent to a "re-education camp" or was he killed during the 1972 Easter Offensive or the 1975 takeover of South Vietnam? I'll never know.

Morale and Welfare, Circa 1971

The primary methods to connect with family and friends back home was either by a "phone patch" over a short-wave radio called MARS (Military Affiliate Radio Service), or letters through the U.S. Postal Service. For music and news, many of us used transistor radios. My mother occasionally sent me taped messages from home she recorded on a portable cassette recorder. The Armed Forces Radio Service (AFRS) kept us linked to events in the country and back in "the world," our term for the United States, the only world we knew before Vietnam. By 1965, AFRS was operating 24 hours per day. In addition to music, it provided command information spots on malaria pills, mosquito nets, R&R sites, venereal disease, the black market, and illegal war trophies.

In Vietnam, we connected with songs like "Paint It Black" by the Rolling Stones, "We Gotta Get Out of This Place" by the Animals, and "Fortunate Son" by Creedence Clearwater Revival; but for me personally, the song "American Woman" by the Guess Who resonated more. It expressed my feelings of denial about my relationship with Nancy and any girl I ever dated. I had "more important things to do."

When it came time to schedule my R&R, I asked other agents about the best places to visit. Some guys went to Japan or Australia, but one agent had recently returned from Hawaii and said the island of Maui was a great place for a getaway. He described it as a quiet, out-of-the-way place without the commercialism that existed in Honolulu. It sounded good to me, and I knew there were palm trees in Hawaii. Palm trees reminded me of spring break in Florida, senior year in college. Despite my attempt to deny any feelings for Nancy, we wrote to each other regularly and seemed to grow closer through our letters than when we were together. I wrote to her and asked if she would meet me in Hawaii. I was excited when she agreed, so I reserved an efficiency apartment on the beach in Maui.

On the day I was scheduled to leave, I boarded a Huey gunship (UH-1 helicopter equipped with 50-caliber machine guns and/or rocket pods) at Long Binh and flew to Tan Son Nhut Airport. It was the only time in Vietnam I flew on the iconic Huey helicopter. I was almost disappointed the door gunner didn't fire at some Viet Cong as we flew over the countryside. From Tan Son Nhut I caught a military flight to Hickam Air Field in Honolulu and reported to the R&R reception station. I caught a cab and checked into a hotel in Honolulu until Nancy arrived. The next day I met her at the Honolulu airport and we spent a night at the hotel before we booked an island flight to Maui for the remainder of my R&R.

On Maui, I rented a car and we enjoyed a week of sun, sand, and surf. We left the beach long enough to travel around the island and take in the sights. Our sightseeing included a train ride through the sugarcane fields near Lahaina, a visit on the sailing ship featured in the 1966 movie, *Hawaii*, and a drive to the peak of Haleakala Crater. One evening we had dinner at a restaurant near our hotel. Nancy decided to order a steak. When the waiter brought our order to the table, Nancy looked confused and asked the waiter if she received the wrong order.

The waiter replied, "It's shark steak, miss."

To a girl born and bred in Kansas, it was completely foreign to her. She apparently chose the wrong kind of steak. I reminded her she wasn't in Kansas anymore.

I eventually realized Nancy was more than just another girlfriend. She truly cared about me, sent regular letters and cards, and flew out to meet me in Hawaii at her own expense. Before leaving for R&R, I thought about what I wanted to do with my life after Vietnam and, besides having a good career, I knew I wanted a family and become the father I never had. I decided to propose to Nancy during R&R but I didn't have a ring to give her, so I did it with song lyrics I typed on a piece of paper before I left for Hawaii. The song was "More," by Kai Winding, a popular love song in 1963. At the end of the lyrics I typed, *Will you marry me?* I left it on her nightstand so she would see it when she woke up. The next morning, she read it and said yes.

I felt lucky she would take a chance on me. I would be gone for several more months and had no job prospects when I returned. The loneliness I felt in Vietnam was amplified by my desire to settle down someday and start a family. Fortunately, Nancy was willing to wait. We exchanged a romantic goodbye at the airport. The next day I reported to the R&R reception station for my return flight to Vietnam to complete the last few months of my tour. Nancy's heart was the biggest 'win' of my life.

An Assortment of Duties

During my year in Vietnam I wrote dozens of reports for higher headquarters as a result of my contacts with our confidential sources. I had no idea how valuable my input was to the overall intelligence effort, but I approached each interview seriously and wrote my reports as if each one was important. I made frequent visits both inside and outside the base to interview sources. When we went "outside the wire", our weapons were locked and loaded. We never encountered the enemy, but the potential was always there.

On one mission, I traveled with three other agents in a Jeep to interview a Vietnamese informant at Bear Cat, about 30 miles east of Long Binh. Bear Cat was one of the larger U.S. bases in Vietnam and was accessible by a paved highway. The road was eerily quiet, bordered on each side by dense forest about 100 yards from the road. We were in full uniform with web gear, helmets, and packs. I sat in the back seat with my M16 locked and loaded. My job was to watch our right flank. In case of an ambush our plan was to speed up and move out of the kill zone as fast as possible. We were lightly armed and no match for a determined enemy attack.

During the Tet Offensive three years earlier, the Viet Cong had massed hundreds of fighters in the Bear Cat area as part of their offensive. By 1971 the area had been cleared and it was relatively safe for travel, but we were still cautious. Our counteroffensive during Tet virtually annihilated the VC and they were no longer an effective fighting force. We arrived at our destination without incident and interviewed a female South Vietnamese informant. As a junior special agent, I wasn't directly involved in the interview and don't recall the specifics, only that she was questioned about her knowledge of a Viet Cong sympathizer in the area. Afterward we hopped back in the Jeep and returned to Long Binh to send in our report. I merely acted as a warm body to fulfill the force-protection requirements.

One evening the base was placed on high alert, due to information that an attack was imminent. We weren't ordered to battle stations, so our weapons remained locked in the arms rack. Apparently, our commander decided we wouldn't be needed to defend our area, so we were instructed to wear helmets and flak jacket and hunker down in our billets. We huddled in a room for most of the night while we talked, drank beer, and played cards. The next day it was reported a couple mortar rounds landed inside the base, several hundred yards from our barracks. They caused some minor damage, but no one was injured.

I had some extra time one day and decided to take a drive off base in my Jeep (which I nicknamed Nancy). I don't recall why I went; maybe it was just to escape from work and enjoy a bit of freedom. I drove down an unfamiliar dirt road and suddenly realized there was no other traffic around. This was unusual because there was always some military or civilian traffic in the area. My instinct told me to get back to base before I ran into an ambush or a road mine. I made a U-turn in the middle of the road and returned to the base. It was the only time I ventured off base alone.

Sometimes personal-security measures became too relaxed on an American base. During an afternoon trip to Bien Hoa to pick up classified documents, we stopped at a bar on the base for drinks and to relax before we returned to Long Binh. I didn't give a thought that classified documents and alcohol don't mix; apparently neither did the other agents. I carried the classified documents in a folder and put them on a chair next to me while I had a beer and discussed our day with another agent. There were a few locals in the bar; so, always taking the opportunity to improve my Vietnamese, I struck up a conversation with a young woman. After about 15 minutes the senior agent signaled it was time to leave. I went out to our Jeep and suddenly realized I had left the folder with the classified documents in the bar. I ran inside to retrieve the documents and found the folder on the chair where I'd left it. I looked through the papers to make sure nothing had been removed or disturbed and, satisfied nothing was compromised, I returned to the Jeep where the other agents waited. I received some good-natured ribbing from the other agents about how a woman distracted me, but they didn't seem concerned I'd forgotten the documents, because I got them back safely.

Contraband, Sex, and Drugs

We routinely assisted the MPs with base security. One of the threats we faced was infiltration by Viet Cong sympathizers working on the base. Although Vietnamese civilians were vetted before they were hired, there was no way to be certain of their loyalties. I would occasionally take a turn monitoring the gates at the end of the workday when the Vietnamese laborers left to return to home. They were employed mostly to clean barracks and do laundry. We worked with the MPs to check for contraband, especially for any official or classified documents and any hand-drawn maps of the area. Most of the items we confiscated consisted of cleaning products, toiletries, snack foods, and some U.S. currency, usually received for sexual favors. It was common knowledge some female workers solicited soldiers for sex and they might be paid in U.S. currency, which had more value than the Vietnamese piastre or đong. Those who were caught were dismissed from employment, but to my knowledge there was no formal punishment for the soldiers.

Some of us played cards occasionally at detachment headquarters and one day the supply sergeant came in with a *mama san* (older woman). He got our attention and said she was willing to give blow jobs, only twenty dollars. We took one look at her as she smiled and revealed a nasty-looking set of teeth that had turned black from years of chewing betel nut, a habit popular among older Vietnamese. We shook our heads in disgust and continued with our card game. None of us was that desperate for sex, but it was available for anyone willing to look for it.

There was a steam bath on base that once served as a pleasure palace. Some of the Vietnamese girls who gave massages were also prostitutes, and anyone who wanted to pay for it could get sex with their massage. The Army closed the operation down around 1970 and purged it of corruption before reopening the facility as a legitimate steam bath and massage parlor. Off base, however, sex was readily available, particularly in Saigon. Unprotected sex often resulted in STDs. Unfortunately, it was a common occurrence at the medical clinics, who treated STDs as routinely as they would someone with a common cold.

At one point during my tour I was assigned to investigate the source of illegal drugs used by our soldiers. I was sent to the base rehabilitation center, where soldiers could voluntarily admit themselves to detoxify without repercussion. I was reminded of the Paul Revere and the Raiders song, "Kicks," which became the first anti-drug song. It proclaimed drugs didn't bring peace of mind and they led to an aimless life. Message notwithstanding, I found it futile to identify the drugs' source because the soldiers were in a state of withdrawal and their speech was often incoherent. I didn't press too hard with my questioning, choosing to give them a break for trying to get detoxified.

Return of a POW

In October 1971, I was involved in an incident that held more significance than I realized at the time. Our detachment took custody of a U.S. soldier held prisoner by the North Vietnamese. Sgt. John C. Sexton was the first American POW released in more than two years. I was outside our headquarters building when he arrived with an MP escort. His uniform looked disheveled and he appeared to be in poor physical condition.

Sexton carried a note with him when he arrived. It would have been difficult for me to translate because it was written in the North Vietnamese, or Hanoi, dialect. I had only a cursory introduction to the Hanoi dialect at language school, so I gave the note to one of our ARVN counterparts to translate. It was from the North Vietnamese, offering to release Douglas Ramsey, a Vietnamese-speaking State Department officer, who had been held by the communists since 1966 (and whom they believed was a U.S. intelligence officer), in exchange for a high-ranking North Vietnamese intelligence officer named Nguyen Tai.

Tai was the highest ranking North Vietnamese officer ever captured in the Vietnam War. He was captured by the South Vietnamese in December 1970, and at the time he was the chief of security for the Saigon-Gia Dinh Party Committee. The United States released a North Vietnamese officer in Cambodia as a reciprocal gesture in the hope the move would spur the liberation of more U.S. POWs.

Negotiations for a prisoner exchange of Douglas Ramsey for Nguyen Tai quickly broke down, but the note Sexton carried apparently made Tai's South Vietnamese captors realize he was too valuable to put his life in jeopardy, so they immediately stopped his torture and interrogation. Tai claimed the North Vietnamese Minister of Interior, Tran Quoc Hoan, told him after the war was over their leadership realized the chances for an actual prisoner exchange prior to a final peace agreement were poor, but their immediate objective was to "make it impossible for the Americans and their puppets to kill me"

After he was released to us by the military police, Sgt. Sexton was transported to an Army hospital in Saigon for recuperation and observation. Several of us took turns as armed guards at his bedside to record anything he might say, in case it could be used for intelligence purposes.

According to a book by Monika Jensen-Stevenson, *The Last Secret of the War in Vietnam*, Sgt. Sexton purportedly said that once he reached American lines, "no one on his own side was interested, other than to impress upon him that he was to keep his mouth shut." Sexton believed his own government was convinced he had been turned (as a spy) by the communists and that was why his captors (the North Vietnamese) released him. There was never any proof he had collaborated with the enemy.

I doubted that no one on the American side was interested because I witnessed his arrival at the 702nd MID and sat with him for several hours during his recuperation in the hospital in Saigon. In my opinion, we were quite interested in him and what he had to say, and to my knowledge no one–at least in the 702nd MID–had told him to keep his mouth shut.

During my tour, I had the opportunity to take a three day in-country R&R at Cam Ranh Bay. Cam Ranh was a huge military installation on the coast about a quarter of the way between Saigon and the North Vietnamese border. It had a deep-water port and an inland lake the Americans called Tiger Lake. It was a popular area for U.S. military personnel to take a break in the country. I took full advantage of the recreation activities there and water skied, swam in the lake, and visited a nightclub on base. At the nightclub, I shared a pitcher of beer with a couple of other soldiers as scantily clad Vietnamese go-go girls entertained us on stage. The attractive dancers held our attention as they cavorted to popular American songs. The soldiers I sat with were from an infantry unit. As we talked I was struck by the glaze in their eyes that reflected the "thousand-yard stare," a phrase used to describe battle-weary soldiers. For me, the visit to Cam Ranh Bay was a brief respite from my duties, which often resembled an office job more than combat duty. For them, it was a break from the stress of combat and day-to-day survival.

The next day I spent some time at the beach on Tiger Lake and listened to a Vietnamese rock band mangle the Creedence Clearwater Revival song, "Have You Ever Seen the Rain?" I chuckled to myself as they mimicked English lyrics to the song. Rain was pronounced "wain." It was especially interesting to me as a student of the Vietnamese language.

When I wasn't on duty, I could relax and enjoy some semblance of a normal life. Long Binh had several morale, welfare, and recreational activities available to us, including the typical amenities of a large U.S. military base: an in-ground swimming pool, a weight room, a volleyball pit, an Oriental-style restaurant, barber shop, and a large PX. One of my favorite diversions was to visit the ice cream truck that traveled around the base. It was a nice touch of Americana.

As one of the main centers of American operations in Vietnam, Long Binh hosted several USO shows. I attended two of them during my tour. Bob Hope performed there on his Christmas tour in 1970. I was involved in a mission that day and caught the last part of his show from a distance as I returned to base. In August 1971 the reigning Miss America, Phyllis George, came to Long Binh with a troupe of women to entertain us, escorted by a military police detachment. That time I was able to see the show and get close enough for some pictures.

Another diversion presented itself when a small brown mutt wandered into our area; we named him Drufus and adopted him as our mascot. One of the guys outfitted him with a shirt he cut out from a khaki uniform and sewed stripes on it. Renamed Sgt. Drufus, the dog remained with us for the duration of my tour.

I become more immersed in the Vietnamese culture and sampled the local food while speaking Vietnamese every day. I acquired a taste for Nuac Mam, a popular spicy fish sauce used for dipping and to flavor many dishes. It was eventually brought to America by Vietnamese immigrants. I also sampled a bottle of Ba Moui Ba (33) beer at a bar in Saigon, just for the experience. It was the only beer produced in Vietnam. Nicknamed "Panther Piss" by American GIs, it was bitter and had the clarity and body of a bad urine sample; the worst beer I ever tasted, but it was cheap.

For souvenirs, aside from a photo album I put together, a ceremonial sword in a wooden sheath was my only reminder of my time in Vietnam. I used it to mimic a photo of my estranged father taken while he was in the Pacific Theater during World War II. He posed bare-chested with a sword in each hand, so I had a photo taken of me, bare-chested, holding the sword I purchased. Like father like son. Sort of.

Everyone who spent time in Vietnam had a different experience. Dale, who served in Vietnam with the 3rd Marine Division, participated in Operation Dewey Canyon during 1969, the last major offensive by the U.S. Marine Corps in Vietnam. He also spent some time at Khe Sanh. I considered myself lucky to have avoided combat, but Dale was blessed to have survived it. The contrast between our tours became obvious when I sent home a picture of myself cleaning my M16 rifle at a picnic table outside our wooden two-story building. My mother showed it to Dale, who asked if I was really in Vietnam because it didn't resemble anything he'd seen over there.

Late in 1971, I received orders for an early release from active duty due to the ongoing reduction of troops. I was offered a $10,000 bonus to stay for another year, but I didn't want to press my luck. I just wanted to go home, get a regular job, marry Nancy, and start a family.

During my tour of duty, I made one attempt to get employment after I returned home. I liked investigative work and thought the FBI would be a great place to work, so I sent a letter to FBI headquarters in Washington, D.C. I explained I was a special agent doing counterintelligence work in Vietnam and had a bachelor's degree in business. In response, I received a personally signed letter from J. Edgar Hoover in which he explained attorneys did their investigative work, but I was welcome to apply for a position as a fingerprint clerk when I returned from overseas. I was excited to receive a response from the director himself, but realized it was a far stretch for me to qualify for the position I wanted. When I returned home I looked into going to law school and took the Law School Admission Test in Buffalo. I scored too low to get accepted and I made no further attempt at law school. The closest I came to working in the legal system was about 15 years later, when I served as a deputy court clerk with the U.S. District Courts.

I was eventually placed on a flight manifest to leave the country during the first week of December 1971. During my final days in Vietnam I received my first decoration, an Army Commendation Medal for meritorious service; the most notable thing about it was the citation was signed by Gen. Creighton Abrams, commander of U.S. forces in Vietnam during my tour of duty.

Gen. Abrams had built a reputation as an aggressive and successful armor commander during World War II. His service record was so remarkable that when the Army developed its next generation main battle tank, they called it the M1 Abrams. He implemented President Nixon's Vietnamization Program, which gradually turned over all operations to the South Vietnamese and started the American withdrawal. From 1972 to 1974, he served as the Army Chief of Staff. Gen. Abrams was also known for conceiving the Abrams Doctrine, which became the basis for the Total Force Structure implemented in the post-Vietnam years. A research report by Lt. Col. Brian D. Jones dated May 2004, titled "The Abrams Doctrine: Total Force Foundation or Enduring Fallacy?" stated the intent of the Abrams Doctrine focused on an active and reserve "force structure balance ... to insure the *relevance* (emphasis added) of the reserve component" by using them as round-out units to fill the requirements of the active component. The Abrams Doctrine would affect me years later during my service in the Army Reserve, when my unit was "capstoned" to an active-duty division as a round-out unit.

Although I never personally met Gen. Abrams, many years later I met his son, Brig. Gen. (Ret.) Creighton Abrams, Jr., at an annual meeting of the Army Historical Foundation. I introduced myself and mentioned his father personally signed my citation for the Army Commendation Medal. He replied I was lucky because he couldn't even get his father to sign his report cards when he was in school.

On March 30, 1972, about three months after I left Vietnam, the North Vietnamese launched the Easter Offensive and managed to get inside the perimeter at Long Binh before being repulsed. As the largest and one of the most-secure bases in Vietnam, it seemed to me it would be almost impossible to penetrate the perimeter. It was one of several times I was blessed with good timing.

Reflections on Vietnam

Long Binh became obsolete after the U.S. Army left in 1975. According to an article that appeared in the *Army Times* dated October 1996, there was virtually no evidence Long Binh Post had even existed by then. After the war, it became a large industrial park, where tennis shoes, bikes, and clothing were produced. Saigon was renamed Ho Chi Minh City and Vietnam was united into one country.

From time to time, I reflected on the meaning of our involvement and the sacrifices of the 58,267 Americans who died there–and the hundreds of thousands who served there. According to statistics released by the Vietnam Veterans of America, 304,000 returned home seriously wounded, 31% experienced post-traumatic stress disorder (PTSD), and 2.6 million affected by Agent Orange cope with debilitating illnesses such as prostate cancer and diabetes.

Did they die in vain, in a futile cause, as many who protested our involvement in Vietnam claimed? I don't believe so. I believe we were there because of a commitment we made to South Vietnam, and our involvement was for a good cause: to preserve the freedom and independence of the South Vietnamese people. Gen. William C. Westmoreland, who preceded Gen. Abrams as commanding general, U.S. forces Vietnam, stated, "I do not believe that the men (and women) who served in Vietnam have been given the credit they deserve. It was a difficult war against an unorthodox enemy."

That the war was a series of tactical victories followed by a strategic defeat was pointedly illustrated by a North Vietnamese colonel in a verbal exchange with an American colonel in Hanoi during April 1975.

The American colonel said, "You know you never defeated us on the battlefield."

The North Vietnamese colonel pondered it for a moment and replied, "That may be so, but it is also irrelevant."

In his book, *In Retrospect, the Tragedy and Lessons of Vietnam*, Robert McNamara, the U.S. Secretary of Defense during Vietnam, admitted a series of fragmented decisions by our political leaders with no unifying goal or exit strategy ultimately led to the poor prosecution of the war. The Johnson administration misjudged the possibility of Chinese involvement, the will of the North Vietnamese regime to unify the country, and the damage caused by a corrupt and ineffective South Vietnamese government. McNamara was one of the architects of the Vietnam War and one of President Johnson's advisors on the prosecution of the war. In that book, McNamara admitted he was terribly wrong in his assessment of the situation.

In a new perspective published in *The American Legion* magazine dated July 2016, William Stearman suggested we have failed to view Vietnam from a historical perspective. Stearman, a retired U.S. Foreign Service officer and author, served on the White House National Security Council staff under four presidents. He served in Vietnam from December 1965 to September 1967. He asserted one of our original objectives in Vietnam was to prevent a "domino effect" in Indochina, which was put forth by President Dwight D. Eisenhower in 1954. The theory was if we didn't confront Communism in Vietnam, it would spread to other countries in the region. Stearman wrote it was generally overlooked that our purpose in Vietnam was to prevent the fall of other countries in Southeast Asia to Communism, and we succeeded.

History has shown there was no domino effect and Communism did not spread as feared. Although Vietnam is a still a communist state, it has become more of a free-market economy, which has greatly improved because of American presence and influence.

Long Binh, December 1970

Enjoying the Hometown News, 1971

Special Agent at Work, 1971

My Aston Martin Coupe

Nancy on Maui During my R&R from Vietnam, 1971

With Nancy at Vietnam Veterans of America Chapter dinner, Dec. 2017

Chapter 5
Marriage and the Search for a Career
(1972-1975)

My flight out of Vietnam took me to Fort Lewis, Washington, after a refueling stop in Alaska. Before I left I received a routine security debriefing, in which I was reminded not to disclose any classified material and I was not to attribute any statements made to me to any person or document.

At Fort Lewis, I was given a new dress-green uniform, served a complimentary steak dinner at the mess hall and issued a plane ticket to New Jersey, where I reported to Fort Dix for a discharge physical and out processing from active duty. I felt like I'd been in a time warp for 12 months. There were new clothing styles in the stores, new movies that came out over the past year, and new songs. When I returned home I felt alienated in a country that didn't acknowledge or appreciate Vietnam veterans. As a result of the 12-month rotations, many soldiers returned home individually rather than with their units. I was given an early discharge after three years of regular Army service but would remain in the inactive Reserve for the remainder of my six-year enlistment.

I was met at the Rochester airport by my mother, grandmother Orsino and a cousin, Bob Osborne, who served with the Marines in Korea. My family was glad to have me home safe, but they remained quiet about Vietnam. I was just happy to be home and didn't talk much about it.

After I settled in at home, I purchased my first new car with money I sent home to my mother while I was in Vietnam. My savings fell short of the cash needed for the car I wanted, a 1972 Camaro, so I paid $3,000 cash for my second choice: a silver 1972 Chevrolet Vega GT. I ordered it equipped with a posi-traction rear axle and four-on-the-floor manual transmission, chrome-magnesium wheels, and an innovative aluminum-block engine.

Soon afterward I called Nancy, who lived in Virginia and was employed with the General Service Administration. We set a wedding date for June 1972 in Penn Yan. We discussed moving to the D.C. area after the wedding, but as it turned out, Nancy was unhappy with the work conditions and ended up quitting her government job. We spent Christmas together in Penn Yan, then drove to Maryland to visit Dale and his wife, Susan. I gave Nancy a diamond engagement ring at Dale and Sue's place on New Year's Eve. After January 1, I rented a U-Haul truck and loaded Nancy's belongings for the trip back to Penn Yan. She lived in my grandparents' home with my mother and my sister, Rosemary, until the wedding. I had no prospects for employment and shared an apartment with my brother Gene in a two-family house behind my grandparents', which they also owned. I vowed to have a job and a place to live before we were married.

In May of 1972, the month before we were married, I found work as a security guard with Doyle Detective Agency in the Rochester area. Assigned to the Xerox plant in Webster, east of Rochester, I found an apartment to rent in nearby Fairport.

We were married June 10, 1972, at St. Michael's Catholic Church in Penn Yan, where I was baptized, received my First Communion, Confirmation, and was an altar server in my youth. Several members of Nancy's family came from Holton, Kansas, for the wedding. They included her parents, her maternal grandmother Olds, her youngest brother Steve and her brother John, who served as the ring bearer. All my family and several relatives attended. Nancy's maid of honor was Darlene Curtin, her best friend while she worked in Washington, D.C.; they'd met while working for the government. Dale was my best man.

Two relatives from the Gigliotti family in Geneva attended our wedding: Uncle John and his sister-in-law, Aunt Sue, who years later helped me connect with my estranged father. My mother arranged the reception at the VFW hall in Penn Yan. Sadly, Grandpa Orsino's health had gradually deteriorated from the stroke he suffered in 1968 and he passed away the day before our wedding. After the wedding, we drove to our new apartment in Fairport and enjoyed a short honeymoon in Alexandria Bay, New York, which included a tour of the Thousand Islands area.

Scott Banfield, a cousin on the Condella side of my family who sang professionally, performed "We've Only Just Begun" at our wedding ceremony. The lyrics to that 1970 tune popularized by The Carpenters, were embraced by many newlyweds in the early 1970s. Nine and a half months later, our first child, Gregory, arrived in March 1973.

In the fall of 1973, I received a letter from the Department of the Army. I still had three years left on my enlistment contract, so I was placed in a control group of service members available to be called up if needed. The letter advised me I could join an Army Reserve unit and get paid as an active reservist. I would attend training one weekend a month and perform two weeks of active-duty training each year. As newlyweds with a small child, the additional income would supplement what I made as a security guard, so Nancy agreed we could try it for a year.

In December 1973, I was assigned to Headquarters Company, 98th Division (Training), based in Rochester. I retained the rank of sergeant, and once I started attending weekend drills, I found I enjoyed being in a military outfit again. Part of the attraction was the pace was more laid back and less stressful than my time in the regular Army. I was assigned as an intelligence analyst, a field marginally related to my duties in Vietnam. Analyst duties were more administrative in nature than my previous role as a counterintelligence agent. In theory, an analyst would review information gathered from various sources in the field to determine its usefulness and aid the tactical commander to make decisions. However, in a domestic peacetime reserve, there wasn't much to analyze, so I assisted an officer who inspected the internal security measures of our subordinate units. The inspected items included control measures for keys, procedures for arms-room access, and security procedures used to handle and store classified information. I'd learned my lesson about proper handling of classified documents in Vietnam.

Job Hopping

By the latter part of 1973 I had advanced within the Doyle Detective Agency to the rank of sergeant. I was given more responsibility and more interesting assignments, but eventually I felt compelled to look for another line of work. I decided to leave after I inadvertently botched a surveillance assignment to discover thefts of Xerox property.

I received instructions to position myself in one of the buildings where I could not be seen and observe employees who might steal tools or equipment. One evening, dressed in civilian clothing and posing as an employee, I climbed unseen to an upper level, to the heating and air conditioning units overlooking the work floor. The chief security officer suggested it as a good observation post.

When I reached the observation post, I discovered an employee sound asleep there. I should have aborted the surveillance, but I had been given orders and wasn't about to retreat from such an intriguing assignment. I assumed a prone position to reduce my profile and began to observe activities on the floor with a pair of binoculars. After a half hour passed, the sleeping employee woke up and spotted me. When he asked what

I was doing, I thought quickly and told him I was assigned to observe safety measures, but my position had been compromised, and he alerted the employees on the floor. I left the area and reported the incident to my supervisor. Our "spy game" had failed. Embarrassed, the next day I resumed my uniformed security patrols at the plant.

Soon I began a search for other employment more in line with my business degree, the kind of position my grandparents had envisioned for me. After several inquiries and a few interviews, I had no offers, so I hired an employment agency to find me a position with a better income.

I eventually signed on with the Rite-Aid Corporation as a management trainee at one of their drug stores in Rochester. After I completed an on-the-job training program through the GI Bill, I was assigned as the manager of a small Rite-Aid retail store in downtown Rochester. The store had no pharmacy and employed two part-time clerks. To my surprise, I was asked to suggest a salary to them and I naively said $140 per week. It was the only time I had the chance to name my salary and I blew it! I based the figure on something I read, that a weekly salary should be at least one fourth of my monthly rent or mortgage payment. Unfortunately, I didn't consider deductions for taxes, Social Security and living expenses. If I had done more research, I would have known the average income at the time was around $200 a week and bargained for a higher amount. Still, the title of manager, along with the increase in pay from security work, was enough to satisfy me at the time. I worked 60 hours a week and did everything from unloading trucks and labeling merchandise to stocking shelves, operating the cash register, and making deposits.

After several weeks, it became apparent shoplifting was a problem in the store, so I focused my attention more on the shoplifters than management of the store. I never prosecuted anyone because the few people I caught had only taken an inexpensive piece of merchandise, such as a pain reliever or cold medicine. I simply took it away from them and returned it to the shelf, unaware people could abuse over-the-counter drugs. I was so paranoid about shoplifting, I rationalized if there was less merchandise on the shelves, there would be less to steal. I deliberately reduced the stock of some commonly shoplifted items. My failure to keep the store fully stocked became a point of contention with my supervisor, who visited on a regular basis to check on store operations. Modern anti-theft technology did not exist yet and I was told there wasn't much I could do to prevent it; regardless, I was directed to keep the shelves fully stocked.

One of the duties I hated most was the weekly Saturday-morning cigarette inventory before the store opened. As a non-smoker, I resented the sale of cigarettes. It seemed counterintuitive to sell cigarettes in a store that featured health and beauty aids.

One evening about midnight I received a call at home from the police, who informed me I needed to come to the store right away. A drunk driver had lost control of his vehicle and crashed into the front of my store, breaking a large plate-glass window. I rushed to the store and obtained a tarp to place over the opening. I spent the rest of the night guarding against looters until the company replaced the window. I swatted away the hands of a few would-be looters who reached inside the tarp during the night. The operation and management of the small store was essentially a one-man task. I became frustrated and felt I couldn't manage everything to my satisfaction, so I resigned about a year later. The experience ended my attempt at a business career.

Nancy and I, along with our infant son Gregory, moved back to Penn Yan in 1974 where I found a position with Heywood Wakefield, a furniture-manufacturing company that had recently relocated there. I caught on to the work quickly and was given responsibility for operating a double-end tenon saw, the largest and most-complicated saw in the plant. After a while, I became concerned about the poor working conditions and lack of benefits, so as a business major with a couple of labor and management courses under my belt, I spoke with some fellow employees during our breaks about starting a union to improve work conditions and increase benefits.

When I returned to work after Christmas break, I was informed that I was fired for poor workmanship and insubordination. It came as a complete shock; my work had always been acceptable, and I never disobeyed my supervisor.

I told my mother, who informed her uncle Pat Condella (one of Grandma Orsino's brothers), who happened to be a union steward at a local clothing plant. He contacted the National Labor Relations Board, which sent an investigator to Penn Yan to interview me. Upon investigation, he found other workers had also been dismissed. We signed sworn statements and the company was charged with unfair labor practices. Further investigation revealed Heywood Wakefield was a "runaway" company that fled Massachusetts to avoid unionization. The company settled out of court and all the dismissed employees were given back pay from the date of dismissal with the stipulation they would not return to work for Heywood Wakefield. In retrospect, the company managed to rid itself of a few union rabble rousers in exchange for a few thousand dollars. It was a good deal for them.

My next employment venture involved part-time police work. In 1974 there was no requirement for part-time officers to attend a police academy. In Penn Yan, I received on-the-job training on the New York State Vehicle and Traffic Law, dispatch procedures, and fingerprinting. I was issued a uniform, a badge, and a .38-caliber pistol, with which I had become familiar during the counterintelligence-agent course at Fort Holabird. Strangely, I was never required to qualify with it as a police officer. I was assigned to a full-time officer for a day or two of training and sent into the streets, primarily for traffic enforcement.

My job with the Penn Yan Police led me to another part-time position with the Dundee Police. Dundee was a small village about 10 miles south of Penn Yan with one full-time officer who acted as the police chief. He was a middle-aged good 'ole country boy whose home doubled as the police office. The village had one patrol car, which the other part-time officer and I shared.

Dundee's weekly newspaper covered the local news, and we were soon featured in a full-page article. During my interview with the reporter, I stated I was "just a small-town boy at heart," which became the headline for my interview.

Dale and Gene worked together for a time as deputies with the Yates County Sheriff. Ironically, the three Mitchell brothers were then all involved in police work, following in the footsteps of our Grandfather Gigliotti, who retired as a sergeant with the Geneva Police Department, and our great uncle, Frank Condella, a dispatcher for the Yates County Sheriff.

While on patrol in Dundee one night, I stopped a vehicle on a rural stretch of road outside town and radioed it in to the county dispatcher in Penn Yan. I pursued the vehicle for speeding within the village limits before it stopped about a mile outside of town. Dale was on patrol with the Sheriff's Department and happened to be in the area when he heard my radio call. He pulled up behind my patrol car and waited while I wrote a speeding ticket; then I walked back to thank him for the backup. It felt good to have him there in case anything went wrong. He was aware a routine stop could go wrong at any time. Dale was an experienced and decorated law-enforcement officer who joined the Baltimore Police Department after the Marines and received a citation for bravery before he and Sue returned to Penn Yan.

Earlier in 1974 I transferred to the 770th Engineer Company in Penn Yan, so I wouldn't have to make the one-hour drive to Rochester each month. The unit's primary mission was to build roads and airfields. Our two-week annual training in the summer of 1974 was held at Fort Pickett, Virginia. We spent most of the time on bivouac in the field to practice defensive tactics. The nights were hot, so I slept in my underwear that first night. We were camped in a heavily wooded area that was home to a critter I'd never encountered before. Even training for Vietnam couldn't prepare me for the forest.

The next morning, I woke up in my tent and noticed several small bugs embedded in my arms and legs. I showed them to someone who informed me they were ticks. One of the guys tried to burn them out with a cigarette. When that failed I was taken to the medical clinic, where a medic used a pair of tweezers to pull out about 12 ticks that had engorged themselves with my blood. After that I was careful to cover up more and used an insect repellent on my skin.

In summer 1975 Nancy and I awaited the birth of our second child, Stephen, who was born August 1 at Geneva General Hospital, the closest hospital with a maternity ward. At the time, I held three part-time jobs; with the Penn Yan Police, the Dundee Police, and a night job at a grocery store in Penn Yan. I began a search for a full-time position to give my young family a regular source of income and was hired by a local company that built bus bodies. One of my duties was to operate a forklift, but I considered the job temporary until I found something more fulfilling. I enjoyed police work but there were no full-time positions available, nor was any civil-service exam scheduled for prospective candidates.

I eventually learned about a vacancy as a police officer with the Veterans' Administration (VA) Hospital in Syracuse. I submitted an application and was interviewed by the chief of the Bath VA police. Bath was about 30 miles South of Penn Yan, but the chief lived in Penn Yan. The chief of the Syracuse VA police asked him to interview me on his behalf since he was near me. I was hired in August 1975 and began a career with the federal government that would last until my retirement.

Because I was moving my family to the Syracuse area for my new job, I decided to leave the 770th Engineer Company in Penn Yan and quit the Reserves. My unit administrator encouraged me to find another unit in the Syracuse area and said if I continued I could get a pension after 20 years of credible service. He added it would be a shame to throw away the time I spent in the service up to that point. I told him I was done with military service and wanted to concentrate on a civilian career that offered more opportunity.

In July, I drove to Syracuse and met with Richard Salisbury, the chief of police at the VA Hospital. A retired Air Force chief master sergeant, he had an outgoing, congenial personality and looked younger than his years. Chief Salisbury had established a great rapport with the hospital administrator and was a progressive leader who fought to eliminate the perception of us merely as security guards. He did much to raise the credibility of the hospital police as a legitimate law-enforcement agency. A fellow officer, Tom Simpson, and his wife, Rose, offered to let me live at his house in Camillus for a nominal rent until I was able to find a place for my family.

I commuted back to Penn Yan on weekends and eventually found an apartment in Camillus. In September, Nancy and I moved from Penn Yan with our two young children. Several weeks later I was sent to the VA Police Academy in Little Rock, Arkansas. The two-week course consisted of criminal law, investigative and arrest procedures, and practical exercises on the use of handcuffs and Mace, a spray irritant used to subdue uncooperative or violent suspects. In order to appreciate the physical effects of Mace, we were required to be sprayed with it. We concocted a poetic phrase for the exercise, "Sprayed in the face with Mace." It stung my eyes and sinuses for a few minutes and reminded me of an incident I had in Vietnam.

One sunny day I drove into Saigon to visit Military Assistance Command Vietnam headquarters and encountered a street demonstration. The Vietnamese police had just fired tear gas at the demonstrators to control the crowd. The wind caused the tear gas to drift and it stung my eyes, blinding me momentarily. I had to pull my Jeep onto the side of the road for a few minutes until I could see clearly enough to continue.

After my graduation from the hospital police academy, I was given a regular day shift at the VA Hospital in Syracuse. I enjoyed police work and began what I thought would be a long career. After about a year, however, I realized I had limited opportunity for promotion. Chief Salisbury was relatively young and would be there for several more years, so I applied and was hired for a position in the medical-administration department of the hospital. I worked there for several months but gradually became annoyed with the number of cigarette smokers in the office. I even wore a face mask to avoid the secondhand smoke but decided the only way to get away from it entirely was to look for other employment. A conversation with a fellow VA police officer led me back to the Army Reserve full time.

Wedding Day, June 10, 1972

Grandma Orsino, Me, Nancy, Mom

With Nancy's Grandma, Flora Olds, and parents, Erma & Bill Riley

First federal employment, 1975; Receiving VA Hospital Police Academy graduation certificate

Chapter 6
Dual Careers and a Commission (1976-1986)

That fellow officer, Wayne Coye, and I became friends at work; we sometimes got together socially with our wives, usually at each other's homes. When I mentioned my dissatisfaction with the amount of smoking in the medical-administration office and desire to look for other work, Wayne said his Army Reserve unit had a full-time civilian position open for a supply technician. It was a civil affairs unit with several officer slots available.

That last bit of information piqued my interest. I tried twice to obtain a commission, and by 1976 had pretty much given up on the idea. First, poor grades washed me out of the ROTC program at Bowling Green. After I enlisted, I applied to officer-candidate school but was turned down. I didn't know anything about the civil affairs branch but I was interested in the job vacancy, so I decided to follow up on Wayne's tip. I visited the 403rd Civil Affairs Company during the summer of 1977 and spoke with Carl Liberatore, the unit administrator, who was a retired colonel.

Carl, as he preferred to be called, was about 5'6" tall with a solid build and formerly served as the unit commander. He was married to a tall, elegant-looking German woman he met while on Occupation duty after World War II. Carl had a dynamic personality and ran the unit on a day-to-day basis, but the unit commander was a Reserve officer. I filled out an application for the unit-supply technician and Carl screened me for the commander. During my interview with Carl I inquired about the officer slots Wayne had mentioned. He said my business degree and prior active-duty service in counterintelligence made me a good fit for the civil affairs branch. The supply technician was a

105

dual-status position, which meant I also had to be a member of the Reserve unit where I worked as a civilian. Carl said if I were hired he would discuss the possibility of a direct commission for me with the commander. The position sounded like a great opportunity. It paid more than I made at the VA Medical Center and I would work in an office where no one smoked. An added benefit was that my prior federal service, accrued leave time, and retirement benefits earned from the VA would transfer to the new position.

I was referred to the commander, Lt. Col. Robert E. Gale, an attorney with a private practice in Syracuse. He had the final authority to hire full-time employees into the unit and assign unit members to positions on the organizational chart. Bob Gale was a career Reserve officer with previous active-duty experience. He came across as an aloof, introspective man who spoke deliberately, as if he mentally processed the impact of each word before he spoke it.

The interview went well, and I was hired as unit-supply technician at the 403rd Civil Affairs Company in Liverpool, New York. I later suspected his decision was based more on Carl Liberatore's recommendation than on his assessment of me during the interview. As the former commander and current unit administrator, Carl wielded considerable influence in the unit. Because I was classified as a dual-status civilian employee for the Army, I had to re-enlist in the Army Reserve. I was assured I wouldn't have to go through basic training again and I could keep my former rank, so I re-enlisted as a sergeant. In September 1977, I began what became a career in the Army Reserve. During my active-duty time I had never heard of the civil affairs branch, so I rode a sharp learning curve to understand it.

Lt. Col. Gale told me I would be a "key" person in the unit – but I didn't realize the word had a double meaning; I carried keys to virtually every area of the reserve center. I was issued keys to the building, keys to the unit's office, keys to the maintenance building and tool cages, keys to the key control box, and keys to the supply room and equipment cages. I was also entrusted with the combination to the arms-room vault. During the week I was a civilian employee of the U.S. government, and one weekend a month I served as a sergeant in the Army Reserve. I enjoyed the work and felt I had an important role: managing the supply and logistics functions for the unit so it could perform its mission on active duty if it was ever mobilized.

Carl Liberatore was my civilian supervisor, which gave us daily opportunity to get to know each other. He was quite personable and I felt more at home when, during talk about our families, I explained I came from an Italian family. He told me he was also Italian and was originally from Geneva. I mentioned my father's family was from Geneva and my grandfather Gigliotti was a police officer there for many years. He recognized the name and told me about an encounter with him when he was a boy. My grandfather caught young Carl attempting to steal a watermelon from the front of a grocery store, whereupon he was scolded and sent home. I thought it was an amazing coincidence. It eventually became apparent Carl had a mind like a trap. He could recall personnel details and Army regulations that amazed me, but his typically congenial personality masked a bulldog-like tenacity to get even if someone crossed him. He was a friend and mentor to many people in the unit and he knew how to expedite matters through the Army's bureaucracy.

During weekend training as a reservist, I was under Lt. Col. Gale's command, but as the supply sergeant I reported directly to Capt. Julius Balogh, the unit-supply officer. As a civilian, Jules taught industrial arts at Liverpool High School. His family emigrated from Hungary when he was young and he possessed a strong work ethic. We called him Jules for short. He was a former enlisted soldier who became an officer through the Empire State Military Academy. Jules had excellent critical-thinking skills and could break down a problem and develop various courses of action to solve it. He mentored me on supply operations during training weekends and I often looked to him for advice, even after he was promoted and reassigned to another position in the unit. We would become–and remain–friends through the years.

Soon after I began work I followed up with Carl about the officer vacancies Wayne had mentioned. After I re-enlisted and served more closely with officers, I became more aware of the weight they carried as leaders along with their additional responsibilities and privileges. Admittedly, the dignity and respect they held was part of my motivation for becoming an officer. Also, as a college graduate, I felt a certain entitlement to a higher income and I wanted the ability to drive the decision-making process. I believed from an early age I had the ability and potential to become a leader, possibly a trait of being the first-born. As a pre-teen I was tasked to make sure my younger brothers' bedroom was clean and given my own room, which I viewed as a status symbol. While in the Cub Scouts and Boy Scouts, I took on minor leadership roles as a den leader and patrol leader. During basic training I never refused a chance to lead fellow trainees. In Vietnam I worked independently for the most part and managed my own time. After Vietnam I managed a retail drugstore. As an officer in the Reserves I would be given new opportunities and responsibilities, along with some difficult challenges.

The 403rd Civil Affairs Company was a rank-heavy unit with a ratio of 60:40 enlisted personnel to officers. Several officers in the unit joined during the Vietnam era to avoid the draft. As we withdrew from Vietnam and the draft ended, many officers left the Reserves, which resulted in several vacancies. Carl said if I was interested he would help me apply for a direct commission when the time was right. I could be commissioned directly from the enlisted ranks without having to attend the traditional officer academies like West Point, ROTC, Officer Candidate School, or the Empire State Military Academy. My college degree fulfilled one of the prerequisites for a commission. During the summer of 1977, Carl scheduled me to take the officers' qualification test and, after passing, I was interviewed by a commissioning board. The board consisted of an active-duty officer, a Reserve officer, and a senior NCO. Thanks to Carl's guidance I was better prepared than I was for the officer-candidate board years earlier. In January 1978, I received notice that I was recommended for a Reserve commission. I was among 12 enlisted members Carl had assisted with direct commissions in the Army Reserve during the mid-1970s. He realized the future of the unit depended on its leadership. It's said the true test of a leader is the ability to recognize leadership potential in others and then help them develop it. Carl Liberatore had an intuitive ability to spot and develop potential leaders. Many of us who served in the 403rd CA Company owe our military careers, and even our civilian careers, to Carl. Although the extent of his influence is debatable, I believe it was more than coincidence the unit produced two judges, a state senator, a mayor, and a police chief after serving with the 403rd Civil Affairs.

On January 31, 1978, at age 31, I was commissioned a first lieutenant, reserve, in the U.S. Army. It was the realization of a dream I'd long thought was out of reach. Promotion as an officer from sergeant made me a Mustang, a term given to military officers who began their careers as enlisted service members and had continuous service from enlisted to officer. The term originated around the time of World War II and initially applied only to enlisted soldiers who received battlefield commissions. One notable Mustang was Audie Murphy, the most decorated soldier of World War II. The term literally refers to the Mustang horse. While it could be tamed, it retained its wild streak. By the same token, since the Mustang was by nature a wild and free animal, it might be more capable and have a better survival instinct than a thoroughbred. Mustang officers were typically older and more experienced than their peers.

From 1978 to 1979, I took two qualification courses for my civilian job as a supply technician. In May 1978, I graduated from the Administrative Supply Technician Course at Fort McCoy, Wisconsin. In June 1979, I completed the supply-technician refresher course, also at Fort McCoy. The courses qualified me to operate and manage a supply section. Lt. Col. Gale soon appointed me as the unit supply officer when Capt. Balogh was promoted.

During drill weekends I carpooled to the Reserve center with three other unit members; Doug McLaughlin, Jim Angelica, and Ken Mereness. Jim and Ken were experienced NCOs with prior active-duty service. Ken was a decorated Vietnam combat veteran and Jim served in the Navy submarine service. In December 1977, only two and a half months after I joined the unit, Ken was killed in an automobile accident. It was a tragic loss for the unit, and I felt a personal loss, even though I'd only known him a short time. Ken was an outstanding soldier who set a quiet but strong example for everyone in the unit. The following year the 403rd initiated an award in his memory for the outstanding soldier of the year. It was awarded to a unit member who best demonstrated Ken's excellence in soldiering skills and service to others.

Our other carpool member, Sgt. 1st Class Doug McLaughlin, was a mainstay in the unit and had been a member since 1965. Aside from basic training, Doug never served in the regular Army, but he possessed a wealth of knowledge about the history of the 403rd and always had an anecdote to tell about past training exercises or former unit personalities. Doug had a good sense of humor and would often bait people with a story which led an unsuspecting listener to a surprise punch line. In civilian life Doug was a skilled draftsman who later designed the unit crest after he served with the unit during Operation Desert Storm.

The Civil Affairs Branch

In March 1981 I graduated from the civil affairs officer-qualification course held at Fort Bragg, North Carolina. Branch qualification was a commissioned officer's first educational requirement and formed the foundation for future promotion and educational requirements. The Civil Affairs (CA) branch of the Army was created in 1955 as a result of military government operations conducted in Europe and Japan during and after World War II. It is the primary branch for the conduct of civil-military operations in each phase of military operations, from low-intensity activities (humanitarian assistance, civil administration and educational assistance) to high intensity activities (stability and support operations, and population and resource control).

In simplest terms, its purpose is to win hearts and minds. I think lyrics to the theme song from the popular television series *Cheers*, expressed the image of civil affairs personnel. People were glad we came and they knew our name. Doug McLaughlin, in his inimitable style, called us the screen-door company. Perhaps it was his folksy way to describe the soldiers engaged in civil affairs work: the doorway to a friendly and informal group of people who were there to help.

CA soldiers coordinate assistance to people in areas where the U.S. military operates. Local civilians whose needs are met are less likely to interfere with military operations. CA soldiers organized into specialty teams may be found at various levels of command and deployed according to the needs of the mission. CA soldiers are trained to address a variety of civilian issues and to develop an individual rapport with people. The specialties included public health, economics and finance, government, public facilities, dislocated civilians, civilian supply, civilian labor, public works, public administration, public transportation, and public education.

Modern civil affairs functional teams are more varied than those sent to Vietnam, which focused mainly on refugee control and civil projects. The Army draws about 90% of its civil affairs expertise from members of the Army Reserve. They practice many of the specialties in their civilian occupations and are among the most frequently deployed troops in the Army. For the remainder of my military career, civil affairs operations would be my primary specialty.

Because of the complex nature of its mission, which includes the need to meet and negotiate with high-ranking civilian officials, civil affairs units consisted of several field-grade officers at the rank of major and above. However, the enlisted civil affairs specialist's role is routinely integrated with that of the officers. Many enlisted specialists are well educated and possess mission-critical civilian skills. They include teachers, police officers, clerks, electricians, carpenters, and building contractors, to name a few.

Supply Technician Duties

As a new supply technician, I struggled to keep up with the constant supply requests. I made the mistake of trying to be everything to everybody. During the week I could work at my own pace; but on training weekends the pace was hectic and the supply cage was one of the busiest places in the unit. With so many officers in the unit, sometimes the chain of command became blurred. As a first lieutenant I often answered to several higher-ranking officers. On Mondays after a drill weekend, I faced a mountain of paperwork to process. It seemed all the work created by the reservists was left for me to finish during the rest of the month.

Overwhelmed by the amount of work left behind, I attempted to train others in the supply section to finish some of the work. I delegated the best I could, but there was never enough time to make much of a dent. The priority on drill weekends was unit training, which almost always pre-empted work in the supply section. One day my frustration came to a head when a senior officer asked me to make some copies. I turned quickly to the nearest sergeant–who, unfortunately, happened to be my friend, Wayne Coye–and told him do it.

When he left I remarked, within earshot of several others, "Why should I do it? I'm an officer."

I felt bad for Wayne, who had told me about the opportunity at the 403rd in the first place and I apologized for making him the object of my frustration. I realized I had a lot to learn about leadership and tact.

My stress level declined during annual training. For two weeks everyone was a full-time soldier and more help was available. In 1978, during the middle weekend of annual training at Fort Indiantown Gap, Pennsylvania, I was even able to go home for a while. Doug McLaughlin and I transported all the weapons back to the Reserve center after we finished firing for qualification.

Driving a 2½-ton truck with all that firepower in back must have affected my libido because I believe Nancy became pregnant that weekend. On May 8, 1979, our third child, Catherine, was born–about a week before our next drill weekend.

Overjoyed to have a daughter, I purchased 100 pink cupcakes and brought them to the Reserve center to distribute during our noon meal on Saturday. It inspired me to nickname my baby girl Cupcake, a moniker she grew to despise and which I dropped during her teen years.

Between 1979 and 1981 I had assembled a field desk with several office supplies and various supply forms for use during field exercises. I became the go-to guy for supplies in the field. However, what I thought was my new niche in life started to wear on me. I realized it was futile to attempt any administrative tasks during drill weekends, so I concentrated on them during the week when there were fewer interruptions, but it still seemed I never had enough time to get everything done. Maintenance of our 18 tactical vehicles ate up much of my time. Routine maintenance could not be completed during weekend drills, so during the week I'd drive vehicles to the maintenance shop (about six miles away) for scheduled care. I waited there and drove them back to the Reserve center when the work was finished. I enjoyed the time away from my desk and developed a good rapport with the mechanics, but it took a lot of time away from my administrative tasks.

A Civilian Career Change

After three years as a supply technician, I realized there was little opportunity for advancement to a supervisory position. Carl was firmly seated in his position and no turnover was foreseeable among the other unit administrators at the Reserve center. I became restless and considered other employment, but I enjoyed the camaraderie of the military environment and wanted to remain in the Reserves. Early in 1981, I learned of a job opening when Nancy invited our new neighbors, Jim and Denise Tassone, for a visit. Jim and I were close in age, we each had young children, and we both came from Italian families. Denise was a homemaker and part-time hairstylist. Jim worked as a Deputy U.S. Marshal in Syracuse.

During our visit we talked about our backgrounds and jobs. I mentioned wanting something with more upward mobility. Jim said the clerk's office at the U.S. District Court in Syracuse was expanding and needed to hire more court clerks; and, he added, they were paid really well. I was interested, so Jim gave me the contact information and offered himself as a reference. I sent in an application and a couple weeks later I was offered an interview. In early March 1981, I went to the clerk's office at the federal building in Syracuse and met with Clerk of Court Joseph Scully, a tall, mild-mannered, heavyset man in his mid to late 40s. After a short interview with him, I was brought before two U.S. District judges, Howard G. Munson and Neal P. McCurn, for a more in-depth interview. This procedure confirmed an interview process I first noticed when hired as a supply technician with the 403rd. A prospect was first screened to determine qualifications and suitability for the position. If passed by the screener, the prospect was sent to a second interview with the decision maker. The process of a deputy-clerk candidate being interviewed by a federal judge was later discontinued and interviews were conducted solely by the clerk of court.

The judges were distinguished-looking gentlemen, both more than six feet tall. Judge Munson had a formal, judicial demeanor with a deep, resonant voice that was somewhat intimidating. Judge McCurn appeared more laid back and had a dry sense of humor, which put me at ease. For the interview I consciously presented an upbeat, confident attitude, but I was in awe of their standing as federal judges. They noted I had a bachelor's degree in business and had completed the LaSalle correspondence course, *Law for Business Leadership*, something I took while contemplating a law career. Judge McCurn remarked that while he was in private practice his firm often had their paralegals take the same course. To prepare for my interview I read up on the federal court system to appear knowledgeable about it. I said I was aware the district court was a court of original jurisdiction for matters involving federal law and the Constitution. Then I made a misguided attempt to discuss federal law and asked a question about the Posse Comitatus Act. I asked if it prohibited my employment with the federal courts if I was ordered to active duty as an Army reservist. I thought in case I had to enforce some law it would create a conflict of interest as a court employee.

Well, not exactly. The Posse Comitatus Act was enacted in 1878 to prevent U.S. military personnel from acting as law-enforcement officers on U.S. soil. The text of the Posse Comitatus Act, which was still in effect, reads: "Whoever, except in cases and under circumstances expressly authorized by the Constitution or Act of Congress, willfully uses any part of the Army or the Air Force as a posse comitatus or otherwise to execute the laws shall be fined under this title or imprisoned not more than two years, or both".

The law had nothing to do with my ability to work at the federal courts if called to active duty, and I certainly would not be the person who made the decision to use the Army or the Air Force to execute the laws. After I posed the question, judges Munson and McCurn looked at each other as if perplexed, then looked at me with some pause. I was confused by their reaction and wondered whether I had asked it correctly, or worse, exposed my ignorance and blew my chances for the position. Judge McCurn finally said it was not a problem. As if my question prompted them to wonder about my mental condition, next they noted I served in Vietnam and asked whether I ever used drugs there, or at any other time. I answered no and stated before I returned from Vietnam I had to give a urine sample and it tested negative. Judge Munson gestured at the papers strewn on his desk and said he needed help to get organized. I said he probably knew where everything was (I later discovered he didn't. Although he was a brilliant jurist, he wasn't terribly organized).

When they asked where I was from, I said Penn Yan and thought I should explain Penn Yan was a small village in New York State, not somewhere in China. Before I could explain, Judge McCurn said when he ran for congress on the Democratic ticket in 1970, he made a campaign stop in Penn Yan where a local union hosted him. He said a union representative escorted him around town and I promptly mentioned it might have been my uncle (my great uncle), Pat Condella. Judge McCurn recognized the name. I was amazed he recalled the visit more than a decade later. I survived the interview despite my Posse Comitatus gaffe and the stigma of Vietnam veterans as drug-using baby killers. Both judges had prior military service, which may have helped my cause. Judge Munson served as a medic in the Army during World War II and Judge McCurn served in the Navy Reserve.

A few days later I received a phone call from the clerk's office in Albany and was offered a position with the U.S. District Court in Syracuse. I was elated and immediately accepted. The first person I called was my mother. I told her I thought it could be my big break, and mentioned one of the judges had even met Uncle Pat. I gave my two-weeks' notice to Carl Liberatore but told him I wanted to remain a member of the 403rd.

As a court employee I would be classified as an Excepted Service appointee with the courts. Joseph Scully assured me my court appointment was considered a continuation of my federal service. Excepted Service meant I remained under the Civil Service System for leave and retirement benefits, but I was considered an at-will employee, without many of the employment protections of the Civil Service Act. On March 23, 1981, I began a new career with the U.S. District Court as a deputy clerk. I remained there for the next 27½ years.

The U.S. District Court for the Northern District of New York encompassed 32 counties, excluding the New York City area. It was bordered generally by Canada on the north, Cayuga County on the west, the Pennsylvania border on the south, and the states of Vermont and Massachusetts on the east. Geographically, it covered the largest area of the four federal districts in New York. It also held the distinction of being the mother court, or the first court ever convened under the sovereignty of the United States, when Judge James Duane held court in Albany on November 3, 1789.

Supply Accountability vs. Responsibility

In 1982, I was promoted to the rank of captain in the Army Reserve. After I accepted employment with the U.S. District Court, I no longer had responsibility for daily supply matters, but I was still assigned as the supply officer and remained accountable for all unit supplies and equipment. One of the principles of Army property accountability stated a commander could delegate accountability, in which someone was charged with physical control of items receipted to them. However, the commander could never delegate responsibility, which was the overall duty to implement and enforce measures necessary for proper management and control of supplies and equipment.

As the accountable officer, I ensured each soldier signed for their personal issue of clothing and equipment, to include their field gear and chemical-protective clothing. To pass down accountability for certain unit equipment (including weapons, vehicles and trailers), hand receipts were issued to the officers in charge (OIC) of each functional team. They in turn could further hand receipt equipment to the user level. Weapons remained secured in the arms-room vault and were only signed out during weapons qualification or cleaning. Vehicles were secured in a parking area at the Reserve center, enclosed by a chain-link fence with a padlocked gate, and signed for as needed. Only designated individuals (e.g., the supply officer, supply sergeant, the motor pool sergeant, and the civilian administrator) had access to the vehicle keys. Individual clothing and equipment were itemized on a list and signed for by each unit member. They were given a wall locker to secure those items until they were needed. I delegated physical accountability for unit supplies and equipment to the actual users of the supplies and equipment.

I compiled a good record for taking care of unit property, but there were a few occasions when I accepted liability for lost or damaged property. Once I backed up a 2½-ton truck behind the Reserve training center to unload some supplies and damaged one of the side-mounted rearview mirrors. Officially known as the truck, cargo, 2½ ton, 6X6, M35, it was a workhorse in the Army inventory of tactical vehicles. It was used to carry troops, cargo, and to tow trailers. After the accident I went to Sgt. 1st Class John Hopkins, our full-time supply sergeant, to tell him about the broken mirror and offered to pay for it. He said he could write it off as an operational loss. I told him I was responsible for the damage and insisted he write up a cash-collection voucher, billing me for the cost of the mirror. It only cost about $35 but it cleared my conscience. I didn't want it to appear I used my rank to avoid compensating the Army for damage I caused, even though it was accidental.

I paid for missing or lost equipment on two other occasions. Some blankets were unaccounted for at the Reserve training center during an inventory, and once during annual training, I paid for some missing kitchen utensils during an inventory. Little things seemed harder to control than the bigger ones. Nonetheless, I considered myself to be fairly good at accounting for property. At least no sensitive or high-value equipment was ever lost during my tenure as supply officer.

Camaraderie during Training

Between 1978 and 1986 we performed annual training together as a unit. At least one week of our two-week training period was spent in the field, practicing tactical skills. Our time training together helped develop unit cohesion and built teamwork. The *Army Common Task Training Manual* was used for most of our field training and we were tested on our proficiency at each level, beginning with skill-level one through skill-level four.

In my experience, training as a unit rarely progressed beyond skill-level one because the personnel turnover was so great, which diminished the unit's overall training level. In the reserves, people moved or left the service for job relocations, promotions, or they left due to interference with their civilian job or family responsibilities.

Individual training was different. Reservists had to pass the skill level equal to the rank they held. Some of the tactical skills included identification of terrain features, navigation with a compass and map, weapons qualification, familiarization with the

M60 machine gun, the hand grenade, the anti-personnel mine, the use of camouflage, and reaction to enemy fire and chemical attack.

We understood the seriousness of the training, but there was always some humor to add a bit of levity. One event many of us looked forward to each summer during annual training was Capt. Ray Meier's impression of Johnny Carson as Carnac the Magnificent. In civilian life, Capt. Meier was an attorney with a great sense of humor whose act provided us with laughs and a welcome diversion from field training. It usually occurred at the midpoint of our annual training exercise. Ray would wrap a towel around his head and, with help from another officer, he was presented with sealed envelopes, which he pressed to his head one at a time and, using his "psychic powers," gave the answer to a question inside the envelope. For example, he might say, "Run like hell," then he'd open the envelope and inside it read, "What do you do when you're out of ammunition?"

During one exercise with our chemical-protective masks, I decided to put the mask to a more practical use and wore it in the portable john to avoid breathing the fumes; it proved very effective. During night operations we used trip flares to guard the perimeter against other unit members who played the enemy. One night a unit member (who shall remain anonymous) decided to urinate near a tree, during which he accidentally set off a trip flare. This literally exposed him to a nearby female soldier. Another time, during a party in the field, I drank too much and a couple of guys drove me back to our barracks to sleep it off. On the way into the building, somehow my wedding band fell off my finger. The next morning a chaplain found it on the lawn and checked with the building occupants to locate its owner. I thanked the chaplain for finding it and told him the ring was a little big for my finger but didn't confess I was drunk at the time.

My favorite meal in the Army was breakfast. While training in the field, a hot breakfast was a great morale booster. Soon after we were out of our tents, the smell of diesel fuel floated through the thick morning air as the deuce-and-a-half trucks were started. The familiar smell of diesel inspired us to borrow a phrase from the movie, *Apocalypse Now*. We'd often emerge from our tents with the words, "I love the smell of diesel fuel in the morning". It became associated with the start of the day's training.

Although we managed to insert some fun into our training, the veterans among us realized tactical training was intended to prepare us for real combat situations. We trained to do things I never had to do in Vietnam. We dug fighting positions, established sectors of fire, applied camouflage paint and placed local vegetation on our helmets to blend in with the area. Maj. Duncan Green, a Vietnam combat veteran, gave a class about noise and light discipline. He conducted a night class during which he demonstrated how sound traveled farther at night, and how the slightest noise is amplified. Much like someone who is blind, in the dark our sense of hearing becomes more acute to compensate for the inability to see.

While I trained for the possibility of going to war, in 1983 the United States launched Operation Urgent Fury to invade the Caribbean island of Grenada. President Ronald Reagan ordered the invasion in response to an appeal from the governor general of Grenada and a request for assistance from the Organization of Eastern Caribbean States. The mission was to oust the People's Revolutionary Government from power and to protect U.S. citizens and restore the lawful government. The United States feared Grenada would become a Communist beachhead after a communist who had close ties with Cuba deposed the prime minister. In the aftermath of the coup, riots broke out, resulting in a general breakdown of civil order. In addition, the safety of 800 American medical students at St. George's School of Medicine was a serious concern for the United States.

The invasion, led by the U.S. Marines, took place October 25. I was gratified to know the invasion was successful because two days earlier in Beirut, Lebanon, 241 U.S. Marines were killed in a suicide bombing. The Beirut bombing affected me so much I wrote a letter to my congressman to give my two cents about how to utilize our forces in future situations. In my opinion the Army was better equipped to defend a stationary position than the Marines, whose doctrine was geared toward offense and maneuver, not occupation.

A Rambo Imitation

During our annual training in the summer of 1985, I had my first experience with an M60 machine gun. A member of a nearby unit brought one into our bivouac area for a show-and-tell demonstration. The M60 is a 7.62-millimeter, belt-fed automatic weapon with a rate of fire of 600 rounds a minute, or 10 rounds per second; a lot of firepower. We loaded a belt of blank ammunition and several of us took turns firing. I tried to imitate a scene from one of my favorite movies, *Rambo: First Blood Part II*, starring Sylvester Stallone. I was fascinated by the scene where Rambo landed a UH-1 Huey helicopter gunship in the middle of an area depicted as a North Vietnamese POW camp. He ripped the M60 from its mount and began firing it with one arm while he fed ammunition with his other arm, killing a horde of enemy soldiers before he rescued several American POWs. When it was my turn with the M60, I realized, weighing in at about 23 pounds, it was too cumbersome for a mere mortal like me to hold with one arm. So much for my dreams of Rambo-like glory.

Research Project

Early in 1986, the 403rd CA Company was tasked by our higher command, the 352nd CA Command, to produce a supplemental case study of the Dhofar War, which occurred in the country of Oman between 1965 and 1975. The initial study was conducted a year earlier by Maj. David Tagg of the 403rd. I led a team of three other members from the 403rd CA Battalion to Carlisle Barracks, Pennsylvania, to conduct research during a split two-week period, one in March and one in June.

Members of the team were first lieutenants Thomas Downs and Mable Richardson, and Staff Sgt. Nonnie Holliman. Carlisle Barracks was home to the U.S. Army War College and had an extensive research library. We familiarized ourselves with Maj. Tagg's study and began to address comments made by the 352nd CA Command. The United States maintained a strategic interest in Oman because of Yemen and Iran, two nearby countries known to harbor terrorists. Our supplemental study concluded that although the United States had an access agreement with Oman to allow U.S. armed forces to enter the country during a crisis, it was not yet possible to enter into a formal civil-military cooperation agreement. Four years later Oman would provide access to the United States during Desert Storm, still without a civil-military cooperation agreement which would allow us to interact with government officials to coordinate a more detailed support agreement.

Company Command

By 1986, I had nine years of service with the 403rd Civil Affairs Company. I made many friends and we developed a great team rapport, but time inevitably brought change. I almost completed enough time in grade as a captain to be considered on the next promotion board for major. Too much time in one unit raised a red flag to a promotion board. Homesteading, as it was called, gave the appearance of an officer with no desire to advance and develop his/her potential. The Army promotion policy dictated steady advancement or get out.

Unfortunately, at the time there were no foreseeable vacancies for a major in the 403rd, which meant if I were promoted, I would be reassigned to an inactive control group without pay. A fellow officer, Ed Magdziak, who left the 403rd for a company command, told me about another company command vacancy in his new unit. I followed up on his tip and applied for a command slot at the 3rd Battalion, 389th Engineer Regiment in nearby Mattydale. I had prior experience with another engineer unit, the 770th Engineer Company in Penn Yan, and the commander of the 403rd CA Company gave me a good recommendation. My prior civilian experience as a unit supply technician also helped. I interviewed with the battalion commander and was selected as one of his company commanders.

Chapter 7
First Command and a Key Promotion
(1987-1989)

The 3rd Battalion, 389th Engineer Regiment was a One Station Unit Training (OSUT) unit. I was given command of Company D, consisting of 16 cadre members. In addition to the commander, it consisted of a first sergeant, a training officer, 12 drill sergeants, and a supply sergeant. The core of the unit was its drill sergeants. The remainder of the company was rounded out with basic trainees during annual training each year at Fort Leonard Wood, Missouri, where engineer recruits were trained. OSUT was a program in which recruits took both basic combat training and advanced training at the same location before assignment to units around the country. Usually a soldier went to another Army post to complete advanced training, but OSUT created a more seamless transition from trainee to qualification in a chosen military specialty.

Command assignments were the goal of every commissioned officer, but as a direct commissioned officer, I wasn't confident about my potential to rise high in the ranks. I had no illusions about becoming the next Eisenhower or Patton. In the officer-promotion system, successful command time, completion of the education requirements, and good evaluation reports were key factors in assessing an officer's potential; but the origin of one's commission carried some weight, similar to someone's pedigree. I also had an issue with the evaluation report system, even though it worked well for me.

Prior to my first weekend drill with Company D, I received a phone call from 1st Sgt. Greg Webster, who welcomed me to the unit and informed me of the date and place of the next drill. On my first day I walked into the orderly room with my civil affairs branch insignia on my uniform collar. One of the first comments I heard was an apparent sarcastic remark about a civil affairs officer in command of an engineer company. I took it as a challenge and was determined to convince the unit members I could lead an engineer training company.

Although the members of Company D deferred to my rank and position, I had to earn their trust and respect as a leader. I had the wisdom of age (40 was old for a captain, but not so in the Reserves) and I possessed a broad range of experience. I used these qualities to summon confidence in my abilities. My first duty, as I saw it, was to build a team. Typically, in a Reserve unit, members lived in the same general area and many knew each other outside the Reserve center. I was blessed to have a good amount of experience spread among members of the company. 1st Sgt. Webster was a veteran soldier with a good feel for the pulse of the unit.

My previous experience as a junior officer in a rank-heavy civil affairs company gave me the chance to observe the senior officers' demeanor and leadership styles, much of which I imitated in my first command assignment. I met privately with each member of the unit to get acquainted and spoke at length with the first sergeant to get familiar with the unit's mission. The first sergeant of a unit typically had the best insight into the morale and abilities of unit members and was the best person to consult about issues needing to be addressed by the commander.

Our annual training in 1987 took place at Fort Leonard Wood, in mid-July. Nancy was expecting our fourth child, but her due date wasn't until late August. She felt uneasy about my absence for two weeks but I said I'd be home before the end of July. I obtained permission to drive there in case she called me or I received a notification from the Red Cross, so I could be home in less than 24 hours. That wasn't much comfort to her, but she agreed to let me attend annual training when I assured her I would be free to leave if necessary. I left home early in the morning and arrived at Fort Leonard Wood the evening before training began. The next morning, I assumed command of a basic training company of engineer recruits who were at the midpoint in their training cycle. 1st Sgt. Webster was on a school assignment so Dave Cowburn, the first sergeant from a sister company in the battalion, was assigned to Company D for annual training.

A few days into training, I was confronted with my first discipline problem. It did not involve one of the recruits as I would have expected, but one of our drill sergeants. Several concerned trainees reported he was asleep under a tree in the field in the presence of those he was supposed to supervise. With the assistance of 1st Sgt. Cowburn, we took sworn affidavits from several trainees. We presented them to the battalion commander, Lt. Col. Bill McGuire, for his guidance. As a result of a preliminary investigation into the matter, we contacted the criminal investigation detachment and conducted a search of the drill sergeant's locker, where we found traces of marijuana. As a company commander the level of punishment I could impose was limited, but I decided to offer the drill sergeant an Article 15. Under the Uniform Code of Military Justice (UCMJ), an Article 15 is a form of non-judicial punishment imposed for minor offenses. The punishment could include a loss of pay, restriction to barracks, and/or a reduction in rank. The soldier could either accept the Article 15 or choose to have a court martial hearing. After the soldier was advised of his rights, he consulted with a military lawyer at the Judge Advocate General's (JAG) Office. He decided to take his chances with a court martial, so I deferred the case to the battalion commander who had more sentencing authority. The drill sergeant was ultimately found guilty of dereliction of duty and reduced in rank, with the loss of one month's active-duty pay. It was the first time a soldier in the battalion was prosecuted under the UCMJ. The soldier was unaware of my legal background with the courts. Admitting his error in rejecting my offer of an Article 15, he said to me, "You never know who you're up against".

As the company commander, one of my duties was to inspect the trainee barracks. I was briefed beforehand by Staff Sgt. Frank Hrynio, one of our drill sergeants. He advised me I should be strict with them to reinforce the discipline imposed by the drill sergeants. Sgt. Hrynio would accompany me during the inspection.

As we entered the barracks Sgt. Hrynio yelled, "ATTEN-SHUN!"

This prompted the trainees to scramble and stand at attention next to their beds. The barracks was a white building with clapboard siding, typical of those on other posts, except it had one level instead of two. There was a latrine at one end of the building; the rest of the area was an open bay with beds lined up in neat rows on both sides of the room. Next to each bed was a metal wall locker to store uniforms, hats, boots, and field gear. On the floor at the foot of each bed was a wooden footlocker to store toiletries, uniform accessories, underwear and socks. First, I inspected the latrine. I knew from my experience in basic training there was always something not quite clean enough in the latrine. Sure enough, I found a couple of things to make remarks about. As I walked through the barracks area, I stopped to inspect each soldier's bed and locker area. The bed covers had to be tight enough to bounce a dime when dropped, and they had to use hospital corners to tuck the bedding in at the foot of the bed. Everything in the wall lockers and footlockers had to be neat and folded properly. I made a couple of comments on neatness and lifted up the blankets on a couple of beds that weren't made properly but I wasn't being tough enough for Staff Sgt. Hrynio.

He took me aside and said, "Sir, you've got to be tougher on these recruits and put the fear of God in them. You need to tear their beds apart and dump things out of the lockers if they aren't in perfect order".

I understood, but subconsciously I may have sympathized with the trainees as a result of my own basic training. During the process of building discipline in basic training, the trainees needed to know standards were strictly enforced and even a slight deviation was unacceptable. The philosophy was to tear down their previous notions of order and discipline so they could be re-educated in the Army way of doing things. I wasn't a strict disciplinarian by nature, but as a result of Hrynio's advice I adjusted my approach and resumed the inspection. I reluctantly summoned my dark side and tore some bedding completely apart, dumped the contents of a couple of wall lockers on the floor, and yelled at a trainee whose area was especially poorly maintained. My primary concern was that they learned something from the inspection. The goal of basic training was to teach discipline and teamwork.

It was in my nature to be with the troops, not behind a desk, so I was out at the training areas to observe almost every day. One day the recruits were learning to rappel from a 50-foot tower. I spoke to one of the drill sergeants at the site and suggested it might set a good example if they saw the commander rappel off the tower. I'd once rappelled 20 feet from the roof of the Reserve training center and enjoyed it, but after climbing the 50-foot tower, I looked down and a sense of fear crept over me. Fifty feet was a lot higher than the roof of the two-story Reserve center, and I started to have second thoughts–but I was at the point of no return. I had to rappel or embarrass myself in front of trainees. One of the sergeants instructed me on the procedure and I donned my harness and gloves. When he gave me the "go" sign, I grabbed the rope and stepped off the edge of the platform, placing my feet on the side of the tower. It was a strange feeling as I leaned out at a 90° angle with my back toward the ground and nothing but a rope to keep me from falling to certain death. With encouragement from the instructor, I pushed off with my feet and gradually bounced my way to the bottom. I was exhilarated after landing safely on the ground so I went up the tower again. However, the second time I became overconfident and descended too fast. I landed on my feet but suffered a nasty rope burn on my wrist. I decided I'd set enough of an example for one day and gathered the trainees for a short motivational talk before I left. I enjoyed addressing the trainees and imparting some of my wisdom and experience. It also fulfilled my inner teacher.

Another time I led them on a five-mile road march. During my first command assignment I began to develop my leadership style. I learned to lead by example and never asked another soldier to do anything I wouldn't do. The remainder of the two weeks' training was completed without incident and I returned home to my still-pregnant wife.

On August 21, 1987, Kevin was born, and I managed to keep my birth-attendance record intact.

At the Reserve center during regular training weekends, I continued to build rapport with unit members as we performed the usual administrative and training tasks necessary to run the unit. We conducted mission-related training, held classroom instruction on various soldier skills, conducted weapons qualification, physical-fitness training, and I wrote individual evaluation reports for members of the unit. The major difference in training requirements from the 403rd CA Company was the engineer mission was based more on technical skills than cultural knowledge. There was no requirement for tactical training because the 3/389th was a training unit and would not deploy anywhere outside the United States.

By my second year of command, I was comfortable in the position and more confident in my abilities. I sensed a level of respect by some drill sergeants who had earlier doubted my suitability to command an engineer training company. One of my favorite training activities was physical fitness, and it was my responsibility to train members of the unit to pass the annual physical fitness test. It consisted of timed sit-ups, pushups and a two-mile run. Confident in my fitness level, I offered a case of beer to anyone in the company who scored higher than me. No one beat my score, even though I was several years their senior. Staff Sgt. Hrynio, who assisted with barracks inspection at Fort Leonard Wood, came closest, so I bought him a beer after our drill weekend.

One of the senior NCOs in the 3/389th Regiment was also a full-time unit technician. He was Sgt. 1st Class David Long, who served as the battalion training NCO. Dave was one of the most knowledgeable and dedicated people in the unit. His passion was taking care of soldiers. He ensured our individual training records were up to date and all battalion training requirements were met. Once, as he examined the results of the Army Physical Fitness Test, Dave asked why I consistently achieved the maximum score when the standard was just to pass. I told him it was because someday I wouldn't be able to and I wanted to do my best while I was able. As I recall, he just shook his head in amusement.

I figured he must have passed it off as showboating and when it came time to leave the unit, I would be remembered as just another officer who passed through the unit before moving on. I must have left an impression on him because 11 years later he contacted me unexpectedly about another opportunity–one that led to the pinnacle of my military career.

Promotion to Field Grade Officer

On August 25, 1988, I completed the Command and General Staff Officers' Course administered by the U.S. Army Command and General Staff College at Fort Leavenworth, Kansas. It was the next level of education required for all Army officers after their basic branch course, but it was impractical for most reservists to attend college in person because of civilian employment obligations. Our options were either to take correspondence courses or attend weekly classes at a Reserve center. Both choices included two weeks' active duty at a satellite location under contract with a college or university. I took classes at the Reserve center in Mattydale because I didn't believe I had the time or discipline to muddle through voluminous amount of correspondence materials without the aid of an instructor. From my experience in college I knew I needed structure to succeed academically.

The class met once a week during the fall and winter months. Each summer for the next three years I attended a two-week phase at one of the satellite locations. One phase was conducted at the University of Southern Mississippi in Hattiesburg, and two of them were at Wesley College in Dover, Delaware. Completion of the course as a captain was unusual, but thanks to Carl Liberatore's emphasis on professional education at the 403rd CA Company, I was convinced to take the course as soon as I was eligible. Completion of half the course requirements was a prerequisite for promotion to lieutenant colonel, so I was ahead of many of my peers in that regard.

In January 1989 I was promoted to major. It was an important rung in the ladder of advancement because it signified my transition from a company-grade officer to a field-grade officer, the civilian equivalent of a middle-management position. It also meant I had to leave my position as the company commander because I exceeded the rank for the position. I was given a small promotion ceremony at the Reserve center with Nancy present to help pin on my new rank, a gold oak leaf. Ironically, the officer who read my promotion order was Maj. Benjamin Gigliotti, assistant chief of staff for personnel for the battalion. His family was from Utica, and he may have been a distant relative, although I learned in Italy Gigliotti was as common a surname as Smith in America.

The promotion meant I had to find another unit, as no vacancies existed for a major in the battalion. Two months later I was assigned as the plans and operations officer with the 1209th U.S. Army Garrison, also in Mattydale. Its mission was to operate an Army post in the event the regular Army garrison was deployed overseas. The 1209th Garrison also acted as the major subordinate command for several Reserve units in Upstate New York.

Soon I was selected to take the Mobilization Planner's course at Fort McCoy, Wisconsin, and was appointed the mobilization officer. I already had a substantial background in mobilization planning from my assignment with the 403rd CA Company, and from completion of the Strategic Mobilization Planning Course at Fort Eustis, Virginia, in 1983. It became an area of expertise for me, one which I put to practical use in future assignments.

Chapter 8
Desert Shield/Desert Storm (1990-1993)

In August of 1990, Iraq invaded the tiny country of Kuwait, on Iraq's southeast border. The massive Iraqi Army, battle tested from the war with Iran in the 1980s, easily overran the Kuwaiti defenses and occupied the country on August 2. President George H.W. Bush demanded the complete withdrawal of all Iraqi forces, but the Iraqis pushed their advance to the edge of the Saudi Arabian border. This caused President Bush to draw an imaginary line in the sand, across which the Iraqis must not advance. As part of contingency planning for the use of force, the president's military and civilian advisers debated the role of the reserve component as they prepared for war. There had been no major activation of the reserves since World War II.

According to Assistant Secretary of Defense for Reserve Affairs for Desert Storm Stephen M. Duncan, military leaders did not think the reserves would be called up, for political reasons. They believed activation of reserves would be perceived as a draft, which would be politically unpopular. There was also a policy consideration: According to Title 10, Section 673b of the United States Code, Congress could only authorize the president to call up reserve units for a maximum of 90 days. Duncan recommended the 90-day activation limit be changed. By the time a reserve unit was called upon to fill any vacancies, validated for deployment, and arrived in the theater of operations, at least 30 days had passed and their actual use to the theater commander would be less than 60 days. Congress acted unusually fast and amended the section to allow the president to call up the reserves for 180 days, or six months.

Reserve readiness was another concern. Vietnam veterans still in the military recalled how National Guard and Reserve soldiers who were activated during Vietnam were soft and undisciplined. Some people joined the Reserves to hide from the draft, and training during the 1960s was inconsistent and substandard. By the mid-1980s, however, the mindset of the Reserve leadership had changed to a train-as-we-fight attitude. In other words, training should be as realistic as possible. Training agreements were formed with regular Army units they would to support in the event of a mobilization. Reserve units designated high priority trained with their active-duty counterparts and traveled beyond the confines of their Reserve centers to obtain more realistic training.

Eventually more than 260,000 Guard and Reserve soldiers were activated for Desert Storm; by most accounts the regular Army commanders were pleased with their performance. Col. Allen Irish, with whom I later served at the 354th Civil Affairs Brigade, was a reservist activated during Desert Storm. He was quoted in an article published in *The Officer*, the journal of the Reserve Officers Association of the United States, that there was initially a lot of worry about use of the reserve components because it wouldn't be politically acceptable, but because the reserves performed so well, that worry decreased after Desert Storm. Not only would negative feelings about the reserve components dramatically decrease, but the reserves would become an operational necessity in later years as the go-to force, transformed from a strategic reserve to an operational reserve.

After Desert Storm, regular Army professionals and politicians alike knew they could depend on the reserve components. The Abrams Doctrine, conceived by Gen. Creighton Abrams in the early 1970s, and later adopted by Defense Secretary Melvin Laird as the Total Force Doctrine, professed America should never go to war without substantial mobilization of the reserve components. Abrams believed the reserves represented America at its heart and they were a visible representation of our armed forces in the homes, factories, farms, and offices across America.

When the invasion of Kuwait occurred, Nancy and I were on vacation with our kids in Penn Yan at the family cottage on Keuka Lake. My mother, Dale, Gene, Rosemary and I shared time at the cottage with our families. We could each set aside up to two weeks during the summer to enjoy the lake. About two days after we arrived, I received a phone call from the staff administrative assistant at the 1209th Garrison, who asked me to return to the unit as soon as possible. He said I would be given orders to inspect the mobilization files of certain units within the 1209th to ensure they were prepared in case of a mobilization.

I initially balked because it meant losing my time at the lake, but I was told that, due to my position as the garrison's mobilization officer, the commander had asked for me by name. When I first joined the Army Reserve in 1973, I knew I could be called to active duty, but given the history of rare mobilizations of the Reserve the possibility seemed remote. Annoyed at the interruption of my vacation, I nevertheless understood life was sometimes overcome by events beyond my control. We packed up, left Penn Yan, and drove 75 miles back to Syracuse.

I was given orders to inspect the mobilization files for two units, one in Schenectady, and one in Mattydale. After my visits I submitted a report for each unit to the commander of the 1209th Army Garrison. The reports detailed their training and maintenance records, their personnel-manning rosters and determined the number of qualified personnel available for deployment. I also identified the number and types of equipment considered mission capable and ensured the units had an adequate procedure for notifying unit members. From what I observed, each unit appeared ready to mobilize, with minor tweaks. I felt confident they could muster enough personnel and equipment to get to their mobilization station. After that, the process of validation and approval for deployment rested with the mobilization assistance team at their mobilization station.

Mobilization consisted of four phases: (1) Preparation, or the ongoing phase conducted during weekend inactive duty training and annual active duty training; (2) Alert and Assembly, when a unit is alerted by higher command and all unit members are directed to report to their Reserve training center for records processing and issuance of equipment; (3) Movement to Mobilization Station, when the unit travels to a pre-designated military base for final processing, training, and validation for deployment; and (4) Deployment, when the unit travels with all validated personnel and authorized equipment to a designated area of operations.

My job was to ensure the units had performed appropriate training, to check their personnel and equipment-readiness status, and that duty appointments were made to the key positions necessary to initiate the mobilization process.

The 1209th Army Garrison was deactivated in the fall of 1990, as a result of force restructuring by the Department of Defense, and neither of the units I inspected was activated for Operations Desert Shield or Desert Storm. The garrison was no longer needed because there was an active Army garrison in place at Fort Drum. Enlisted personnel in the 1209th were automatically reassigned to other units within commuting distance of their homes. Officers had four options: find a position compatible with their current rank in another unit, be reassigned to the inactive control group in a non-pay status, retire if eligible, or resign their commission.

If the Army issued a "stop-loss" order, all retirements and resignations were put on hold. My status remained in limbo for a few weeks after the unit deactivated as I considered my options. Then I received a call from the same staff administrator at the 1209th who called me away from my vacation. He offered me an assignment with another unit in Ithaca.

I was assigned to Headquarters, 3rd Brigade (Engineer OSUT), 98th Division (Training), as the assistant training officer. The brigade was the higher headquarters of my former outfit at the 3/389th Regiment. I was grateful for the assignment because it meant I no longer had to fear transfer to a non-pay control group. By that time Nancy and I were in the Reserves for the long haul and the second income came in handy.

Shortly after I was reassigned I was given an opportunity for a temporary tour of duty at Fort Devens, Massachusetts, during Operation Desert Shield. Fort Devens was a mobilization station for many Army Reserve and National Guard units in the Northeast and I would be assigned to work in the Emergency Operations Center (EOC) to facilitate the mobilization of units as they arrived for deployment to the Middle East. The EOC was the center of gravity for all base operations. It received and disseminated non-classified and classified information, monitored threat levels, coordinated the arrival of mobilizing units and assigned mobilization-assistance teams to validate units for deployment. It also scheduled their departure when they were ready. During routine operations the pace was often slow, but during a massive mobilization like Desert Shield, it was a high-tempo, high-stress environment. It operated 24/7, 365 days a year. I was well prepared for the assignment because a year earlier the 1209th sent me to Fort McCoy, Wisconsin, to take a mobilization planners course. I fared well enough to be placed on the commander's list, reserved for the highest-scoring students. I drove to Massachusetts the day after Thanksgiving to begin my assignment at Fort Devens.

All hell broke loose at home the day I left. Our youngest, Kevin, developed a high fever. Nancy took him to the pediatrician, who diagnosed an ear infection. She stopped to fill a prescription and when she arrived home, she heard what sounded like a waterfall in the kitchen. Our second oldest, Stephen, was in the shower upstairs. Water had spilled onto the bathroom floor, seeped through the ceiling below and into the kitchen. While I was away, Murphy's Law was in effect. If anything could go wrong, it would.

At Fort Devens I quickly became acquainted with another temporary-duty officer. He suggested since we were on active duty during a real operation not classified as training, it would benefit us to have an officer evaluation report (OER) issued to rate our performance and document our service during Operation Desert Shield. Someone in the chain of command, preferably an officer with direct supervision over me, would be my rater. Another officer at least two grades above me would act as my senior rater. OERs in the Reserves were typically issued once a year but I was advised if I served on active duty for at least 18 days, I could request a special OER. My orders had been issued for only 12 days, so I phoned the Reserve center in Mattydale to request an extension to 18 days. It was granted due to the size and anticipated duration of the mobilization.

To get started in my assignment, I met with the civilians and the other soldiers at the EOC and began work as an operations officer. They all seemed friendly enough and I soon settled into a regular work schedule. I slowly developed a rapport with everyone and after I felt comfortable with my new duties, I requested an OER be issued at the end of my assignment. I was encouraged to find out I would be rated by the deputy director of the EOC, a senior civilian employee. I had occasional contact with him but since he was a civilian, I felt more comfortable with him as my rater. He knew I was a reservist and would identify more with my background.

During one of my shifts at the EOC, while browsing through the list of Reserve units mobilized around the country, I noticed the 403rd Civil Affairs Company was activated. I'd served with that unit for nine years and had many friends there but felt left out because they were going to war without me. I called the commander of the unit, Lt. Col. John Butler, whom I knew from my assignment with the 403rd, and asked if he could request me by name for their battle roster so I could deploy with them. John said he'd like to have me in the unit but higher headquarters filled all unit vacancies with members from other civil affairs units to bring them to full strength. Since I was no longer in the civil affairs chain of command, there was no chance to be attached to the 403rd CA Company. It was disheartening to know I couldn't join the people I knew and served with for so many years.

I soon learned my senior rater would be the installation commander, Col. Richard Hoover, a regular Army engineer officer. The rater was supposed to be someone who knew how the rated soldier performed on a daily basis. The senior rater was usually someone who knew the person at least casually and based his or her rating largely on information provided by the rater. The senior rater's evaluation was important because he or she graded the rated officer on a pyramid-type scale that compared the officer with other officers of the same rank whom the senior rater had graded that year.

Because I was new to the EOC, the colonel asked to meet with me to discuss my job performance and get to know me better. Our meeting was cordial and my past experience as a company commander in an engineer training unit may have helped create some rapport with him. I was pleasantly surprised to get a top-block rating on the population curve of Reserve majors he rated although, who knows, I may have been the only one. The following is Col. Hoover's comments on my performance:

Maj. Mitchell excelled in every endeavor and demonstrated the best of professionalism throughout his tour of duty... His ability to conduct research and produce factual staff papers with logical recommendations is second to none. He leads by example and is in peak physical condition. (I had received the maximum score on the physical fitness test while at Fort Devens.)

I rate his potential as unlimited. Promote immediately. He is ready for battalion command now.

I was elated to receive such glowing remarks from an active-duty colonel, but how important was the OER in the advancement of my career? It would be another six years before I was promoted, and nine years before I received a battalion command.

Practically speaking, it only helped me keep up with my peers, who also "walked on water", and my career progressed at a normal pace.

The long wait for promotion worked to my advantage, because in the Army Reserve, officers who lobbied for early promotion were usually unsuccessful unless they had political connections in the unit or were West Point graduates. The mandatory-promotion system required seven years in grade for promotion to each grade at captain and above. Officers risked the chance their careers would be cut short if they were promoted too fast, because opportunities for promotion dwindled at the top. Retirement was mandatory after 28 years' commissioned service or at age 60, whichever came first, so someone who wanted to stay in the Army until mandatory retirement was wise to take promotions based on time in grade and not seek early promotions.

When my assignment at Fort Devens ended, I drove home to spend the holidays with my family and watched the successful outcome of Operation Desert Storm on television. I wanted to make more of a contribution, to give me a sense of closure after the disappointment in Vietnam.

Several years earlier, U.S. Magistrate Judge Edward Conan, for whom I first clerked at the U.S. District Court, asked if it frustrated me not to have used my training for a real mission. I said yes, but at least I felt ready if I was ever called up. My short time spent at Fort Devens in support of Desert Shield in 1990 provided me the satisfaction of contributing to a real mission. I couldn't know that within three years I would have a role in a real mission which would put me in harm's way.

After our decisive victory in Desert Storm in 1991, our armed forces received their first welcome-home parade since World War II. I felt only a remote connection with the troops because I didn't deploy with them; but at least I assisted in getting them to the fight. Meantime, a song from 1984 regained popularity during Desert Storm. Lee Greenwood's "God Bless the USA," resulted in a new swell of patriotism.

Transfer Within the Courts

During the spring of 1990, I accepted a voluntary transfer to the clerk's office in Binghamton, about 80 miles from home. A coworker, Larry Baerman, had become the chief deputy and headed up that office. He offered what I felt was a great opportunity as the courtroom clerk to Judge Thomas McAvoy. I'd known Larry since I started working with the court. He was personable, had a great sense of humor, and was personally driven. He was also a talented golfer who excelled as a scholastic athlete and a young amateur. I believe he could have gone on the pro tour, were it not for his attachment to Upstate New York and his family roots there.

My new position required me to drive 90 minutes each way, but it was a promotion–and it came with a pay raise. Nancy and I made plans to move to the Binghamton area. After several weeks, we still couldn't find a house we liked in our price range; because the housing market was depressed, we didn't feel we could sell our house for enough money to make the move worthwhile, so I resigned myself to the long daily commute.

Judge McAvoy ran an accelerated court docket and was noted for his quick disposition of cases. I put in many extra hours to keep his schedule filled. It was my most difficult assignment with the court. The amount of work involved overwhelmed me and I eventually got reassigned to another position. For the first time since getting fired from the furniture company in 1974, I was told my performance was unsatisfactory. There had been allegations of unfair labor practices at the furniture company, but this time I just couldn't keep pace with the workload.

Adding to the increased stress in my new court position was my second job in the Army Reserve. My newest assignment with Headquarters, 3rd Brigade, in Ithaca, required me to attend training meetings every Wednesday from 6 to 10 p.m., instead of one weekend a month. Every Wednesday after work I drove 40 miles from Binghamton to the Reserve center for the training meeting. I stayed overnight at the cheapest motel I could find (I was not on orders and had to pay for it out of pocket). The next morning, I drove back to Binghamton. My previous training and experience with reserve mobilization led me to once again assume duties as the mobilization officer with the 3rd Brigade headquarters. I took the initiative to update their mobilization files, and I planned and conducted a brigade-level mobilization workshop, at which I acted as the brigade's senior representative. My assignment there lasted just more than a year, until November 1991, when a chance encounter at a court social function in Syracuse renewed my acquaintance with Lt. Col. John Butler from the 403rd CA Company.

In civilian life John, a local attorney, was admitted to practice at the U.S. District Court. As I recounted my previous time with the 403rd CA, he informed me the unit would be reorganized into a battalion. The change to a higher echelon unit included more positions at the rank of major, and he asked whether I wanted to reprise my role as supply officer with the unit. It took me a mere second to say yes.

Back to Civil Affairs

I was excited to be back with the 403rd CA. Several officers in the unit had been informal mentors when I was a newly commissioned officer. John knew my history with the 403rd and assigned me as direct-support team chief with additional duties as battalion supply officer overseeing inventory. In conjunction with the reorganization, the unit transferred from the training center in Liverpool, to a larger, more-modern facility in Mattydale, about eight miles away–where the former 1209th Army Garrison had been before its deactivation. The direct-support team was responsible for providing support to the commander at the tactical level and advising the commander on civil-military operations within a specified area. I still commuted to Binghamton every day for my civilian job with the courts, but it was a relief to no longer drive to Ithaca during the week and pay for an overnight motel stay.

The reorganization to a battalion may have been the result of a change in the Army's organizational structure. In October 1985, about a year before I left the 403rd, the U.S. Army Reserve

Special Operations Command (USARSOC) was created and given operational control of all Army Reserve Civil Affairs and Psychological Operations units. This began a paradigm shift in the way civil affairs units trained and operated. During 1990, in the midst of sending soldiers to the Persian Gulf during Operation Desert Shield, USARSOC was re-designated the U.S. Army Civil Affairs and Psychological Operations Command (Airborne), or USACAPOC(A). This was significant because it eliminated the words "Army Reserve" from the title and it became an airborne command. USACAPOC(A) joined all Reserve civil affairs and psychological operations units with their active counterparts. It was more in line with the total force concept Gen. Abrams envisioned and had the effect of giving civil affairs more credibility.

By 1991 some new faces had appeared in the 403rd, but I still knew many people from my previous assignment between 1977 and 1986. During my first year back, I took responsibility as the planning officer for annual training at Camp Smith, a short distance from West Point Military Academy. I planned the convoy movement that included driver assignments, the vehicle order of march, and identified checkpoints along the way without the benefit of computers (which were still a few years from being introduced in reserve units). Camp Smith was used primarily as a National Guard training area; it occupied 2,000 acres in southeastern New York State. Approximately 85% of the land consisted of rugged, hilly terrain with the remaining land as former farmland on a plateau overlooking the Hudson River. It was one of two bases where West Point cadets participated in air-assault training; the other was at Fort Campbell, Kentucky.

Our training plan called for a tactical field exercise at Camp Smith. To ensure training went according to schedule, I published a matrix to track the time needed for each phase of the exercise. The training was physically and mentally challenging, but it was necessary for our new role as a priority unit. As part of the Army Special Operations Command, our chances for mobilization increased. Special Operations forces were often among the first sent into a conflict.

By 1992, Nancy was expecting our fifth child. She was not as far along in her pregnancy as she was with Kevin when I left for Fort Leonard Wood in 1987, so she wasn't as nervous about my absence when I left for Camp Smith. Our last child, Scott Anthony Mitchell, arrived January 3, 1993. To put his birth in perspective, Scott was born almost 20 years after our first child, Gregory. At Scott's birth, Nancy was 42 and I was 46. Despite my absences for Reserve training through the years, I was present for the births of all our children.

Physical Fitness School

The Army Physical Fitness Test (APFT), administered at least once a year, consisted of three facets: pushups, sit-ups, and a two-mile run–done in that order. For the pushup and sit-up events, soldiers had two minutes to do as many correct repetitions as possible. For the run, each soldier was timed to see how fast he or she could complete the two miles on a flat course. Raw scores were converted to a graduated scale, from 0 to 100, according to age groups. A passing score was 70 in each event, but in the U.S. Army Special Operations Command, the standard was 80 in each event. A score of 70 was still considered passing because individual commands could not change the Army-wide standard, but they were free to set internal goals. Civil affairs units were encouraged to meet the higher scores. Alternate tests were given for those with medical or physical profiles. These alternate tests included walking, bicycling, or swimming.

Back in 1986, as an incentive, the Army established the Physical Fitness Excellence Patch. To qualify for the patch a soldier must score at least 90 in each event, for a total of 270 out of a possible 300 points. I always maintained a high level of fitness and earned a Physical Fitness Excellence Patch every year. Unusual for a reservist, I maintained a regular personal-fitness regimen in addition to any physical training during weekend drills.

In the spring of 1993, the 403rd CA had a quota to fill a slot for the Master Fitness Trainer Course conducted by the U.S. Army Physical Fitness School. The goal was to have a master fitness trainer in each battalion-size unit to manage physical training for the commander. The school was at Fort Benning, Georgia, but that year they held a course for reservists at Oceana Naval Air Station, Virginia. The active duty course was four weeks but was condensed into two weeks for the reserves. When the soldier initially selected to attend the course couldn't go, I volunteered. Some unit members questioned why a major should attend, since it was usually attended by NCOs or junior officers. Course graduates acted as the commander's adviser on physical-readiness matters and administered the unit's fitness program. I received some support when someone noted I always scored high on the APFT and would be a good candidate. It was the most practical course I ever took in the Army.

When I arrived at Oceana Naval Air Station, I was weighed and administered the APFT again, to satisfy the school I met the Army standard under their direct supervision. Some test administrators, especially in the reserves, would falsify scores to keep otherwise-good soldiers from being flagged, or barred, from promotion and possibly subject to discharge from the service.

I was about to experience the difference between Army life and Navy life. We were assigned to enlisted billets, which were equal to an officer's billet on an Army base; a nicely furnished room with a private bath. Meals in the dining facility bore little resemblance to the ones we endured in the Army. I had heard stories through the years about the difference in quality of life in the Navy, and my time at Oceana verified them. When our class met for the first time, I was identified as the senior-ranking student so I was appointed the class leader, a position I had hoped to avoid, because it raised my profile with the instructors. They would scrutinize me because of my rank, to ensure I wasn't some slacker just looking for a couple weeks' extra pay.

We were advised at the start that the academic phase of the course was the primary focus and physical exercise was secondary. The instructors emphasized we would cover the same material as the four-week active duty course. There would be no short cuts for reservists. We were warned the classroom instruction would be highly concentrated; it focused on anatomy, muscle physiology, the principles of exercise, and nutrition. Targeted exercises to reinforce classroom instruction were intended to improve our physical conditioning and flexibility.

The instructors injected some fun into the exercises with an "Olympics" competition. Class members were assigned to teams that competed for token awards. I received an official Army Physical Fitness plastic water bottle for the pushup event, at which I originally became proficient through forced repetitions during basic training. Written tests presented the biggest challenge for those who weren't prepared for the amount of classroom work and the study requirements. To assist classmates who needed help, I organized a study group and took pride in the class achieving a 100% graduation rate. I returned home in late June 1993, with a certificate awarding me the title of U.S. Army Master Fitness Trainer.

As much as I enjoyed and advocated physical fitness training, there was one training requirement imposed by the Army Special Operations Command I found unnecessary. Once each year we were required to complete a five-mile road march. I thought it was a waste of time and it did more harm than good. We were required to carry 45 pounds or a third of our body weight, whichever was greater, in a rucksack and complete the five miles within two and a half hours. I usually carried weights from home totaling 55 pounds and put extra cushioning in my boots to absorb the shock on my knees. Carrying that amount of weight for five miles was brutal on the legs, feet, and back. Practically speaking, I could think of no reason for a soldier in the modern Army to march five miles carrying that much weight. In my opinion, there was no benefit from doing it only once a year and the resulting blisters, back pain, and knee damage outweighed any benefit.

Chapter 9
Mogadishu, Somalia (Nov. 1993-March 1994)

In 1992, halfway around the world on the Horn of Africa, ongoing famine and power struggles had reduced Somalia to a state of anarchy and clan warfare. The events that led to my deployment to Mogadishu were detailed in an unclassified publication by the Center for Military History, *The United States Army in Somalia*. It provides the background for the United States' involvement and explained how mission creep developed, which led to the battle depicted in the book and the movie, *Black Hawk Down*. I've included a summary of that publication in the following paragraphs:

The ongoing feud between warlords resulted in U.N. Resolution 814, which considerably broadened its mandate to intervene in another country's affairs, and the U.N. began to intervene militarily in a peacemaking role. It became involved in peace *enforcement* (italics added), and not merely peacekeeping. By May, the United States initiated Operation Continue Hope in support of U.N. Operations Somalia (UNOSOM) and provided a substantial logistics structure consisting of about 2,600 troops and a small special-operations element. The U.S. also provided a 1,100-soldier quick reaction force (QRF) from the 10th Mountain Division based at Fort Drum.

The relief operations went well at first, and it seemed some measure of normalcy returned for the Somali people. Markets reopened, travel became more common, and hope of restarting a Somali national police force met with some initial success. However, U.N. diplomats began to press for a more active military role in confiscating weapons from the clan armies and forcing some kind of political settlement. "Mission creep" began to enter the vocabulary of those serving in Somalia, and after the United States turned over the mission to the U.N. in May, the situation started to unravel.

The most powerful warlord, Mohamed Farrah Aidid, had little respect for UNOSOM or the U.N. On June 5, his forces ambushed and killed 24 Pakistani soldiers; another 44 were wounded. In response, the U.N. Security Council approved Resolution 837, which adopted a more aggressive military policy toward Aidid. From June 11-17, Aidid's forces came under attack, during which two weapons storage facilities were destroyed and Radio Mogadishu, Aidid's propaganda station, was rendered ineffective. His vehicle compounds were also destroyed. A warrant was issued for Aidid's arrest with a $25,000 reward.

On August 8, Aidid's forces detonated a mine under a passing U.S. Military Police vehicle, killing four U.S. soldiers. As the situation worsened, the U.N. Secretary-General Boutros Boutros-Ghali asked President Clinton to assist him in capturing Aidid. The U.S. soon deployed a joint special-operations task force to Somalia. The task force, named Task Force (TF) Ranger, had the mission to capture Aidid and his key lieutenants and turn them over to UNOSOM forces.

During August and September, the task force conducted six missions into Mogadishu, all of them tactical successes. On September 21, Osman Atto, Aidid's chief financial aide and close adviser, was captured. The operation went smoothly, but for the first time the U.S. Rangers received mass rocket-propelled grenade (RPG) fire from Somali militia.

On October 3, TF Ranger, under U.S. command, conducted its seventh mission, this time into Aidid's stronghold near the Bakara Market, to capture two of his key lieutenants. The Rangers came under increasingly heavy enemy fire, more intense than during previous raids. The assault team captured 24 Somalis and was about to load them onto the convoy trucks when a circling Black Hawk helicopter was hit by an RPG and crashed nearby. A six-man element, a small assault helicopter and a modified Black Hawk carrying a 15-man combat search-and-rescue team, were deployed. They evacuated two wounded soldiers, but their copter was also hit by an RPG. Somehow the pilot managed to keep the helicopter steady and nursed it back to the Mogadishu airport.

Ground fire struck two more Black Hawks; one went down less than a mile from the first downed helicopter, while the other made it to safety at the airport. A Somali mob overran the second crash site and, despite a heroic defense effort, killed everyone except one of the pilots, Michael Durant, whom they took prisoner. Two defenders at this location, Master Sgt. Gary Gordon and Sgt. 1st Class Randall Shughart, were posthumously awarded the Medal of Honor, the first awarded since Vietnam.

Meanwhile, after loading the detainees on trucks, the convoy attempted to reach the first crash site but was unable to find it among the narrow, winding alleyways. They came under small-arms and RPG fire and, after suffering numerous casualties, returned to the airport.

Back at the airport, a relief column was slowly being formed. The coordination time was significant because it was a complex, multinational force operation under U.N. command. After hours of planning and collecting forces, a 60+ vehicle convoy finally moved out with Pakistani tanks in the lead. As dawn broke on October 4, all the casualties from the first crash site were loaded onto the armored personnel carriers. The remainder of the force ran to safety inside a soccer stadium in what became known as the Mogadishu Mile. The main force of the convoy arrived at the stadium around 0630 hours on October 4. It was one of the bloodiest and violent urban firefights since the 1968 Tet Offensive.

Task Force Ranger lost 16 soldiers; another 57 were wounded during the battle. The 10th Mountain Division's 2nd Battalion, 14th Infantry lost two and had 22 wounded. Various estimates placed Somali casualties between 500 and 1,500. Two Black Hawks were downed, and two others were damaged but managed to reach the airport.

U.S. military presence in Somalia increased significantly after the October 3-4 battle. These forces were organized under a new Joint Task Force Somalia. Gen. Thomas Montgomery's guidance was to protect the force, protect the U.N., and bring our forces out with a minimum of casualties. President Clinton directed that all U.S. forces would withdraw from Somalia no later than March 31, 1994. After intense negotiations, Aidid agreed to release the wounded pilot, Michael Durant.

Among the U.S. soldiers involved in Somalia were Army civil affairs and psychological operations forces. The 96th Civil Affairs Battalion at Fort Bragg deployed a CA tactical-support team and six direct-support teams to provide critical support for relief operations.

Deployment to Mogadishu

My involvement in Somalia was the result of President Clinton's decision to increase U.S. presence there. I was outraged and disturbed as the media released news of the battle and streamed graphic video clips showing our dead soldiers' bodies being dragged through the streets like animals. The barbaric and offensive display by the Somalis would have to be avenged by the United States, and I felt compelled to be part of it. On October 8, less than a week after the battle, the 403rd CA Battalion received an order from USACAPOC to provide personnel for Joint Task Force Somalia in support of Operation

Continue Hope. I told Nancy I felt a personal duty to volunteer. She looked at me in disbelief and asked if I had a death wish.

I told her I needed to contribute whatever training and experience I had gained through the years. I thought back again to Judge Conan's question years earlier; if I felt frustrated about not using my training in an actual mission. I saw Somalia as my chance to use it in a larger role.

After convincing Nancy I was serious, I called my unit to volunteer. On October 13, I was placed on orders to report to Fort Bragg for pre-deployment processing and training. One of my fellow officers asked me why I volunteered for an apparently thankless and dangerous mission. I told him I wasn't needed for Desert Storm and it was my turn to go.

Two other members of the 403rd, Capt. Shannon Kennedy and Staff Sgt. Tony DeFoster, also volunteered. Together we became part of a specialized team assembled from various civil affairs units to relieve members of the 96th CA Battalion who'd been in Somalia for several months.

Nancy and I sat down and reviewed our finances, wills, and life-insurance policies. I executed a power of attorney, so she could act on my behalf while I was gone. I arrived at Fort Bragg on October 25 and went through the mobilization process I had studied and planned for the past several years. It was no longer a paper exercise. I underwent medical and dental exams, received immunizations and had a psychological interview to determine my mental fitness for possible combat, which was a sobering thought to say the least. I also had to provide a DNA sample, so I could be identified in case of my death because Somalis were known to mutilate enemy dead. Nancy may have questioned my sanity when I volunteered, but the Army declared I was mentally and physically fit for duty. I had to qualify with the M16A1 rifle and the 9mm semiautomatic handgun and received general cultural training about Somalia, its people, and their language. I easily passed the physical fitness test and weight standards. Finally, I was issued desert camouflage uniforms, boots, web gear, an M16 rifle and 9mm Beretta pistol.

At Fort Bragg I met the other members of the civil affairs operational-planning team that would become part of the task force from the 18th Airborne Corps. The other members included Col. Michael Deegan, the officer-in-charge, Lt. Col. William Deane, Sgt. 1st Class Dennis McTighe of the 414th CA Battalion from Utica, and Sgt. Thomas Burrell of the 401st CA Battalion from Webster, New York.

I was selected to be the operations officer, responsible for planning and executing missions and ensuring we complied with the operations plan from USACAPOC. It would be my first deployment as a civil affairs officer. We were given the mission to conduct stability operations to protect the force, which involved interaction and coordination with numerous international and private relief organizations, and coordination of medical and engineer civic-action projects. To keep us updated on the current situation in the country, we received daily sitreps (situation reports) from the CA team in Mogadishu.

One of my duties was to conduct mission briefings. My first briefing was to Maj. Gen. Campbell, the commander of the U.S. Army Civil Affairs and Psychological Operations Command. The briefing map of Mogadishu was color coded with the position of U.S. forces indicated in yellow. In a poor attempt at humor, I pointed to our position and stated the color in no way represented the status of our troops. The general remarked that the statement was unnecessary and inappropriate. Ten years later I would encounter the general again, while he was employed as a civilian in Baghdad during Operation Iraqi Freedom. Fortunately, he didn't remember my gaffe during my briefing on Somalia.

Arrival in Mogadishu

After we completed our deployment training and were validated by the Mobilization Assistance Team at Fort Bragg, we boarded a bus to Dover Air Force Base in Delaware for our departure flight. While we waited, two members of my higher headquarters at the 352nd CA Command in Riverdale paid a visit to see us off. Late that night we boarded a C-5A cargo jet, the largest aircraft in the U.S. Air Force. It was configured with passenger seats to make our trip more comfortable. After a long flight that included a three-hour stop in West Cairo, Egypt, we landed at the Mogadishu Airport at 0600 hours the following morning, November 3.

It was exactly 30 days after the battle in Mogadishu. As I stepped off the aircraft onto the ground, the air hit me like a blast from a furnace. I had never experienced heat that intense so early in the morning – not even in Vietnam. As we waited at the airport in the sweltering heat for a convoy to pick us up, I wondered what challenges we would face in the days and weeks ahead. Our convoy arrived about an hour later and we met some of our counterparts from the 96th CA Battalion. They were the guys we would relieve. We rode in the back of three Humvees, one equipped with a mounted M60 machine gun. The floor of the cargo area was covered with sandbags intended to reduce or prevent injury by absorbing the blast from a bomb that might go off in the road.

Somalia was bordered on the east by the Indian Ocean and on the west by Djibouti, Ethiopia, and Kenya. The capital, Mogadishu, was about 200 miles north of the equator. The area outside the city was almost barren. It was mostly sand with little vegetation and an occasional umbrella tree that offered a small amount of shade. The economy was based on livestock, although fishing was important along the coast. There was no water or sewage system, and only a few local generators stood to provide electricity to residents. As we drove toward our destination in the city, a few Somalis and their children waved at us. It was as if nothing had happened four weeks earlier. It took us about 15 minutes to arrive at a building that once housed the National University of Somalia. It was circular and U.S. troops dubbed it "the doughnut." A defensive perimeter had been established around the campus with concertina wire, barricades, and guard towers. Concertina wire came in coils that could be deployed quickly and stacked in multiple levels to form an instant barrier. It looked like a Slinky toy when stretched out, except it could tear clothing and cut into the skin of anyone who tried to breach it.

    I was initially assigned to live in a large Pakistani tent with five other U.S. soldiers. We were given the rest of the day to catch up on sleep, but the heat was so oppressive even routine activities like unpacking my duffel bag made me drip with sweat. The next morning, we met with the other team members for a situation update. Most of them were Army Special Forces soldiers from Fort Bragg who were also qualified in civil affairs. I worked closely with Maj. (Promotable) John Whidden. Before Col. Deegan's arrival Maj. Whidden was the senior CA officer in Mogadishu. I was assigned as his assistant operations officer. Some background on Maj. Whidden deserves mention.

    John Whidden had earned his Ph.D. and was qualified in virtually every soldier skill imaginable: airborne, ranger, special forces, pathfinder, and medic. He was an iconic personality who gained legendary status at USACAPOC during his time in Mogadishu. One report related a time he pulled out a knife and cut a Somali civilian when a crowd pressed in too close during a medical-assistance visit. Already in Mogadishu for several months, John had established himself as the primary staff officer for civil affairs operations. He was diligent and highly committed to the mission in Somalia, but by the time I arrived he showed mounting effects of stress from his long deployment. However, he was deemed so essential to the CA mission, his orders were extended when most other CA soldiers rotated home. As time went on, his temper grew short and he often became impatient, even belligerent, with other officers.

As an officer on the promotion list for lieutenant colonel (hence the designation "Promotable"), he tried to use it as leverage to push the CA mission with units we supported. By January, reports of his erratic behavior had made their way to the chief of staff, who summoned John for a meeting. As his assistant, I was requested to accompany him. After a stern lecture, he was referred for counseling and advised to be more considerate with others.

Consideration became John's mantra and I was directed to accompany him wherever he went and report any outbreaks of temper directly to the chief of staff. As a result of the meeting, John went out of his way to be considerate. After he met with someone with whom he was particularly annoyed, he would turn to me and sarcastically ask whether he had been considerate enough. At times I joked that maybe he was too considerate. John and I would become friends and go on many missions together in Mogadishu.

During my first week of duty I attended civil affairs staff meetings, found a place to run within the perimeter, and helped pile sandbags around our tent for protection against mortar blasts. About one week later I was notified Capt. Kennedy and Staff Sgt. DeFoster had arrived at the airport and were awaiting pickup. By that time, I was fully immersed and knowledgeable of the force-protection requirement and rules of engagement. I organized a convoy of two Humvees and met them at the airport. It was great to see familiar faces. Shannon Kennedy was a bright, amiable guy of Irish descent who served in the Navy during Vietnam and would help anyone who asked. Tony DeFoster was a decorated combat veteran of Vietnam and a good marksman. He found humor in almost everything, often sarcastically, and he always lightened up a conversation.

Everything appeared peaceful after my arrival in Mogadishu, but the force-protection rules required caution. We had to travel with a minimum of two vehicles, one equipped with an automatic weapon. Each vehicle had to be occupied by at least one other armed person in addition to the driver. We could use deadly force to protect weapons, classified information, and against hostile threats or acts, but with the minimum necessary force to repel a threat. We were to avoid casualties to unarmed civilians who might be intermingled with armed individuals by shouting warnings, using pepper spray, or firing warning shots to disperse crowds. If there was no time for crowd dispersal, we had to minimize collateral damage by avoiding the use of grenades or machine guns and engage armed individuals with our personal weaponry (M16 rifle or 9mm pistol). If we were fired upon but could not see muzzle flashes or did not know the location of the attackers, we were to move out of the area as fast as possible and report the incident.

It was apparent a response to a perceived threat required quick decision making to use the right amount of force and avoid collateral damage. The first seconds of an encounter were critical in deciding the appropriate amount of force if it was called for at all.

I settled into a daily routine that included staff meetings and coordination meetings with other units, with U.N. officials, and with humanitarian-relief organizations. I wrote daily situation reports with the laptop computer I was issued and used the internet to send unclassified reports back to Fort Bragg. One of my first assignments was to write a CA estimate for Mogadishu. The CA estimate was a detailed report that evaluated the status of various civil functions in the area and their possible impact on the mission. They might include the available labor market, type of education system, agricultural resources, economic-development needs, public-safety conditions, public-health needs, and dislocated persons, refugees and evacuees. I thought its usefulness was marginal at best. It was a long-term planning tool for nation-building purposes and it was clear we weren't there to conduct nation building ... or were we?

The temperature hovered around 110° every day and the amount of equipment we were required to carry made it imperative to stay hydrated and in good physical condition. I carried bottled water on trips outside our compound. To stay in shape, I ran around the inside of the perimeter and did pushups and sit-ups. I was thankful for the master fitness course I'd taken the previous June. As a preventive-health measure, once each week we took a pill to prevent malaria, which often resulted in a bout of diarrhea.

Portable johns were positioned at several places around our compound. After a few days the stench became so strong, I held my breath as I walked past them. It was especially bad when the "honey wagon" came around twice a week to suck out the waste. If I'd had a chemical mask available then, I would have used it inside the portable john, as I had several years earlier.

One of the major impacts we had was the trust we built among the Somali people. They knew the civil affairs detachment was the place to go for assistance. It was how we attempted to win hearts and minds in Mogadishu.

In November a Somali couple arrived at the main gate of the university compound, complaining their son had been injured by a truck belonging to Brown & Root, the company contracted by the U.N. to provide construction and support services; incidents like that damaged our trust-building efforts. The couple had been referred to our CA team. Through an interpreter, I interviewed them to get details of their complaint, in hopes of facilitating a solution. I advised them of their right to submit a claim against Brown & Root, then referred them to the staff judge advocate's office to file their claim.

Some satisfying moments in Somalia gave me hope we were making a difference. We were invited by a former professor at the university to visit the Children's Language Institute. I organized a convoy and we traveled in three Humvees with an M60 machine gun mounted on one of the vehicles. When we arrived, about 100 children greeted us. Several of them expressed their gratitude in broken English for the humanitarian assistance the United States provided. As the senior officer present, I was asked to say something to the children. I spoke a few words through our interpreter and ended by thanking them in Somali for the invitation. During deployment training I learned some rudimentary Somali vocabulary words. The students applauded with approval and I felt like we had taken a small step in creating a favorable image of U.S. forces.

On another occasion we delivered medical supplies to a clinic, and school supplies to one of the local schools. Throughout our deployment, we assisted Somalis lined up at the front gate to find work. I even wrote a recommendation letter for a clan chief to give him direct access to UNOSOM officials so he could request employment and humanitarian assistance for his people. Those activities encouraged me that maybe we could win over some of the people. Primarily, though, my interactions with the children gave me hope they would remember our kindness as they grew up.

Tensions Remained

In Mogadishu we resurrected the Animals' Vietnam-era song, "We Gotta Get Out of This Place". After several weeks we were frustrated in our efforts to improve basic public services and to establish the rule of law. It was virtually impossible to get the U.N. to act on any requests we made for support, because they operated within a huge bureaucracy that impeded progress. Adding to our frustration was the clan rivalry, which remained a constant threat to civil order. One day, inter-clan fighting in the city killed four Somalis and wounded two. Mogadishu reminded me of the Wild West, where everyone had a weapon and wasn't afraid to use it. It remained a tense and hostile environment. In mid-November we learned an American soldier traveling in a U.N. vehicle was killed in an ambush. It demonstrated the potential for violence still existed in the city. Gunfire was an everyday occurrence, mostly between rival clans; but occasionally it was directed at coalition compounds scattered throughout the city.

Friendly fire is always a concern in a combat environment when soldiers are on edge and ready to pull the trigger. On December 15 a Tunisian soldier was killed at the university compound as his convoy exited the gate. A U.S. soldier's M60 accidentally discharged from the guard tower. Upon investigation it was learned, in violation of force-protection rules, the weapon's safety was off. The safety was to be on unless a visible threat presented itself. This was especially true inside our compound. It was a tragic example of the continued tension. I was among the CA officers dispatched to the Tunisian headquarters as a diplomatic gesture and to apologize. The Tunisians were among our most staunch partners in Somalia. Although grief stricken, they accepted our apology and understood it was an accident. I participated in a memorial service at the airport for the fallen soldier and we assured the Tunisians measures had been taken to prevent another such accident.

Five days later I narrowly avoided a friendly-fire incident of my own. I'd just started to doze off one evening when an officer came running down the hall, shouting for everyone to get to battle stations with weapons locked and loaded. Years earlier I'd escaped combat in Vietnam; but when a machine gun on the roof suddenly opened fire, I thought I might not be as lucky this time.

I threw on a shirt and pair of trousers, grabbed my Kevlar helmet and M16, then ran out to the center of the doughnut, the open area that connected the two wings of the buildng. I was pointed to a stack of sandbags and told to station myself there. We were told an armed group of Somalis attempted to breach our perimeter but were given no other information that might have told us about friendly troops in the area. I loaded a 15-round magazine into my M16, pulled back the charging handle to insert a round into the chamber, then took the rifle off safe because of the threat and switched it to "three-round burst." The soldier nearest me was about six feet away. The moonlit sky provided our only visibility as I peered into the darkness for signs of movement. The evening brought some relief from the heat but I was more concerned with the intense volume of fire put out by the machine-gun emplacement on the roof above us.

I scanned the darkness and soon noticed two silhouettes approaching our position. I wrapped my finger around the trigger and put the figures in my sights. I couldn't identify them yet and knew I had to ensure they were hostiles before firing. Despite all the machine-gun fire, they appeared to be out for an evening stroll, so I held my fire until I could identify them. I continued to watch for some clue and realized no one else along our defensive line was firing, except that damn machine gun above us, so I held my fire with my finger still wrapped around the trigger. As the two figures came into view, I identified them as Egyptian soldiers with rifles slung over their shoulders. They smiled and said hello as they passed, apparently unaware they were a trigger pull away from being shot. I breathed a sigh of relief, but it took me a little longer than usual to get to sleep that night.

The Civil Military Operations Center (CMOC)

The CMOC was the civilian version of a tactical-operations center, or the heartbeat of the coalition effort. It was where representatives of the various international-aid organizations and the U.N. gathered to plan and coordinate humanitarian assistance, to include long-term plans for nation building. It made me wonder, *If we were only there until March, why was nation building being discussed?* Something was going on at many levels above me to indicate our presence in Somalia was more than a humanitarian mission set within a stability operation.

I visited the CMOC once a week to keep updated on their activity, to coordinate CA operations with the humanitarian-aid organizations and report my actions to higher headquarters. Travel to the CMOC took us through the stronghold of Farah Aidid's Habr Gedr Clan. As a precautionary measure, I traveled there and back in an armored Mercedes SUV belonging to our German coalition partners. Its body and windows were bulletproof, and it was equipped with run-flat tires. However, the vehicle's armor offered little protection against RPGs, which had been the weapon used to down two Black Hawks in October. The driver was accompanied by an armed civilian in the front passenger seat and usually three or four passengers in the back. My first few trips were routine until one morning an ambush delayed the vehicle on its way to pick me up. After it arrived I noticed the driver's side was pock marked with several bullets. No one was injured, but the incident caused the command to discontinue my weekly trips to the CMOC.

Removal of Displaced Persons

A major portion of my time was devoted to removal and relocation of a small clan of Somalis situated between two compounds (one occupied by Americans and the other by Pakistanis). They'd been forced from their usual location as a result of inter-clan fighting. On November 12, Col. Deegan tasked me to remove the camp of approximately 300 people to open a path for a show of force through the area. I was told a classified operation was planned to move through the area with tanks and other armored vehicles, to deter any clan militia from an attack on the coalition compounds. I organized an armed convoy for an initial assessment of the area and met with the elders to discuss their relocation. I took Ayan, our female interpreter, with me and advised the elder clan members they were in danger of being fired upon if hostile activity in the camp threatened either of the coalition compounds. I was accompanied by Col. Perkins from the 46th Combat Support Hospital. He checked out the area for a possible Medical Civic Action Program (MEDCAP).

The people lived in makeshift shelters constructed of sticks, cardboard, cloth, plastic sheeting, and pieces of canvas. Many Somalis were nomadic people who moved whenever resources in the area became scarce or when their safety was threatened. They had been in that location for several weeks. Col. Perkins informed them that after they moved, his unit would conduct a MEDCAP at their new location. The Somali people had little access to medical care, so the offer was a strong incentive. The meeting went well and we returned to the university compound to begin plans for the move.

They seemed like a peaceful group of people who weren't bothering anyone. When I volunteered for Somalia I wanted to kick some Somali ass, but these weren't the people who attacked us in October. They were more likely victims of the inter-clan rivalry, the ones who had food stolen from them by the militias.

I asked Col. Deegan for clarification about why they had to be moved.

He shot back, "Terry, you were told to move them. *Just do it!*"

I answered, "Yes, sir," and marched on.

It would be a significant undertaking. I coordinated with other units for security, supplies, engineer, and transportation support. On November 17 I surveyed a relocation site with an engineer officer. It was a vacant, rectangular lot about 100 yards long and 50 yards wide, bordered on one side by a six-foot-high concrete wall. The ground was sandy with desert shrubs throughout the lot. The engineer officer agreed to clear the shrubs, grade the lot, and dig a drainage ditch.

On November 29, I made another trip to the camp with our interpreter, Ayan, and met with the clan elders again. I explained, without revealing anything classified, that for their own safety, they had to move to another area. I said we would provide transportation, food, discarded canvas, some folding cots, and surplus rations to compensate them for the move. After some discussion I thought we had an agreement for them to move on December 1st.

I published a "frag" order, or fragmentary order, which supplemented our operations order, and distributed it to the units tasked to support the move. On December 1st we assembled a convoy and moved out toward the Somali camp. I arranged with the quick-reaction force (QRF) to have a security element present at the site for force protection. The road to the camp was paved, which gave us good visibility, unlike the sand-packed roads outside the city that caused vehicles to kick up thick clouds of dust. As we approached the refugee camp in the distance, I noticed plumes of black smoke rising into the sky. As we got closer, we noticed the Somalis had set several tires on fire in the middle of the road. A pre-deployment briefing indicated Somalis burned tires as a signal for others to swarm to the area for support. It was the same tactic used during the battle almost two months earlier.

Will this end in another battle? I felt a rush of adrenalin in anticipation of a firefight. I worried we might get overrun by a mob and have to fight our way out. In the back of each Humvee we kept a box containing hand grenades and extra ammunition. It was called the *"oh shit"* box. Small groups of Somalis had gathered on the side of the road and shouted angrily at us as we drove by. We sped up, so no one could rush the convoy and board the vehicles.

After we negotiated our way around the burning tires, we arrived at the entrance of the camp. As my Humvee neared the entrance I shouted to our driver to slow down so Ayan and I could get out while he found a safe place to park. The Humvee slowed to a crawl near the line of security troops already in place, and Ayan and I jumped out. The security force was in a defensive position across the entrance to the camp with weapons at port arms, held diagonally in front of the body.

I wanted to avoid any violence and instinctively stepped in front of the troops to address the crowd of Somalis across the street. I felt as long as I was in front of our troops, there was less chance one of them would open fire at the crowd. By this time the Somali crowd had grown to more than 100 people who continued to shout and throw rocks. I was hit in the shoulder by one rock; another hit my helmet. They were obviously angry, but I didn't see anyone with weapons. We weren't there to threaten them, but it must have felt that way to them. It was a paradox civil affairs soldiers faced. We dressed like combat troops but had to appear non-threatening. Our objective was to win their trust and approval ... but this didn't seem to be moving in that direction.

  I pointed my rifle toward the ground and told Ayan to call out for any clan elders to step forward and talk. Seconds later, three Somali men emerged from the crowd and walked toward us. Ayan introduced us to each other and I invited them to join us inside the camp area under the shade of a tree. I chose the tree because I knew it was a Somali custom to have important talks under a tree. I explained through Ayan we weren't there to harm anyone, but we needed them to move for their own safety, to avoid an accidental shooting from one of the adjoining compounds. I said we would provide food, canvas, and folding cots, and we had another location picked out for them. After about 30 minutes of discussion, the clan leaders agreed to disperse the crowd. We postponed the move until December 11, so the elders could spread the news we were on a peaceful mission.

  We reassembled our convoy and returned to the university compound without further incident, thankful we had avoided an escalation of violence. Before the move the engineers had cleared the area and strung concertina wire around it as a security measure. I issued a revised frag order and on December 11 we drove to the camp, accompanied by cargo trucks carrying the promised provisions. This time no burning tires and no angry crowd met us. The only security at the site was a Bradley Fighting Vehicle (named for former General of the Army Omar

Bradley of World War II fame), a tracked armored personnel carrier armed with a 25mm chain gun capable of firing 200 rounds per minute and equipped with a coaxial 7.62mm machine gun. The QRF commander decided on the size and scope of the security force. It seemed he made a prudent decision to forego the presence of troops. The Bradley presented a huge deterrence and reduced the chance someone would get spooked and accidentally fire a round, which could quickly escalate the situation.

About half the people had already left. We helped load the remaining people and their things onto the trucks and transported them to their new area. I was awestruck by their personal possessions and makeshift shelters because they looked to me like rubbish.

At the new location, many Somalis glanced at me as they unloaded their belongings and seemed to be speaking about me. I asked Ayan what they were saying; she told me they believed I was the one responsible for making them move. I smiled at them, hoping I wasn't a marked man in case something went wrong. After everything was unloaded I left with a feeling of accomplishment.

The next day we returned to the camp, to check on the people in their new location. I was surprised and disappointed to find it abandoned. We thought they might have returned to their old camp, so we drove back there. When we arrived, an older Somali male told us he belonged to the group we'd moved. He explained his people had been chased out by another clan who claimed to own the land. The food we'd left in a small building the previous day to deliver to the relocated Somalis had been looted overnight. A couple days later I was advised the planned show of force was cancelled.

After the dust settled, I reflected on what we accomplished. We removed about 300 peaceful Somali civilians from an area to be used as an avenue of approach for a show of force, which might in the end have provoked more violence. Afterward, they were driven from their new settlement by a rival clan and apparently ended up elsewhere. My biggest disappointment was that we lost the food we promised them. I was relieved someone up the chain of command realized the show of force would have done little–if anything–to support the stability operations. The exercise turned out to be "much ado about nothing".

<u>A Day at the Beach</u>

While we planned for the relocation of the Somali camp, we also planned for a MEDCAP (Medical Civil Assistance Program) at Jasiira Village, just south of Mogadishu. Some enterprising members of our CA team along with some medical personnel, planned to do it in conjunction with an afternoon R&R near the village at a white-sand beach on the Indian Ocean. On December 5, we were joined by several personnel from a medical unit and convoyed to the small fishing village for an area assessment ("area assessment" was a valid civil affairs activity, but back at the Reserve center it was sometimes used as an excuse to get out of the center for coffee or do some sightseeing). This time, however, we determined where the MEDCAP should be located, the resources and support we needed, and how it would be set up. Afterward, we drove to the beach.

Mindful we were still in an imminent-danger zone, we set up an observation post atop a large sand dune overlooking the beach. We positioned a Humvee mounted with a .50-caliber machine gun at the top and posted two soldiers with it. They were rotated at 30-minute intervals so everyone had a chance to enjoy the surf and relax on the beach. We stripped down to the swim suits we wore under our uniforms and basked in the sun. After a few minutes, some Somali fishermen approached and offered to catch lobsters and cook them right on the beach. Several of our "beach party" negotiated a price and chipped in to pay the fishermen. I decided to pass because I was skeptical about eating lobsters cooked by Somali strangers over an open pit fire on the beach. Apparently, my skepticism was unwarranted because, according to everyone who participated, the lobsters were delicious.

While the others ate, I walked along the beach and gazed out at the Indian Ocean as the waves washed over my bare feet. I waded up to my knees but hesitated to go deeper because I worried about stingrays and sharks. Afterward, I relaxed in a folding chair to get some sun. It felt exhilarating to be out in the sun without all the equipment we had to wear every day. I looked up and down the pristine expanse of beach and imagined the area someday developed with high-rise condominiums.

If Somalia ever progressed as a civilized nation and respected the rule of law, could American businesses commercialize the country and bring McDonald's or Burger King to Somalia? Realistically, it was a far stretch to imagine Somalia as anything but a lawless, Third-World country. Given its political situation, inter-clan rivalry, poor infrastructure, and lack of a functioning government, I doubted Somalia would ever become a resort destination.

Before we left the beach, one of the Somalis took a photograph of our group in our swimsuits. After our half day of sun, surf, and a lobster feast, we put on our battle gear and convoyed back to the university compound to resume our duties. We rationalized we had performed a valid civil affairs function because we conducted an assessment of the area for our medical assistance project and created some goodwill with the Somali fishermen. We advised them to let the villagers know we would be conducting a medical-assistance project near the village later in the month.

Monitoring the Khat Market

In Somalia a leafy, slow-growing evergreen shrub or tree almost certainly contributed to the aggression and audacity of Somalis during the October 3-4 battle of Mogadishu. The plant is called Khat, and is pronounced in Somali as "cot," although most of the soldiers pronounced it "cat."

Native to East Africa and the Arabian Peninsula, Khat contains an amphetamine-like stimulant said to cause excitement, loss of appetite, and feelings of euphoria. A controlled substance in many countries, it is illegal to import to the United States, but is legal for sale and production in many other countries. Among its immediate side effects are an increased heart rate, an increase in alertness, excitement, and energy. Long-term effects include depression, anxiety, insomnia, constipation, and oral cancer (medical-dictionary.thefreedictionary.com).

Many Somalis chewed Khat in the afternoon to give them a mid-day "lift." The operation in October to capture several of Aidid's lieutenants took place in the afternoon, when the immediate Khat-chewing effects were at their peak. It must have contributed to the Somalis' willingness to fight in the open without apparent fear for their lives.

One of our ongoing missions was to monitor and control activity at a known Khat market just outside the city limits. Our CA team made several visits to observe the activity, and once we flew over in a Black Hawk helicopter to conduct an aerial observation. We usually met with Somali police at a checkpoint near the market to discuss traffic control. Several times we requested they disperse crowds that overflowed onto the road and blocked vehicle traffic. On one visit we observed two Somalis engaged in an apparent argument over some Khat. The argument became so heated, one of them pulled a knife and waved it at the other one. Fortunately, the Somali police broke up the argument before anyone was injured. A crowd had gathered during the confrontation, which the police quickly dispersed. It was beyond the scope of our mission to prevent the use of Khat, which would be impossible. Our purpose was to ensure the Somali police prevented crowds from gathering and to keep the road open for military traffic. The use of Khat was just a fact of life in Somalia.

<u>Increase in Responsibility</u>

On December 8, I was appointed assistant chief of staff for civil-military operations for the 507th Corps Support Group (CSG), part of the 18th Airborne Corps Joint Task Force sent to Somalia to support stability operations after the October 3 battle. My predecessor was an Army Reserve officer returned to the United States when his secret clearance was revoked. A routine background check determined he was previously convicted of child abuse. His career as an officer was most likely finished. My new appointment meant I took on a higher profile and essentially became the face of CA for the commander of the 507th Corps Support Group. One of my new responsibilities was to brief Maj. Gen. Montgomery, the U.S. Forces Commander in Somalia, once a week about CA operations in support of the 507th CSG.

During one of my first briefings to Gen. Montgomery, I mentioned our CA team performed a security assessment of two entry gates, one at the airport and one just north at the port. The assessment revealed several security concerns about which we advised Gen. Montgomery at a weekly briefing before a room full of staff officers.

After I gave my presentation, Gen. Montgomery responded, "That's just the kind of thing a general wants to hear," which elicited some nervous laughter from those present. I wasn't sure if his remark was sarcastic or not.

Afterward his chief of staff took me aside and angrily told me, "You never brief the general before you first give me a pre-brief of what you're going to say so I can approve it."

I apologized but was told I would not brief the general again. Someone else continued the briefing duties. The stand down by the chief of staff shook my confidence as an officer, especially because I was not commissioned through a military academy, but the CA soldiers who did the assessment supported me and would verify my comments. After the briefings ended, several staff officers approached me to say the information about gate security needed to be said. It gave me some vindication but I learned a valuable lesson about pre-briefing the general's chief of staff.

Iconic Characters

A couple people I met were well known in Mogadishu. One was a local Somali called Big Chief Ali. Holder of the garbage-hauling contract for UNOSOM, this jovial, heavy-set man in his fifties obviously was not one of the people we came to save from the famine. It was rumored he grossed $80,000 a month from the U.N. for collecting garbage at the coalition compounds around the city. Upon talking with him, I learned he had 58 children from 100 wives, although he never had more than four wives at a time. Apparently, he needed every penny he made to support all those wives and children.

Another iconic figure was a U.S. Marine, Maj. Mike Collier. He was known as the "Mogadishu Rambo." He stood 6'4" tall, weighed about 240 pounds, and was a heavy cigar smoker. His weapon of choice was a sawed-off shotgun. He operated independently and was considered a loose cannon by the

U.S. command. Collier reportedly would disarm Somali civilians on sight and threatened to kill them if they ever picked up another weapon. John Whidden and I met with him on a couple of occasions to discuss coordinating disarmament efforts, but we decided his methods were too radical for U.N. standards. He wasn't concerned with winning hearts or minds.

MEDCAP

As promised to the fishermen on the beach near Jasiira Village, a MEDCAP mission for the village was held on December 31st. The 46th Combat Support Hospital provided medical personnel and clinical equipment, the 6th Special Forces Group provided security, and the 4th Psychological Operations (PSYOPS) Detachment provided loudspeaker support to announce the MEDCAP.

Our convoy consisted of 20 vehicles carrying 79 U.S. personnel and eight interpreters. When we arrived at the site, a concertina-wire perimeter had been erected that offered security and a path to channel people into the MEDCAP area for treatment. A triage station was set up while PSYOPS loudspeakers announced our arrival. People appeared out of nowhere and lined up to be screened. In my after-action report, I noted the medical personnel treated 331 people for illnesses including diarrhea, worms, bronchitis, sexually transmitted diseases, lacerations, and various infections. The MEDCAP lasted about 3½ hours and was intended as a high-visibility event. It attracted attention from the media and ranking coalition officers.

One of those interested was Brig. Gen. Peter Pace of the U.S. Marine Corps, the deputy commander, Joint Task Force Somalia, under Maj. Gen. Montgomery. He arrived in a Black Hawk helicopter gunship. As the project officer for the

MEDCAP, I went to meet him when he landed. We exchanged salutes and walked to the briefing tent for an overview briefing. We spoke casually on the way and he inquired about my background. I mentioned I served in Vietnam during 1970-71 and was a reserve officer on active duty as part of a civil affairs operational planning team. In an attempt to create some connection with him as a Marine, I told him my brother Dale served with the 3rd Marine Division in Vietnam in 1968. He said he was there about the same time with the 1st Marine Division. After briefing him about the MEDCAP, I accompanied him back to his helicopter where we again exchanged salutes as he departed. Twelve years later, in 2005, Gen. Pace became the 16th Chairman of the Joint Chiefs of Staff. He was the first of two future chairs of the Joint Chiefs I would brief during my career.

"Dead Eye" DeFoster

Sgt. 1st Class Tony DeFoster, one of the volunteers from the 403rd CA Battalion back home, earned his nickname, "Dead Eye." As part of his duties one day, he was visiting an explosives ordnance detachment charged with overseeing a stockpile of unexploded ordnance when he spotted a Somali male, about 100 yards away, attempting to take some of the ordnance from the pile. Tony yelled at him to get away from the stockpile, but the Somali ignored him. Tony fired a warning shot into the air, which didn't deter the would-be thief. Finally, Tony took aim with his M16 and killed the Somali with one shot. Shortly afterward, he was summoned to the commander's office and questioned, per standard operating procedures. After questioning and an interview of witnesses at the site, it was determined the shooting was justified.

Hometown Notoriety on TV

In December, I received an email from Nancy saying the ABC affiliate in Syracuse had broadcast a local update on U.S. operations in Somalia that highlighted my family as they prepared for the holidays without me. The broadcast featured a still photo of Nancy and our five children. Scott, not quite a year old, was shown on his hands and knees, crawling toward the camera. The news spot also showed a map of the Middle East I'd taped to a wall in the living room before I left. The report also mentioned Shannon Kennedy and Tony DeFoster, the other local soldiers deployed with me. It was a heartrending public-interest story that pointed out the sacrifices made by families while their service members were absent.

Continuing Violence

On January 31, during an operations update, we received word a U.S. liaison team in an armed convoy had been ambushed in the city by Somali gunmen. They used a "technical" vehicle (a pickup truck with an automatic weapon attached) to block the road and opened fire on the convoy. There were no U.S. casualties, but eight gunmen were killed and 15 wounded. It was a small measure of revenge for the battle of October 3, but it sent a clear message to the militias that we would stand and fight if fired upon.

Disarmament and Demilitarization

On February 8, 1994, I was able to arrange a meeting between three militia leaders and Mr. Elsheikh of UNOSOM. It resulted from an earlier private meeting I had with one of the militia leaders, Col. Abdi Mohamed Nuur, a former colonel in the Somali National Army. He previously requested a meeting to seek vocational rehabilitation for approximately 1,000 militia members who belonged to various Habr Gedir sub-clans under the control of Farah Aidid. Col. Nuur was a diminutive, rugged-looking, middle-aged man who seemed to be genuinely concerned for his men.

After that meeting I contacted Mr. Elsheikh at the U.N. to arrange a follow-up meeting. Col. Nuur appeared with two other militia leaders and expressed a desire to work with the U.N. to do whatever was necessary to obtain job training for their members. Mr. Elsheikh advised them, through an interpreter, they must first demobilize their militias and turn in their weapons before the U.N. would commit funds for job training. He added they must convince UNOSOM the fighting would stop before money was committed. The militia leaders agreed and mentioned most of their members had families, but currently made their living as hired guns. They wanted to be trained for more useful occupations like carpentry, masonry, and to learn computer skills. Col. Nuur mentioned if the U.N. couldn't assist his people with job training, there would never be peace in Somalia. We were able to provide them with some surplus rations as a goodwill gesture as they left the meeting. Col. Nurr impressed me as a man with a vision for improving his country.

Afterward, I posed for a photo with Mr. Elsheikh and Col. Nuur. I was encouraged the meeting might lead to a start in disarming the militias and stop the inter-clan violence. I saw little hope in accomplishing anything unless the United States was there to move the U.N. to action.

On March 1 Mr. Elsheikh advised me he'd reached an agreement with Col. Nuur for the U.N. to provide building materials so his people could rehabilitate a former military transportation building to conduct classes. One week after delivery of the building materials all but 10 of the weapons possessed by the 100 people under his control had been turned in.

The remainder would be used for self-defense. In addition, the World Food Program would provide food for his former militia members. After all the preparation, virtually nothing was accomplished, and inter-clan violence continued.

Redeployment Home

On March 5, our CA team redeployed to the United States. Our C-5A military aircraft arrived at Dover Air Force Base at 0130 hours on March 6. From there we were bused to Fort Bragg and given some time off to catch up on sleep. We cleaned our weapons and turned them in to the arms room. We had medical and dental exams and turned in our desert uniforms but were allowed to keep our bush hats and desert boots.

During our medical exam, John Whidden requested we both get an additional blood test to rule out his suspicion we'd contracted a form of food poisoning. We had both felt feverish for several days and experienced some abdominal pain with persistent diarrhea. At first, he was brushed off but when he insisted and became antagonistic, additional lab tests were conducted. We were found to have contracted food poisoning, most likely from salads we'd eaten at the Bamburi Beach restaurant while on R&R. Thanks to John's persistence, we were successfully treated. I arrived home March 16, but because I accumulated leave while in Somalia, I wasn't released from active duty until March 27. I returned to work in Binghamton in early April.

In an interview dated March 8, 1994, published in *The Somalia Sandpaper*, the unofficial publication of U.S. forces in Somalia, Maj. Gen. Thomas Montgomery praised the troops for their service saying, "I'd like the troops here to know that they saved hundreds of thousands of Somalis. Their efforts continued the recovery from a terrible famine-not just in Mogadishu but in a large part of Somalia. The vast majority of Somalis are victims who are looking for better lives. We've given them a chance to start on the road to recovery. It's up to them to follow it. I have been most impressed with the professionalism of the troops and their valor to face up to a harsh and unfriendly, dangerous environment without letting that affect them in terms of getting the job done."

He went on to say although the desire for retaliation existed in many soldiers, the protection of innocent civilians was always a primary consideration.

President Bill Clinton added his praises during a visit to Fort Drum on March 16 of that year, after the 10th Mountain Division troops' return. A news article in *The Syracuse Post-Standard* quoted President Clinton: "Our troops helped restore hope and saved hundreds of thousands of Somalis from certain death. Today in Somalia, crops are growing and food and medicine are flowing. No longer are children dying every day." He went on to describe Operation Restore Hope as "an effort to stop one of the great human tragedies of our time."

President Clinton stated the mission was successful even though Somalia has not found enduring peace and added, "Never forget that because of your efforts ... the starvation has ended, and the Somali people have been given a serious chance to build their own future. That's all we or anyone else can provide."

The statements made by Maj. Gen. Montgomery and President Clinton helped to validate our efforts in Somalia, but the future of the country was greatly in doubt. I left with a small sense of personal accomplishment because I provided children with school supplies, delivered food to a starved people, coordinated medical assistance, and even made some friends among the Somali people. However, we were unsuccessful in stabilizing the political situation and suppressing the violence, which left me feeling empty about our mission. Despite our accomplishments and the accolades by Gen. Montgomery and President Clinton, I felt we left behind unfinished business.

On July 24, 1996, Farah Aidid was shot during an inter-clan battle with his former finance officer, Osman Ali Atto, and Ali Mahdi Muhammad, his chief rival. Aidid died about a week later from his injuries. Shortly after Aidid's death, former Special Envoy to Somalia Robert Oakley was interviewed during a PBS *Newshour* show. Oakley stated the U.N. and the United States misjudged the situation on the ground and Aidid's obsession with power. He was seen as an obstacle to the kind of Somalia we wanted. When we tried to marginalize him, Aidid fought back and it became a military confrontation.

Oakley went on to say we learned several lessons from our involvement in Somalia. One was to assess the situation more carefully and not take anything for granted – either militarily or politically. The second was to recognize the interrelationship among political, military, and humanitarian environments, and the economic-development needs. The third was to move with care and not get too deeply involved, try to adapt to the cultures and realities of the situation, and not try to impose too much upon it.

Me, Tony DeFoster and Shannon Kennedy, Mogadishu 1993

Disarmament Meeting with Col. Nuur and El Sheikh of

UNOSOM

Chapter 10
A Time of Transition (1994-1999)

I returned to reserve status in April 1994 and assumed my former position as a direct support team leader with the 403rd CA Battalion. That same month I received my coveted 20-year letter from the Department of the Army. It meant I'd completed the required years of service to be eligible for a pension at age 60. I could retire immediately if I wanted, but I was only 47 and would have to wait 13 years before I could receive retirement pay. My family would miss the income, and despite the hardship of serving in Somalia, I still enjoyed being in the Army. Nancy was not working at the time and there was little chance she would seek employment other than in the music field. Full-time work in music, with enough income to offset the cost of daycare for our two youngest, was rare. She fed her passion for music with volunteer roles in live theater and received a part-time stipend for conducting a senior-citizens chorus. Later she played the trumpet in the Onondaga Civic Symphony Orchestra, also a volunteer gig. I figured with a little luck, good evaluations and some good timing, I could stay in the Army Reserve until I reached 60, the mandatory retirement age.

That summer, a new commander was appointed at the 403rd Civil Affairs Battalion – Lt. Col. Julius Balogh, whom I'd known since I joined the 403rd. Many years earlier, I succeeded him as the unit's supply officer.

Soon after I returned to duty with the 403rd, a vacancy opened for command of the General Support Detachment in the battalion. I would be considered for promotion to lieutenant colonel in 1996 and another command assignment increased my chances for promotion, so I asked Lt. Col. Balogh to assign me to the position. I assured him I had the background and experience necessary. By that time, we had become well acquainted. He was aware of the civil affairs experience I gained in Somalia and my history as a subject matter expert in supply and logistics with the unit. Because it was a subordinate command within the battalion, there was no need for a promotion board to meet. I wasn't aware of anyone else he might have considered, but I was grateful for the appointment.

On July 1, I signed an assumption-of-command letter and accepted responsibility for the General Support Detachment, the largest subunit of the 403rd Civil Affairs Battalion. I also assumed duties as the Master Fitness Trainer for the battalion, acting as the battalion commander's adviser on physical-readiness matters. My duties as a detachment commander involved more responsibility and a larger time commitment. I was required to sign for the supplies and equipment assigned to the detachment and to attend administrative meetings one evening each week. My experience in the supply field helped me reorganize and tighten supply procedures within the detachment. For the remainder of 1994, I attended weekend Reserve training in Mattydale, eight miles from home, and resumed my daily commute to Binghamton for my civilian position with the U.S. District Court.

I put Somalia behind me and resumed life at home when in September I received a phone call at work from Maj. David Hines, the battalion operations officer. A bulletin had been distributed from higher headquarters for civil affairs-qualified soldiers who specialized in judicial administration to deploy to Haiti. The nation's democratically elected president, Jean-Bertrand Aristide, had been overthrown by a military coup nearly three years earlier, on September 30, 1991. The Clinton administration had devised a plan to remove the military regime with a combination of diplomacy and a show of force. As our forces prepared to invade, a diplomatic team–led by former U.S.

President Jimmy Carter, retired U.S. Sen. Sam Nunn, and retired Chairman of the Joint Chiefs of Staff, Gen. Colin Powell–persuaded the military regime to step down and allow the duly elected officials to return to power. Their effort was successful in part because the U.S. delegation was able to point to the massive force poised to invade the country. After leaders of the military regime stepped down, our mission changed from a combat operation to a peacekeeping and nation-building operation that involved deployment of a U.S.-led multinational force in Haiti, a mission tailor made for civil affairs. The mission was named Operation Uphold Democracy. Dave said I would be deployed to help restore the court system, in disarray after the military coup overthrew the elected administration.

It seemed like a natural assignment for me as a deputy clerk at the U.S. District Court. However, it was a voluntary assignment. It was a tempting opportunity because I could apply my experience as a court clerk in a military mission. I also considered that, if successful, I would get a measure of personal closure after our failed effort at reconstruction in Somalia and the misguided strategy of Vietnam. In the end, I turned down the assignment for two reasons. First, I had recently been assigned as the detachment commander and felt a responsibility to the detachment members and the battalion. Second, I did not want to leave home again so soon after returning from Somalia, for what could be a tour lasting six months or more.

Uphold Democracy eventually succeeded in restoring Haiti's democratically elected government, thanks to well-executed political, military, diplomatic, civil-administration and humanitarian operations. I felt some regret at not participating, but in the end, my family was more important. When I joined the Reserves, I never expected to be sent overseas every few months. Regular Army families learned to expect it but Army Reserve families were increasingly called on to sacrifice as their service members served a more active role.

Civilian Job Stress

After I declined the tour of duty in Haiti, my attention turned to reducing my long daily commute to Binghamton. Other employment didn't seem to be an option; a transfer closer to home wasn't likely. Nancy and I decided several weeks after I accepted the position in Binghamton we couldn't afford to move. We hadn't found a suitable house in our price range and the market wouldn't support the price we needed to get for our present home. The 90-minute drive each way from Clay amounted to 800 miles a week and almost $100 a week in gasoline ... plus wear and tear on my car. I became such a frequent customer at an auto-repair shop in Binghamton, the mechanics knew me by name. During my five years of commuting to Binghamton I went through two cars. I often dozed off at the wheel during the long trip, especially on the way home. The time I spent commuting combined with the stress at work probably resulted in some depression, although I never sought help for it.

Fortunately, an FBI agent I knew in Binghamton offered a temporary solution. His mother's health had declined and she moved in with his family, leaving her house vacant. He offered to let me live there for $50 a week, so the house would not look vacant. It saved me the daily drive from home, wear and tear on the car and me, and significantly reduced my weekly gas bill. I spent weekends at home and drove to Binghamton on Monday. Nancy, as always, was supportive and somehow managed to keep our household together and care for our two youngest children.

Our arrangement continued for about five months until early 1995, when Larry Baerman saw an opportunity to get me back to the Syracuse Clerk's Office. Having seen the physical and mental toll the work in Binghamton had taken on me, he found a way to reassign me to the Utica Clerk's Office for a year, after which I would be reassigned to Syracuse.

The Transfer to Utica

Utica was the geographic center of the district, and home to the oldest courthouse in the Northern District. It was the district's repository for all the closed cases before their shipment to the National Records Center in Missouri. Utica was 55 miles from home and it cut my commute by 30 minutes. I was further motivated by the prospect of returning to Syracuse in a year's time.

One morning on my way to work I took a different route through the city, thinking it might be shorter. As I approached an intersection near the courthouse, I slowed down to turn left at an unfamiliar intersection, unaware of the parallel lane of traffic to my left on the other side of a median. Suddenly I heard the screeching of tires; a pickup truck broadsided my 1988 Oldsmobile Cutlass. I had my seatbelt buckled, but the force of the collision tossed me sideways. I must have blacked out because the next thing I remembered was lifting my head up from under the dashboard. Next, I heard someone ask if I was okay. I answered yes, but unknown to me, the force of the impact had catapulted my wedding band from my finger.

A police officer soon appeared on the scene; thankfully, I wasn't issued a ticket. Maybe he thought the damage to my car was enough punishment. I didn't seem to have any injuries, but my car was totaled and had to be towed. My insurance provided for a rental car and the tow-truck driver gave me a ride to the rental office. I called the clerk's office to explain I'd been in an accident and would be late for work. In the confusion of the accident, I didn't realize I had lost my wedding band until the following day. Several days later, I located the garage to which my car was towed. I looked inside the car on the floor and under the front seat, but there was no sign of my wedding ring. I got out of the car, glanced at the ground and saw the ring half buried in the dirt. It was the second time I lost the ring and later found it. The symbol of my marriage seemed destined to survive, despite me.

One of my assignments in Utica was to compose an information pamphlet for the district's new Alternative Dispute Resolution (ADR) Program. After a law clerk in Syracuse reviewed the text for accuracy, I inserted some clip art to illustrate the various ADR options. ADR encouraged settlement of designated civil cases without going to trial. It saved litigants money, and freed judges to concentrate on cases not conducive to settlement. Once the final product was approved and printed, the pamphlet was used for several years as a handout for all ADR-eligible civil cases. It was one of my proudest achievements with the court.

Fort Polk

In April 1995, I volunteered for a three-week tour of duty as the senior observer/controller (O/C) for a civil affairs unit during a major training exercise at Fort Polk, Louisiana, home of the Joint Readiness Training Center. In order to be excused from work, I used the two weeks of military leave I was authorized each year and added one week of annual leave. The exercise included 10 days of field duty under tactical conditions. We were required to wear the Army Battle Dress Uniform (BDU), patterned with wooded camouflage colors (various shades of green, black, and brown). We wore soft BDU caps (to distinguish us from the exercise participants, who wore Kevlar helmets), and we carried notebooks instead of M16s and blank ammunition. The remainder of our uniform consisted of a web belt, suspenders, two canteens, a first-aid case, and two ammo pouches. We also had to wear camouflage paint, something I hadn't done since tactical training during summer camps several years earlier.

Before we left for the field we were briefed on the exercise scenario and the reports we needed to write. We were trained to drive Humvees using night-vision goggles and familiarized ourselves with radio communications protocol and the call signs for the exercise. We were each issued a 10-day supply of Meals, Ready to Eat (MREs) and a supply of bug juice to repel ticks and mosquitoes. Finally, we received our assignments and were sent off to live in the woods. I slept in the cargo bed of my Humvee and used the hood as a table for meals and a desk to note my observations. Our assignment was to observe and comment on the actions of a direct support team from the 450th CA Battalion, based in Riverdale.

On April 19, 1995, in my second week at Fort Polk, the deadliest act of domestic terror in American history occurred. The Alfred P. Murrah Federal Building in Oklahoma City, Oklahoma, was bombed, killing 168 people, including 19 children in a day-care facility on the ground floor. I continued with my duties, shocked by such a horrendous attack on U.S. soil. A suspect, Timothy McVeigh, was quickly apprehended, charged, then tried and convicted of the bombing. He was sentenced to death and executed in 2001, weeks before the September 11 attacks. A co-conspirator, Terry Nichols, was convicted and sentenced to several consecutive life sentences. Two other conspirators who testified against McVeigh and Nichols were sentenced to lesser terms of imprisonment.

Ironically, McVeigh was an honorably discharged U.S. Army veteran awarded the Bronze Star for his service in Desert Storm.

A Heartfelt Family Support Conference

In the summer of 1995, Nancy and I were given the opportunity to attend a two-day family support conference at Fort Bragg, intending to become involved in the 403rd CA Family Support Group. After having been separated for several months during my deployment to Somalia, we understood the challenges and issues that could arise at home when a member of the family was deployed for a long period of time. Conference attendees included family members from around the country who had a connection with the Army Special Operations Command. Our two oldest sons, Gregory and Stephen, lived on their own and shared an apartment, and our teenage daughter, Catherine, chose to stay at home; Kevin, age 7, and Scott, age 2½, came with us. We planned to drive to Florida after the conference to visit Disney World with the boys. During each day's sessions, we placed Kevin and Scott with a registered child-care provider on base; we picked them up when we returned to our hotel in the evening.

During the conference we had the honor to meet the widows of Sgt. 1st Class Randy Shugart and Master Sgt. Gary Gordon, who had each been posthumously awarded the Medal of Honor for their actions during the battle of Mogadishu. Their widows attended the conference as panel members to help lead the discussion of how the Army could better support families. Their husbands fought bravely to their deaths to protect Warrant Officer Michael Durant and his crew after Durant's Black Hawk helicopter was shot down.

Nancy and I introduced ourselves to Mrs. Shugart and Mrs. Gordon and expressed our sorrow for their loss. I mentioned my four months of service in Mogadishu with a civil affairs team a month after the battle to help with stability operations. They thanked me for my service, but inside I was in awe of those young women who had each suffered such a deep and tragic loss.

The conference was arranged to give family members a forum to express their concerns and offer suggestions to the command about how the Army could provide them better communication and support during their soldiers' deployments. Reservists' families had special issues because they often lived long distances from an active military base and information about their soldiers' status and family benefits wasn't communicated well to remote locations. Each Reserve unit was encouraged to form its own support group to keep lines of communication open between the military and the families left behind.

We left with a wealth of information and resources to bring back to the 403rd CA Battalion, and Nancy and I became active members of our family support group.

Before heading home, we spent two days at Disney World with the kids. It was a quick visit because of our limited finances and my leave from work was about to end.

The next year brought significant changes to my dual careers. Promoted to lieutenant colonel, I accepted a position with Headquarters, 354th CA Brigade, based in Riverdale, the next higher command of the 403rd CA Battalion. Assignment to the 354th meant a 360-mile monthly commute to Maryland for Reserve training. Then, after my year in Utica, I accepted reassignment to the clerk's office in Syracuse. For the first time in six years, I only had to drive 11 miles to work each day.

354th Civil Affairs Brigade

I quickly immersed myself into training with the brigade headquarters. During my first year, in the spring of 1997, I led a team of nine officers and NCOs to Fort Bliss, Texas, for a two-week rotation in a field exercise called Roving Sands. Even though the Army Reserve was a part-time commitment, members were expected to be competent in their fields and able to "hit the ground running." It was my first visit to Texas and it was the hottest weather I'd experienced since Somalia. However, instead of tents, we were assigned private rooms in a comfortable hotel in nearby El Paso. Amenities of the Southwestern-style hotel included an outdoor pool, a fitness room, and a daily continental breakfast. They were the nicest accommodations I ever had for a field exercise. Col. David Spinelli, the acting brigade commander, arranged the accommodations. He believed if we were going to spend two weeks training in desert conditions, we should at least have comfortable lodging. It was contrary to the "train as we fight" motto, but after the Spartan conditions in Somalia, and more recently at Fort Polk, I was thankful for the cushy amenities. During our two-week rotation we were responsible for providing civil affairs support to the commander of the 377th Theater Army Area Command (TAACOM), a major Reserve command based in New Orleans. I acted as assistant chief of staff for civil-military operations to the TAACOM commander. In the event we were mobilized, the 354th would be assigned to the 377th TAACOM to provide civil affairs support. In theory, we would deploy overseas with the 377th to their area of operations. The purpose of the exercise was to integrate us with the command staff of the 377th TAACOM and solve various scenarios involving civilians on the battlefield, portrayed by contract role players. I briefed the TAACOM commander on the CA mission and supervised the activities of all the CA soldiers participating in the rotation.

    One incident during the exercise involved a female captain on my team who was fluent in German. She received a call from a unit in the field for a German interpreter to translate for them because they had a German role player in custody. When she informed me of the request, I refused to let her go; she'd just returned from another unit moments earlier and I was concerned she might get overextended if she had to answer to every request for a German interpreter. She was eager to go, but I explained my concern to her, and I wanted to impress upon the unit that in real life you don't always get what you want. After she advised the unit their request was denied, I got an angry phone call from the company commander, who complained I was not adequately supporting the exercise. I listened patiently and let him vent his frustrations. After he hung up I felt some guilt about denying his request but I stood by my decision. Apparently, the young officer used some resourcefulness and came up with another solution, because we never heard from him again. I hoped he learned to always have a backup plan.

The area in and around Fort Bliss consisted of flat, desert-like terrain punctuated by the Franklin Mountain range, which rose just north of the base and continued into New Mexico. It was the most visible geographic feature of the area. I was fascinated with the mountain range because it was barren of any forestation, in stark contrast to the Adirondack Mountains of Upstate New York.

I enjoyed hikes in the Adirondacks, and one of the foothills below the Franklin Mountain range gave me an idea for a hike. I met with members of my team and told them of my plan. They were reluctant at first but most of them agreed to join me. We took along a compass, our field gear with full canteens, and cameras, and rode in Humvees to the base of the hill. It took about 20 minutes to hike to the summit–not a long climb by any standard–but it was good cardio exercise. We took some pictures and walked back down. It proved to be a pleasant diversion from our daily routine.

Another day, when we had a break in our exercises, a few of us walked across the border at El Paso into Cuidad Juárez, in Mexico. For safety reasons, we wore civilian clothes so we didn't attract attention; and we'd been warned not to drink the water. Juárez, as it is commonly called, was considered a seedy place even before the violent drug wars that killed thousands and made it one of the most dangerous cities in the world. We browsed around the shops for several hours and I eventually purchased a hand-woven red-and-black striped throw blanket and a miniature Mexican sombrero as souvenirs. We crossed back into the United States later that day by way of the pedestrian bridge.

Officer Evaluation Reports

That year I had the opportunity to my combine my knowledge of the judicial system with my civil affairs experience when I assisted with the justice portion of a groundbreaking initiative the 354th CA produced to support Army Central Command. It laid out a generic plan for post-hostility civil-military operations in a host country. The document helped solidify my position with the 354th CA Brigade and was later reflected in my annual officer evaluation report (OER), a critical benchmark that measured officers' career potential. The evaluations contained information that demonstrated an officer's potential for advancement and higher-level responsibilities. I thought for years many of the accolades used in a typical officer evaluation were overstated and clichéd. It seemed some officers were so good they "walked on water," an often-used phrase used to describe an officer with an outstanding OER.

My first OER as a lieutenant colonel contained phrases such as, "Lt. Col. Mitchell's performance of duty has been superb"; and "Lt. Col. Mitchell did an excellent job of assisting in developing and writing the justice portion of this groundbreaking effort." My senior rater picked up on both phrases and stated, "Lt. Col. Mitchell is a *superb* officer who has performed his assigned duties in an *excellent* manner" (emphasis added). There was even a manual available to assist raters in selecting adjectives to describe a rated officer's performance. "Outstanding" was, without a doubt, the most-overused adjective in the entire Army vocabulary. I received a top block from my senior rater, a colonel, which meant I must have been among the best lieutenant colonels he rated that year. It seemed the higher an officer rose in rank, the more "outstanding" were his or her accomplishments. It was common in the Army Reserve for the senior rater to use the rater's comments. The rater, pressed for time as a weekend reservist, often told the rated officer to submit his own narrative for consideration. It appeared the 100-officer pyramid diagram was developed in response to the tendency to exaggerate evaluations, so the senior rater had a way to compare the rated officer with others of the same rank whom he or she rated. In my experience, evaluations were driven from the bottom up, so an officer who wrote well could pretty much determine his/her own narrative and, therefore, affect his/her standing on the senior rater's pyramid.

Kudos from a General

In 1998, my second year with Headquarters, 354th CA Brigade, I took on an extra assignment as the unit's mission planning officer for a major staff exercise named Internal Look '98, held at Fort Lee, Virginia. Staff exercises did not typically involve field duty. We worked in a large, air-conditioned building divided into several partitions to accommodate various staff functions such as personnel, intelligence, operations and training, logistics, and civil affairs.

The exercise involved 660 personnel, including members of the Air Force, Navy, and Marine Corps, in addition to the Army. Our accommodations were more basic this time, unlike our posh hotel in El Paso the previous year. We lived in military quarters at Fort Lee and I was assigned to a modest but comfortable room in the officers' housing area. I acted as assistant chief of staff for civil affairs and prepared a CA annex and operations plan prior to the exercise.

The purpose of the exercise was to simulate the high-tempo environment of a Tactical Operations Center, where a staff officer would operate in a real-world operation. Its importance was punctuated by the presence of a three-star general. During the exercise we responded to dozens of action items submitted by the exercise-control group requiring civil affairs input. My experience in Somalia made me aware of the real-world implications of the exercise scenario, so I took the initiative to form a civil-military planning committee comprising officers from the various staff sections. My purpose was to plan for the conduct of a transitional government, which I anticipated would be needed after "hostilities" ended. I presented the committee's plan to the commanding general and it was approved. Our team performed well in my highest-level staff exercise to date.

At the conclusion of the exercise I got a pat on the back and a "Good job, Mitchell," from the three-star general.

It was a great boost to my confidence after the lecture I'd received from the chief of staff in Somalia, a mere colonel.

Chapter 11
Bosnia-Herzegovina (1999)

My next deployment took me to Eastern Europe, where Yugoslavia had erupted in ethnic violence between 1992 and 1995. The main belligerents were the Republic of Bosnia-Herzegovina, and those of the self-proclaimed Bosnian Serb and Bosnian Croat entities within Bosnia-Herzegovina.

A good summary about the origin of the conflict and eventual intervention by the international community was provided in a paper written by Aleksa Djilas printed in *Foreign Affairs Magazine*, dated July/August 1995, titled "Tito's Last Secret: How Did He Keep the Yugoslavs Together?" He stated war came about as a result of the breakup of Yugoslavia after its dictator, Marshal Tito, died in 1980. The main reason Yugoslavia remained unified during Tito's rule was the existence of the powerful communist police and army, which he controlled. Yugoslavia was a pot waiting to boil over. Following the Slovenian and Croatian secessions from Yugoslavia in 1991, the multiethnic Yugoslavian republic of Bosnia- Herzegovina, which consisted mainly of Muslim Bosniaks (43%), Orthodox Serbs (31%), and Catholic Croats (17%), passed a referendum for independence on February 29, 1992. Bosnian Serb political representatives rejected the referendum and established their own republic, the Republic of Serbia. Following their declaration of independence, Bosnian Serb forces supported by the Serbian government of Slobodan Milošević and the Yugoslav People's Army (JNA) attacked the Republic of Bosnia-Herzegovina in order to secure Serbian territory.

Soon war broke out across Bosnia, accompanied by ethnic cleansing of the Bosniak population, especially in Eastern Bosnia. The state administration of Bosnia-Herzegovina effectively ceased to function, having lost control of the entire country. While they formally supported the Serbian declaration of independence, Bosnian Croat forces and Croatian president Franjo Tuđman also aimed to secure parts of Bosnia-Herzegovina for Croatia. The war was characterized by bitter fighting, indiscriminate shelling of cities and towns, ethnic cleansing, and systematic mass rape and genocide. Events such as the Siege of Sarajevo, the Omarska prison camp, and the Srebrenica massacre would typify the conflict.

After the Srebrenica massacre, the North Atlantic Treaty Organization (NATO) intervened during 1995 against the Army of the Republic of Serbia, which internationalized the conflict, but only during its final stages. The war came to an end after the parties signed the General Framework Agreement for Peace in Bosnia-Herzegovina in Paris December 14. Peace negotiations were held in Dayton, Ohio, and finalized December 21. The accords were known as the Dayton Agreement. A 1995 report by the Central Intelligence Agency found Serbian forces responsible for 90% of the war crimes committed during the conflict. (www.en.wikipedia.org/wiki/Bosnian_war)

Initially, it did not occur to me my unit would be involved in implementation of the Dayton Agreement. I continued my Reserve duties and my civilian career and relished my short 11-mile drive to work in Syracuse each day.

Because of the distance to my assignment with the 354th CA Brigade in Maryland each month, on Fridays before the weekend drill I used four hours of annual leave to drive to Maryland and stay at a hotel near the Reserve training center. Occasionally I was able to stay at the officers' quarters at Fort Meade, about 20 miles north. Sometimes Nancy, Kevin and Scott would come along if I could get a room at Fort Meade, as it was less expensive than a hotel room outside the base. We enjoyed the well-appointed quarters given to senior officers at a fraction of what a hotel of comparable quality would cost and took advantage of tax-free purchases at the PX.

During the summer my Reserve duty gave us an opportunity to get away and enjoy the Washington, D.C., area. The downside was Nancy had no transportation while I was at the Reserve center, but I was usually back at Fort Meade by 5 p.m. and there was still plenty of daylight left. Among our side trips were visits with Nancy's best friend, Darlene Curtin, in Maryland, trips into Washington, D.C., a tour of the museum at Fort Meade, and a baseball game at Camden Yards between the Baltimore Orioles and Toronto Blue Jays. One year, Nancy and I made the trip alone during cherry-blossom time, and we rented a paddle boat on the tidal basin.

In the summer of 1998 our brigade headquarters received a warning order we would have to fill troop rotations 7 and 8 to Bosnia-Herzegovina for Operation Joint Forge as part of the Stabilization Force (SFOR). When we were told every eligible member would have to spend six to eight months on active duty, I spoke with Col. Howard Becker, our deputy brigade commander, and requested to be sent in the first rotation so I could be home in time for the holidays. I explained I had already spent Christmas away from home twice (Vietnam, 1971, and Somalia, 1993), and I didn't relish telling Nancy I'd be away for the holidays.

Col. Becker was kind enough to see I was put on the roster for the first rotation the following January.

Mobilization at Fort Benning

After pre-mobilization activities at the Riverdale Reserve center on January 10, those of us set for Rotation 7 flew to Fort Benning to begin our deployment. We were organized into three companies for the mobilization process; I was placed in charge of one of the companies. The process was similar to what I experienced for Somalia, except we were a far larger group of 80 people. We received cultural training specific to Bosnia-Herzegovina and were issued clothing appropriate for the climate: cold-weather gear and insulated boots. We also qualified with our weapons, took physical fitness tests, went through counter-terrorism training and attended several classes in the Serbo-Croatian language. We also had to pass a European driver's test. Even though we were already qualified to drive certain military vehicles, the NATO Status of Forces Agreement required us to be qualified to drive on European highways and be familiar with international traffic signs.

We went through the usual administrative process (financial records, wills, powers of attorney, and medical exams). Two reservists were disqualified during the validation process and sent home. A woman was found to be pregnant during her medical exam, and one man admitted to being homosexual. He was a squad leader in my company and even though I believed him to be a competent soldier, his admission violated the Don't Ask Don't Tell (DADT) policy. It could become an issue that affected the morale and effectiveness of the unit, so the brigade commander sent him home.

President Clinton signed DADT into law in 1993 as a compromise measure allowing everyone to serve in the military regardless of sexual orientation. Prior to its enactment, the official policy found homosexuality incompatible with military service. DADT's "Don't Ask" provision mandated military or appointed officials could not ask about or require members to reveal their sexual orientation. Its "Don't Tell" provision stated a member may be discharged if he/she claimed to be homosexual or bisexual, or made a statement that indicated a tendency toward or intent to engage in homosexual activities. A "Don't Harass" provision was added later, ensuring the military would not permit harassment or violence against service members for any reason (Herek, Gregory; *Lesbians and Gay Men in the U.S. Military: Historical Background of "Don't Ask, Don't Tell Revisited*, 1997; retrieved from www.en.wikipedia.org).

There was an exception in a 1999 FORSCOM Regulation (500-3-3 *RC Unit Commander's Handbook*) for reservists. It allowed active duty deployment of some Army reservists and National Guard troops who falsely claimed to be homosexual, or who were falsely accused of homosexual behavior. It was intended to prevent disciplining reservists and National Guard members who *pretended* to be homosexual to escape combat duty.

President Barack Obama repealed DADT in December 2010. Nevertheless, it remained within a commander's duty and authority to discharge anyone whose behavior adversely affected the good order and discipline of a unit – including inappropriate sexual activity – whether homosexual or heterosexual.

Departure to Bosnia

On January 20, we departed Fort Benning in a U.S. Air Force C-141 Starlifter for Bosnia. The C-141 was a jet aircraft designed for strategic airlift of military cargo such as vehicles and large steel cargo containers called conexes. It was outfitted with webbed passenger seats. I first became familiar with the C-141 during a Strategic Mobility Planning Course at Fort Eustis in 1983, as unit-mobilization officer for the 403rd CA Battalion. It was one of my most interesting courses in the Army Reserve. As part of the course we loaded and tied down a Jeep and a three-quarter-ton cargo truck inside a C-141 and took a short flight around Northern Virginia. For our flight to Germany, the aircraft was configured with the familiar webbed passenger seats along the inside of the fuselage with all its cargo, which made the flight crowded and uncomfortable. Our flight lasted 7½ hours before we landed at Ramstein Air Force Base in Germany.

We stayed overnight in the Hotel Barbarossa in Kaiserslautern, a town boasting the largest population of Americans outside the United States. The next day we returned to the Ramstein Air Force Base for the flight to an air base in Taszar, Hungary. In Taszar we were billeted in temporary wood-framed huts furnished with folding cots and equipped with electricity and gas heaters. Smaller huts used for latrines were nearby. The base was in a remote location, with few recreation facilities. A USO tent housed a movie screen, ping pong tables, and a few computers with internet access. Another building served as a mess hall, but most of our meals consisted of MREs.

Taszar was a Soviet air base during the Cold War. After the collapse of the Soviet Union in 1990, the base was abandoned. A few of us ventured onto the base to "recon" the area and found it had been converted to a NATO base for staging troops in and out of the Balkans. Remnants of the former Soviet base still existed, giving us a glimpse of what life was like for Soviet soldiers stationed there during the Cold War. Some monuments and a MiG fighter dotted a lawn. We remained at Taszar for two days until our buses arrived at the staging area to transport us into Bosnia.

We left Taszar on January 24 in three double-decker buses with all our gear. Our security escort consisted of three armored Humvees mounted with automatic weapons. We carried our individual weapons but could not carry ammunition while in transit. The secretary of defense had declared Bosnia an imminent danger zone, an area where there was no active combat but hostile groups existed, and fighting could break out without warning.

Our trip into Bosnia was uneventful but the scenery along the way was filled with reminders of the devastation left behind by the war. We saw dozens of houses shelled during the war, many with no roofs. One oddity was a McDonald's restaurant that appeared undamaged. I thought perhaps the warring factions stayed away from shelling the iconic American hamburger joint for fear it would cause international outrage. On the other hand, maybe they spared it so they could get a Big Mac during a lull in the fighting. Our trip to Tuzla took about nine hours. Tuzla was in the American sector, designated as Multi-National District (MND) North. Soldiers stationed there disembarked from the buses and we continued south another four hours to Sarajevo, into the French sector of MND South. The trip took us on narrow, paved roads with no shoulders and steep drop-offs that wound through the mountains. My stomach got queasy when I glanced out the window and saw nothing but treetops below us.

It was dark when we arrived in Sarajevo. As we approached the building we were to occupy, the power went out. We disembarked from the bus and had to climb four flights of stairs with our gear to reach our rooms. The building was powered by a large generator (because electricity had been cut off during the fighting), so within an hour power was restored. The building had running water and flush toilets but little heat or hot water. Those not among the first to shower or shave in the morning were left with cold water. I learned to shower and shave in the evening to take advantage of the hot water that accumulated during the day. The showers were an upgrade from the gravity-fed tanks in Vietnam and Somalia.

The next morning, we assembled for roll call and rode by bus with an armed guard to the Residency compound in Sarajevo, which formerly served as Tito's summer home. As we drove through the city many of the buildings were pockmarked with bullet holes and shell fragments. Despite the severe war damage in Sarajevo, I felt fortunate to be stationed in the historic city. It turned out to be the most culturally enriching and fulfilling deployment of my military career.

At the Residency compound I was assigned to the Combined Joint Civil Military Task Force (CJCMTF). The terms "combined joint" seemed redundant, but it meant the combination of multinational forces to serve in a joint civil-military effort. Several international, non-government organizations (NGOs) were also present. I was assigned as senior liaison to the Organization for Security and Cooperation in Europe (OSCE). My job was to coordinate civil affairs operations with those of OSCE.

OSCE headquarters was a five-minute walk from the Parliament building where I was billeted. On the way I walked across the historic bridge where Archduke Ferdinand and his wife were assassinated by a Serb nationalist in 1914. Those assassinations set off a chain of events that led to World War I. I stood at the site on the bridge that spanned the Miljacka River where the assassinations took place and imagined the chaos that must have occurred in the moments after the shots were fired. The only physical reminder of the history-making event was a nondescript marker placed at the end of the bridge. It seemed as if the people of Sarajevo wanted the event buried in history.

At the Residency compound I was introduced to Capt. Davi, the French officer I would replace. He took me to OSCE headquarters and introduced me to the civilian staff. OSCE comprised 55 nations and was the world's largest regional security organization. In Bosnia it had a mandate from the United Nations to supervise the election process, monitor human rights, and assist with negotiations on confidence and security-building measures, and arms control. When the military is involved in a peacekeeping mission, it maintains a close liaison with international civilian organizations like OSCE. Civilian organizations were generally skeptical of military involvement in civil matters, but once they understood the role of civil affairs, they realized we would be helpful in the advancement of civil society, and to promote democratization. I would perform liaison duties between OSCE, the CJCMTF, and SFOR headquarters. It was a plum assignment, which gave me new insight into the role of civil affairs. I learned a Serbo-Croatian phrase that expressed our goal to win hearts and minds: "Zelimo vam pomoci," or "We are here to help you." We were there to implement the Dayton Peace Accords and help rebuild institutions, civil society, and infrastructure.

During my second day at OSCE headquarters I was introduced to Hank Nichols, director of the Joint Operations Center (JOC) for OSCE in Bosnia, who assigned me a desk and computer at the JOC inside OSCE headquarters. Hank was a good source of knowledge about the operation of the JOC, the civilian equivalent of a tactical operations center in the Army. The focal point for plans and operations, it acted as the information center for all OSCE activity in Bosnia. Hank scheduled me for an OSCE orientation where I would meet Ambassador Robert Barry, head of mission for OSCE in Bosnia. I attended daily meetings with Barry and his staff to keep informed about OSCE activities. In return I provided them with situation reports from SFOR headquarters. I also had to attend weekly staff meetings at the Residency to keep updated on CJCMTF activities, during which I reported on OSCE activities.

Badges, and More Badges

In addition to an OSCE badge, I was issued several other badges during the next few days, permitting entry into the various SFOR bases around Sarajevo. The ID badges I carried deserve some elaboration in order to fully appreciate their intent, which bordered on the absurd. They were used not only for identification but dictated where and when I could travel, and whether I could wear civilian clothing or a uniform. I was an example of someone identified to the extreme. I carried a Class One Security card, my OSCE Staff card, SFOR Identification, and a Class C Force Exemption card, in addition to my military ID card. The Class One Security card granted me access to restricted security areas. The OSCE Staff card permitted me access to all OSCE facilities. The SFOR Identification got me into all SFOR compounds. However, nothing compared to the Class C Force Exemption card. That card permitted me to travel alone around the city, unarmed, in civilian clothes, and exempted me from the curfew and force-protection rules while in Sarajevo. The main reason for being unarmed was firearms were not permitted in OSCE facilities. The Force Exemption card was a free pass to roam around Sarajevo at will, which gave me more freedom than most soldiers stationed in the city. It allowed me to survey the area, take in the culture, and generally observe people. I integrated myself into everyday society to collect information for the purpose of civil-military cooperation.

I was issued a blue sedan (the European equivalent of a Ford compact) with official SFOR insignias on the doors and hood. It used diesel, and all fuel, maintenance, and repairs were provided free at a nearby SFOR base. That made it more convenient for me to travel around the city and conduct liaison visits with several organizations. My most frequent destinations were to Butmir and Ilidza, two SFOR bases on the edge of

Sarajevo, and to the Residency, site of the CJCMTF headquarters. I often parked in a public lot near OSCE headquarters so I wouldn't have to walk back to my billets across the river to drive to another location. Each time I entered an SFOR compound, guards scanned the underside of my vehicle with a mirror. It gave me concern that a bomb might be planted under the car because it was easily identified by its SFOR insignia. Sarajevo was fairly peaceful but there was still a danger to SFOR personnel by dissidents who did not accept the Dayton Peace Accords. Whenever I parked outside a secure area, I checked around and under the car before I started the engine for signs of tampering and evidence of an explosive device. Someone at OSCE noticed me checking my vehicle at the public lot near OSCE headquarters and informed Hank Nichols I seemed concerned about security at the lot. Hank arranged an underground-garage parking space for me next to OSCE headquarters. Initially it felt safer to park out of sight since the SFOR insignias made it a soft target for terrorists. I soon realized anyone could drive past the Bosnian garage attendant, so I continued to conduct random checks around and under the vehicle, even when parked inside the garage. It may have been overly cautious of me, but I concluded there was no substitute for performing my own personal-security measures.

    Occasional reminders of terrorist activity remained in the city. On March 16, Deputy Interior Minister for Bosnia Jozo Levtar and his driver were seriously injured when a car bomb exploded about 200 meters from CJCMTF headquarters, where I was. The blast was powerful enough to shake the building. It was later discovered the driver did not follow proper security precautions and left the car unattended. Levtar died from his wounds 11 days later. It reinforced the personal-security measures I used with my vehicle.

In February I began attending an English-speaking Mass on Sundays at the Cathedral of the Sacred Heart. An American couple led the singing with no musical accompaniment, despite the presence of an electric organ. One Sunday after Mass, I approached the priest and offered to play the organ during Mass. He introduced me to Fran and Andy Michaels, who lived and worked in Sarajevo; we would become friends for the remainder of my tour in Bosnia and beyond. They provided me with music for Mass each Sunday and we met once a week to rehearse. I accompanied Fran as she sang; Andy acted as an usher. Fran worked for the International Organization for Migration, a civilian organization that managed and tracked the movement of refugees and displaced persons. The organization also aided in the advancement and understanding of migration issues and encouraged social and economic development to uphold the human dignity and well-being of migrants. Andy was a captain in the Air Force Reserve. We enjoyed meeting socially after Mass, and once, they invited me to their apartment for a home-cooked meal. The cathedral became such an important part of my time in Sarajevo, I purchased a souvenir watercolor painting of it from a street vendor.

My schedule allowed me flexibility to enjoy the city's rich history and the cultural and artistic events. Service in Sarajevo also provided me the opportunity to interact with people from several nations. I served with troops from France, Germany, Italy, the Netherlands, Hungary, and Turkey. I was particularly close with the French troops and brushed up on my high-school and college French. Additionally, Turkish troops guarded our compound, and I had German and Swedish roommates.

One European custom that surprised me was unisex restrooms. The typical public restroom contained a common wash area with separate toilet stalls used by both men and women. It was strange to sit on a toilet and have a woman occupy the stall next to me. I guess Americans were more conservative than Europeans when it came to toilet customs. There was certainly an economy in needing only one public restroom in a building.

Throughout the city red "florets" embedded in walkways and streets in several places marked locations where people were killed by mortar rounds during the war. The city filled the impact craters with red-tinted cement in the shape of a flower, as poignant reminders of the tragedies inflicted by the four-year siege. Many women in Sarajevo colored their hair in various shades of red as symbolic reminders of the bloodshed.

My inside view of Sarajevo gave me the opportunity to interact with the people and their culture on a level few soldiers serving in Bosnia were able to experience. One afternoon I attended a performance at the Sarajevo Cultural Center. The Kolo Bosansko Dance Ensemble put on a wonderful display of traditional dress, music, and dance, performed by Bosnians, Serbs, and Croats. Before the war people of the three ethnic groups often socialized together and even intermarried. It took a few radical nationalists to tear the country apart and destroy many families that had been formed from the interethnic marriages. The dance ensemble was an example of how music brought people together. It was a visible sign of post-war healing and represented hope for better cooperation among the former warring factions.

Chapter 12
The Politics of Peacekeeping

On March 23, OSCE withdrew its international staff from the Eastern Republic of Serbia and closed its field offices there in anticipation of NATO air strikes against the former Yugoslavia in Kosovo. The JOC in Sarajevo went into 24-hour operation with all available personnel on duty. When the Stabilization Force (SFOR) advised me air strikes had begun, I notified the OSCE staff. Aside from the obvious safety reasons, it was considered a political impossibility for OSCE to operate in an active combat zone because of its neutral mandate to promote stability and cooperation. Their continued presence might have given the appearance OSCE condoned the air strikes.

The air strikes were conducted after the International Criminal Tribunal for former Yugoslavia had confirmed the country's security forces were responsible for crimes against humanity and human-rights abuses against the Kosovar civilian population. The Hague tribunal ruled that more than 700,000 Kosovo Albanians were forcibly displaced by Yugoslav forces, with many more thousands displaced within Kosovo. After repeated warnings to Serb and Yugoslav forces to withdraw, on March 24, NATO launched air strikes aimed to destroy their military infrastructure. The air strikes lasted until June 10, 1999 and led to the withdrawal of Yugoslav forces from Kosovo, establishment of a U.N. mission in Kosovo, and put an end to what remained of the former Yugoslavia.

<u>Strike Force Mitchell</u>

The NATO air strikes in Kosovo increased tension among the Bosnian Serbs, who sympathized with their fellow Serbs living there. Several acts of violence erupted against the international community and SFOR units, including public demonstrations, rock throwing, and grenade and bomb attacks, usually directed against NATO facilities, but occasionally at our troops. Two CA officers stationed in Northern Bosnia at Brcko (pronounced *Birchko*) were forced to evacuate their office after their building was trashed by Serbs who stole all their military gear and uniforms. The officers took their weapons with them when they evacuated and confined themselves to their apartment. We were unsure about the current situation there, but reports indicated it had stabilized.

Because those CA officers reported directly to me, our commander appointed me to lead a convoy to extract them and return them safely to Sarajevo. I issued an operations order, which the personnel officer gave the tongue-in-cheek mission title of "Strike Force Mitchell." We assembled a convoy of two Humvees, with four soldiers in each. Force protection rules required us to wear full combat gear and carry loaded weapons whenever we were outside Sarajevo. On April 12, with NATO air strikes continuing in Kosovo, we moved out toward the Serbian city of Brcko, where the two CA officers were. It was one of the few times I had to wear combat gear during my duty in Sarajevo.

We split the trip up into two days and spent a night at the American base at Tuzla. Our trip took us on the same narrow roads in the mountainous terrain our bus negotiated on our way to Sarajevo two months earlier. This time we traveled in daylight and I saw how treacherous the roads were; some places had no guard rails, and only a narrow shoulder separated the road from a steep drop-off. Countless destroyed homes dotted an otherwise-beautiful countryside nestled between the mountains. Eagle Base, the American base in Tuzla, served as the forward headquarters of the 1st Cavalry Division in Bosnia. We obtained housing for the night and enjoyed our first taste of American food since arriving in Bosnia. It was a welcome change from the European-style cuisine in Sarajevo. I remarked I would make the trip to Eagle Base every day just for the food. When we reached Brcko the next day, the town appeared peaceful and people paid little attention to our convoy. The most obvious sign stability had returned was the sight of several soldiers playing volleyball at a Serbian army barracks. We met our two evacuees at the Sava River Bridge, where NATO peacekeeping forces first crossed into Bosnia in early 1996. After taking some photos, we began our return trip to Sarajevo, but not before stopping at Eagle Base again for the night and indulging ourselves with another feast of American food.

Commander Relieved

On April 14, two days after our return from the mission in Brcko, we were called to a special staff meeting where it was announced that Col. O'Dell, the Civil Military Task Force Commander, was relieved of duty and sent back to the States. Col. Joseph Davis of the 354th Civil Affairs Brigade was appointed commander in his place. O'Dell was one of two deputy commanders, each appointed with equal authority. They had been appointed as a political necessity because of the joint command relationship the United States shared with NATO. The other deputy commander was a colonel with the Italian army. As the new deputy commander, one of Col. Davis' inherited responsibilities included oversight of the Strategic Support Team (SST) and the International Organization Support Team (IOST), established to provide strategic assessments and coordinate military support for the international civilian organizations in Sarajevo.

When Col. Davis assumed command, he appointed me as his executive officer to oversee daily management of both teams.

Each team sent me their reports and PowerPoint presentations to be reviewed prior to my briefings to Col. Davis. I also received and consolidated the monthly civil-military status reports from the other liaison officers, who informed SFOR headquarters of our efforts at civil-military cooperation. Those responsibilities were in addition to my duties as the liaison officer for OSCE.

We later found out Col. O'Dell was relieved of duty for communicating classified information over unsecured electronic media. He expressed personal opposition to the NATO air strikes in Kosovo and voiced his opposition directly to the SFOR commander. He believed they would undermine our efforts at civil-military cooperation inside Bosnia and refused to support it. It was determined to be a security violation that could compromise the NATO mission. Col. O'Dell had violated two important military principles: He disobeyed a direct order by the SFOR commander, and he committed a serious security violation.

Free Elections Radio Network (FERN)

On April 21, I again traveled outside Sarajevo. This time I dressed in civilian clothing as an OSCE staff member but carried a concealed 9mm Beretta. The trip was necessary because lack of a multiethnic broadcast station outside Sarajevo threatened the democratization process in the countryside. A hardline Croat element in Western Bosnia advocated a separate political entity for the Croatian people because they feared their ethnic identity would be lost in the new Bosnia.

The Dayton Agreement called for one country consisting of a Croat-Muslim Federation and a Serb Republic. A biased information campaign conducted by the Croatian hardliners did not properly inform the Croat population in Western Bosnia about the democratic process. A week prior, OSCE tried unsuccessfully to obtain access to a British communication base at Mount Ivovic, a small, remote location about 80 miles west of Sarajevo and just 25 miles from the Croatian border. OSCE had dispatched its engineers to conduct a site assessment and set up a transmission station powered by British generators. After they waited outside the base for several hours while OSCE headquarters in Sarajevo attempted to negotiate entry with the British headquarters in Banja Luka (pronounced *Banya Looka*), 80 miles north of the communication station, they were denied entry.

OSCE then requested my help to secure permission from the British for OSCE engineers to enter the base. It took five days to work through the NATO "puzzle palace," but I finally obtained a document from British headquarters in Bosnia that permitted the engineers to enter the base and conduct their assessment. I decided to accompany them in their vehicle to ensure the British honored the document. I carried my OSCE identification to appear as a civilian employee; I also carried my military identification in case I needed it.

About an hour outside Sarajevo we stopped at a shopping mall for some electronic equipment. Designed in typical socialist-communist fashion, the building featured lighting and a warehouse-like appearance. It looked like a low-end version of a home-improvement store. After we purchased the necessary electronic components, we continued our journey. These roads were in better condition than those we traveled to Brcko just weeks earlier. The scenic landscape along the highway consisted of open flatlands bordered by mountain ranges that reminded me of the Adirondacks. The higher peaks were snowcapped, which made me curious about their elevation. I checked our contour map; some elevations were higher than Mount Marcy, the highest peak in New York State, which I'd hiked with Greg and Steve the previous summer.

On our way to Mount Ivovic we passed through several villages. I continued to be awed by the extensive damage to homes. One of the engineers explained the houses on one side of the road belonged to Muslims while houses on the other side belonged to Croats. During the fighting they destroyed each other's homes. It reminded me of an Eastern European version of the Hatfields and McCoys. Road signs at the edge of each town read, "Sretna Put" (Have a good journey). The signs must have seemed ironic for the villagers as they fled their homes, wondering how good the journey could be under the circumstances. Along the way we ate lunch at a restaurant that had been spared during the fighting. Again, it seemed any place that served food was off limits.

At the end of our three-hour trip, we drove about a half mile up a gravel road to the top of Mount Ivovic in Western Bosnia. I introduced myself to the guard and presented the written authorization I obtained from British headquarters, whereupon he admitted us to the base for the engineers' site assessment. I established a point of contact at the base so they could make future visits without me. I felt a sense of accomplishment, having facilitated access for OSCE representatives to the British base. The success of that mission reminded me of a favorite line by Col. John Hannibal Smith, George Peppard's character on the '80s television series, *The A Team*: "I love it when a plan comes together."

German/Hungarian Animosity

I had several different roommates at the Parliament building–from Germany, Sweden, and Hungary. The Swede, a reserve officer, was an environmental engineer in civilian life. He seemed to be the stereotypical Swede: tall, with blond hair, and a laid-back personality. He spoke good English and we enjoyed many conversations. The Hungarian was a young, clean-shaven attorney who enjoyed American movies, which he said improved his knowledge of English. His wife was pregnant with their first child. The German was a stoutly built naval-intelligence officer with a beard and a rigid personality, who spent long hours at the Residency compound.

The relationship between the German and Hungarian officers was tenuous at best. One incident punctuated their political divide. Germany became unified after the collapse of the old Soviet Union and it was admitted to NATO; but Hungary had not yet been admitted. During a cold spell that winter, the Hungarian officer noticed the German had two NATO-issued wool blankets on his bed, while he had none. When the German officer went on leave, the Hungarian took one. When the German officer returned and saw the blanket on the Hungarian officer's bed, he took it back while the Hungarian was on leave. He explained Hungary was not a member of NATO and so he wasn't entitled to it. When the Hungarian officer returned, a contentious verbal exchange ensued, causing the young Hungarian officer to request reassignment to another room. His request was granted and a few days later I had a second German roommate.

Busted in Germany

In May I took 13 days' R&R and traveled home. I boarded a military aircraft in Sarajevo and flew to Rhein-Main Air Force Base in Germany. I spent two days at the 64th Replacement Company's temporary lodging facility before being notified of a commercial flight to the States. While there, I had an embarrassing encounter with the Air Force security police. On my first full day at Rhein-Main, I decided to get some exercise and went for a run. Unfamiliar with the base, I made sure I had my military ID on me, then headed toward an open area that appeared free of vehicular traffic. I ran about halfway across the area when I was suddenly surrounded by police vehicles with flashing lights. Several Air Force security police rushed toward me, so I stopped. One of them told me to turn around, place my hands above my head, lean against a patrol car and spread my legs. As I complied with his order, I smiled at the officer to let him know I was harmless.

He glared back at me and said in a raised voice, "This is no joke!"

After I was given a pat-down search, they examined my ID card and put me in a patrol car, then took me to the security police office for questioning.

I had entered a secure area on the flight line. An Air Force security officer examined my ID and questioned me. I explained why I was at Rhein-Main and said I was unfamiliar with the area and must have inadvertently crossed into a secure area. After about 30 minutes, he concluded it was an honest mistake by an ignorant Army officer and released me. He told me to run along streets where there were sidewalks. In my defense, the secure area didn't appear to be marked or cordoned off to warn persons as they approached, but I wasn't going to make a federal case out of it.

A day later I was scheduled for a flight to the Baltimore-Washington International (BWI) Airport, the closest airport to my home designated for use by the Air Mobility Command. After arriving at BWI, I used my orders to obtain a free commercial flight to Syracuse. My time at home was a needed mental break from duty in Sarajevo. NATO was a complex organization made more so by the presence of the U.N. and a confusing array of international organizations. Added to that was the effort and the patience required to communicate in English with NATO soldiers who spoke with heavy native accents.

R&R at Home

While at home I paid a visit to the U.S. Courthouse to visit my co-workers. Everyone gave me a warm welcome. Nancy and I took a three-day trip to the village of Watkins Glen, on the south end of Seneca Lake, about 80 miles southwest of Syracuse. We hiked two miles of trails at the state park, a geological marvel featuring deep gorges and waterfalls left behind when the Ice Age receded. The following day we checked out some of the stores in town and took a luncheon cruise on the lake, the largest of the Finger Lakes. The trip gave Nancy a break from the challenges she faced at home and gave us some alone time together. I often thought her job at home was more difficult than mine because she had to concern herself with housekeeping, meal preparation, laundry, bills, car repairs, and our two youngest boys, ages 12 and 7. All I had to do was concentrate on my job as a liaison officer in the historic city of Sarajevo. I hardly had to lift a finger because my housing, meals, laundry, and vehicle maintenance were provided free by NATO.

After a wonderful time at home with Nancy and getting back in touch with the boys, I boarded a plane in Syracuse for BWI, then caught a flight to Rhein-Main Air Force Base to await a military hop to Sarajevo. My second visit was less dramatic; to pass the time I toured some of the sights on base. One of the most interesting features was a monument commemorating the end of the Cold War, made from large slabs of concrete taken from the Berlin Wall, which had separated East and West Berlin from 1961 to 1989. The slabs were decorated with colorful graffiti and peace messages. On May 24, I arrived back in Sarajevo, rested and ready to resume my duties.

OSCE Welcome Briefings

In early June the OSCE staff asked me to present an SFOR briefing to new arrivals as part of their orientation program. I gathered information from the Combined Joint Civil Military Task Force (CJCMTF) headquarters and included handouts and a PowerPoint presentation about the role of SFOR in Bosnia. My presentation focused on the role of CJCMTF to assist international organizations with their mission to build civil institutions such as government, the judicial system, and the promotion of democracy. I presented the briefing about twice a month; it became an integral part of the OSCE orientation program.

The CIMIC Course

Every two months, the CJCMTF hosted about 40 new troop arrivals from various NATO countries, including the United States, for a six-day orientation course about CIMIC (civil-military cooperation). CIMIC was the European version of civil affairs. The course was conducted at a building called Army Hall in Sarajevo and was designed to teach people how CIMIC was carried out in Bosnia. Lt. Col. Renelda Peldunas, a fellow member of the 354th CA Brigade, organized the course and acted as its program director. Lt. Col. Peldunas was a bright, highly motivated, and athletic female officer who served as assistant chief of staff for operations and training at CJCMTF. I gained respect for her soldiering skills during a training exercise at Quantico, Virginia, prior to our deployment to Bosnia. Several of us had practiced rappelling from a 50-foot tower. I'd last rappelled 12 years earlier as a company commander at Fort Leonard Wood and was eager to do it again, minus the rope burns from my previous attempt. While everyone rappelled the traditional way, hopping down the tower face up, Lt. Col.

Peldunas used an Australian rappelling technique. It involved descending the tower facedown, essentially walking down the face of the tower. It was an assault technique whereby a soldier was belayed with a rope and faced the ground, enabling them to fire a weapon while descending.

Lt. Col. Peldunas asked me to be a lecturer to explain the role of OSCE to the new military arrivals. I prepared an outline of the OSCE mission and its activities in Bosnia and gave presentations to an audience comprising military personnel from several different countries. It reminded me of a mini United Nations assembly, except everyone was in uniform.

Trip to Bosnian-Serb Territory

On June 9, I embarked on a flight to Banja Luka, in the heart of the Republic of Serbia, to meet with members of the Strategic Support Team assigned there. I flew in an OSCE twin-prop aircraft owned by the Swiss Army. The Swiss provided logistical support to OSCE but remained neutral and avoided the appearance of any connection to NATO. Banja Luka was a modern-looking city compared to Sarajevo. It was largely spared any war damage because the Serbs were usually on the offensive. My purpose was to make a coordination visit with our team members there. The visit was part of my new responsibilities as chief of the Strategic Support Team.

Banja Luka was considered an unfriendly area for NATO troops, so we were advised to exercise caution. Intelligence reports indicated radical elements were in the city and presented a threat to NATO military personnel. Several weeks earlier a U.S. soldier was brutally attacked in the city with a club by a Serb party leader. The soldier shot and killed his attacker in self-defense.

I maintained a low profile and posed as a civilian, dressed in a business suit with only my OSCE badge for identification. As a security precaution I carried a concealed 9mm Beretta semi-automatic inside my coat. Prior to the trip, I loaded a 15-round magazine and placed the weapon on safe. The trip was a James Bond moment for me. I was dressed in a coat and tie, carried a concealed weapon, and arrived undercover on a Swiss aircraft to a dangerous East European city. The only thing missing was having a martini on the plane served by a beautiful flight attendant.

Upon arrival, I met with one of our team members, Maj. Scott Pautz, who also wore civilian clothes, and discussed his activities. In civilian life, Scott was an attorney from the Central New York area, so we had some common ground. We took the opportunity to enjoy ice-cream cones as we talked and strolled through the city. We walked by the parliament building for the Republic of Serbia, a majestic-looking building that identified Banja Luka as the capital city. Later that day, I returned to the airport to check in for my return flight to Sarajevo. I noticed several armed Serb security police inside the terminal – who weren't there when I arrived earlier in the day. NATO air strikes were still in progress against the Serbs in Kosovo and I thought the Serbian police might be alerted to detain anyone connected with NATO. I picked up a Serbo-Croatian magazine nearby and pretended to read it to appear inconspicuous. After several minutes it was apparent I wasn't being watched. Fortunately, no one asked me what I was reading because I had no idea. Once on the plane, I finally could relax. My ordinary features, once necessary to become a counterintelligence agent, apparently still worked for me because I didn't attract the attention of the Serb police.

During my flight, I gazed out the window at the clear sky and enjoyed a panoramic view of the mountains below. When we landed at the Sarajevo airport, I thanked God the trip had gone without incident. I'd had all the mystery and intrigue I could handle in one day.

I entered the airport and noticed a sign with a tongue-in-cheek message about the multinational participation in Bosnia. It read, "Heaven is where the police are British, the cooks French, the mechanics German, the lovers Italian, and it is all organized by the Swiss. Hell is where the police are German, the cooks British, the mechanics are French, the lovers Swiss, and it is all organized by the Italians." I thought it was odd there was no mention of the Americans. I guess Americans are so diverse we can't be stereotyped.

Surprise Email

Technology had improved by 1999 to the point Nancy and I were able to email each other daily. We still wrote letters, but not as often. I felt confident she had everything under control at home, which left me free to concentrate on my duties.

One email from Nancy came as a surprise. She wrote to tell me Sgt. 1st Class Dave Long had called. Dave was the unit administrator for the engineer unit in which I'd held company command more than 10 years earlier. I was puzzled why he would contact me after all that time until I read that he suggested I submit a packet for a battalion command position at Fort Drum. A reserve unit was recently relocated from Pennsylvania as part of a new program that assigned active and reserve soldiers to the same unit to prepare Army Reserve and National Guard units for mobilization.

I was surprised he remembered me and excited at the prospect of a battalion command. He advised Nancy which documents to assemble from the military records I kept at home and offered to submit my packet through channels to the selection board.

I immediately emailed Nancy that I was interested and described where my records were kept, saying she could provide Dave with whatever documents he needed. Command positions were competitive so I didn't raise my hopes of being selected, especially as I was assigned outside the command. I also thought being deployed out of the country would hurt my availability.

The Politics of New Government

Thanks to the Dayton Accords and the presence of the NATO Stabilization Force, Sarajevo appeared to return to normal. Five years earlier Serb artillery had occupied the mountains above the city and killed hundreds of people during a four-year siege. As summer arrived, temperatures in Sarajevo ranged from 85° F during the day to 55° in the evening. The mountains around Sarajevo were lush green as leaves sprouted on the trees. The arrival of warm weather also saw the road crews busy with street repairs and maintenance. Flowers bloomed everywhere and flower carts shared the streets with ice-cream and hot-dog vendors. People were out shopping, working, and relaxing at several outdoor cafés around the city. At a park in the city a large chess board on a concrete pad featured "life-size" chess pieces at which people could enjoy a friendly stand-up game. However, the appearance of normalcy disguised the issues still unresolved with the Tri-presidency, which consisted of a Bosniak Muslim, a Croat, and a Serb.

In a news article, Jacques Klein, the deputy high representative for the United Nations in Bosnia, voiced his concern about government corruption as a major roadblock to progress. I met Mr. Klein a couple of months earlier at one of the many meetings I attended. In the article he wrote, Klein stated Alija Izetbegovic (the Muslim member of the Tri-presidency established under the Dayton Agreement) had dismissed allegations of corruption with the remark, "Show me the swimming pools." Klein stated Izetbegovic missed the point because corruption came in many forms. It could be any kind of advantage gained with one's influence in an official position. Klein went on to say if the corruption continued, money from international donors used to rebuild Bosnia would be withheld. Donors had repeatedly stated continued financial aid to the country depended on the government's compliance with the Dayton Agreement. Klein concluded his article by stating it would ultimately be up to voters in Bosnia to remove corrupt elected officials from office. One of the OSCE mandates was to monitor and certify those elections.

Visit to Medjugorje

On June 27, I left Sarajevo with several other soldiers on an SFOR bus for a morale and welfare trip to Medjugorje. Since 1981, the village of Medjugorje in Southwest Bosnia claimed to be the site of apparitions by the Blessed Virgin Mary to six "visionaries" from the village, with messages for the world. Her mission was said to be one of peace and love. Since the apparitions began, millions of people of different faiths throughout the world visited Medjugorje; many left spiritually strengthened and renewed. People brought back stories of miracles in the form of healings (of mind, body and soul), supernatural visual events, and deep conversions back to God. My mother visited in the late 1980s, so I was interested to visit the place she had spoken of with so much reverence. It was an opportunity to literally follow in my mother's footsteps halfway around the world. We were required to be in uniform but we were unarmed, since it was considered a safe area for travel.

The Catholic Church took no official position and did not sanction pilgrimages to the area, but it also did not deny the apparitions' occurrence. In 1991, Pope John Paul II appointed a commission of bishops to investigate Medjugorje. After a three-year study, they issued a statement that said, "We accept Medjugorje as a holy place, as a shrine. This means that we have nothing against it if someone venerates the Mother of God in a manner also in agreement with the teaching and belief of the Church."

I was curious to see what my mother claimed to see on her visit 10 years earlier. A couple of us walked up a rocky trail to the top of a small mountain where a shrine had been built. I knelt and prayed, then looked up toward the sun, where the apparitions were said to have occurred, but saw nothing. I was skeptical but tried to put it aside as I prayed because I wanted to see a vision. My mother's faith may have been deeper than mine. After some time at the shrine without a vision, we descended the mountain to visit the church in the village where a group of civilians was touring. A young woman approached us and identified herself as an American. She told us how happy she was to see American soldiers there and thanked us for our service. We explained we were there as part of the peacekeeping mission to help implement the Dayton Agreement. It was gratifying to hear an American citizen express appreciation for our service. After taking photos with her, we parted ways, then visited a few souvenir shops in the village. Did the young woman represent a "vision" and the Virgin Mary's message of peace and love? The Lord works in mysterious ways.

On the way back to Sarajevo later that day, we stopped in the ancient city of Mostar for a brief visit. The most notable feature about Mostar was an historic 427-year-old bridge, destroyed in 1993 during the Croat-Bosniak war. The bridge connected two parts of the city separated by the Neretva River. A temporary bridge had been constructed in its place. The original arched bridge was made of stone and was about 98 feet long and 13 feet wide. The only original structures remaining were fortified towers protecting each end of the bridge. The culturally enriching trip gave me a deeper understanding about the history of Bosnia-Herzegovina.

<u>Visit to Croatia</u>

During the summer I had the opportunity to take a three-day R&R within the theater of operations. I teamed up with colonels Joe Davis and Jim Childs from the 354th CA Brigade to rent a car to visit Croatia. As the junior member of the group I drove, so I only caught glimpses of the beautiful coastline along the Adriatic Sea separating Croatia and Italy. We drove north along the Croatian coast to Dubrovnik and stayed at the Excelsior Hotel on the coast. We swam in the ocean and observed some of the women were topless, a cultural norm I first experienced in Kenya years earlier. As Americans we were unaccustomed to that practice but we enjoyed the scenery. It became less interesting when we saw a few topless women with children. After three days of relaxation and sightseeing, including a walk through the ancient walled section of Dubrovnik, we drove back to Sarajevo.

I enjoyed negotiating the winding coastal roads at a good pace, eager to end the long drive and return to our base. As we left one small town onto a long, straightaway, I didn't realize how much I had accelerated. Suddenly a police siren sounded behind us. I slowed down to let him pass but it quickly became obvious he was after me. I pulled onto the side of the road. A Croatian Police officer approached and asked for my identification. When he realized I was an American soldier serving with NATO, he gave me a warning and permitted us to continue our trip. I was lucky to avoid a ticket but embarrassed to be stopped with two senior officers in the car. Fortunately, I was on good terms with them and suffered no repercussions for my speeding, although Joe Davis made a disapproving comment about my driving. I stayed within the speed limit for the rest of the trip.

Exhumation Dig

On July 20, I rode in a combined SFOR/U.N. convoy accompanying a group of Bosnian Muslims (Bosniaks) to Kalinovik, in the Republic of Serbia, about 30 miles south of Sarajevo. Kalinovik was a town in Southeastern Bosnia-Herzegovina. According to information provided by the U.N. International Criminal Tribunal for the Former Yugoslavia, since 1991 Bosniaks were subjected to harassment and physical intimidation by Serbs. In June 1992, Kalinovik was declared a war zone by the Serb armed forces. On June 25 of that year, many Muslim men were arrested and detained at the Kalinovik elementary school where they were allegedly beaten and killed. At the beginning of August 1992, Serb forces shelled and burned the villages around Kalinovik, killing hundreds, including women and the elderly. Kalinovik is also the birthplace of Ratko Mladic, the former chief of staff of the Serbian Army, who was indicted by the War Crimes Tribunal for acts of genocide during the Bosnian-Croat war.

The purpose of our trip was to investigate a suspected mass grave of Bosniaks killed by the Serbs during the war, under Mladic's direction. The Bosnians brought a backhoe, picks and shovels to dig in the area. They had reason to believe several people were executed and buried in the Kalinovik area. I was present along with U.N. officials and other NATO soldiers, to observe the dig and report any findings to CJCMTF. I watched the dig from about 50 yards away and waited for news of any bodies unearthed. We spent about four hours at the site while the dig continued in three or four separate areas until they determined no bodies were buried there. I felt disappointed no evidence of the mass killings had been found. I wanted to report more proof of Serb atrocities like those at Srebrenica in 1995. Nonetheless, it did not rule out the possibility a mass grave existed somewhere in the vicinity. It was estimated more than 30,000 people were buried in mass graves as a result of genocide during the war.

Balkan Stability Summit

Ten days after the exhumation dig, the Balkan Stability Summit was convened in Sarajevo on July 30. Its purpose was to formally declare a policy to establish stability and reconstruction programs for the countries in the Balkan region. The biggest international event held in Sarajevo since the 1984 Olympics, it hosted leaders from nearly 40 countries inside the Zetra Sports Complex, a modern building housing an indoor track, an artificial-turf soccer field, and several offices and conference rooms. It also included an open-air stadium which hosted the inaugural ceremonies for the 1984 Winter Olympics. We were told during the war the Serbs used the stadium for sniper positions. The stadium was completely rebuilt by 1999 and stood as a symbol of the progress made after the war ended. I visited the stadium prior to the summit for a planning meeting. The Federal Republic of Yugoslavia was deliberately excluded from the summit to make it clear that, other than humanitarian aid, no donor funds would be provided while Milošević remained in power. The United States and the European Community would announce their commitment to rebuilding the region based on its progress toward peace and the willingness to build democratic societies. At the planning meeting, U.S. Ambassador to Bosnia-Herzegovina Richard Kauzlarich happened to sit next to me. Noticing my uniform, he shook my hand and gave me a pat on the back. Ambassador Kauzlarich made a strong point during the meeting that a multiethnic face must be presented for the summit.

On the opening day of the summit, I watched on Bosnian television from OSCE headquarters as President Clinton and Secretary of State Madeline Albright arrived via motorcade from the Sarajevo airport. I walked three blocks to the intersection where the motorcade would turn toward the Zetra Stadium and stood in uniform, along with a group of reporters and camera crews, as the president's motorcade passed by. His motorcade was led by a Sarajevo City Police vehicle, followed by armored SUVs, then two presidential limousines, followed by about 20 other vehicles. Special U.S. security forces were flown in from Germany to secure the motorcade route, especially along "sniper alley," which ran from the airport to the city center. Three U.S. Army helicopter gunships outfitted with rocket pods provided aerial cover for the motorcade. Local police had sealed off the streets the day before and even my SFOR vehicle was prohibited from the streets in the center of the city. Announcements made via the local media warned people not to lean out of (or even open) windows, because it could be interpreted as a threat. Pedestrians were barred from some areas. As the motorcade approached the intersection to turn toward Zetra Stadium, I got a glimpse of President Clinton in the right rear seat of his limousine.

The summit lasted three hours. Before it adjourned, leaders from the United States, the European Union, and the Balkan nations pledged to promote political and economic development, and to increase security in the region. The United

States pledged an economic-aid package worth approximately $700 million for post-war reconstruction in the Balkans; no economic assistance was offered to Serbia, whose leadership remained the subject of intense criticism by President Clinton and other Western leaders. The United States was among several nations restricting aid to Yugoslavia's main republic until Yugoslavian President Slobodan Milošević left office.

The French Connection

I formed an especially close rapport with the French, who comprised the primary NATO force in the Sarajevo area. The first French soldier I met was Captain Davi, whom I replaced as liaison officer at OSCE. I eventually interacted with French soldiers on a daily basis. I tried to remember my French from high school and college. Next to Vietnamese, it was probably the foreign language I was most familiar with, but it had been several years and I'd forgotten most of the vocabulary. The French officer with whom I had the most contact was Commander Thierry Domin, chief of staff for operations at CJCMTF. When we met, we discovered our first names were pronounced alike. That amused him, but he declared since he outranked me, he should receive preference to be called Thierry, and I would be referred to by my last name. Conversation among staff officers was often on a first-name basis, but I agreed it would create less confusion for them to call me Mitchell.

A group of French soldiers I became acquainted with invited me to go for a run with them. They had been in Sarajevo long before I arrived and had established a secure running route. Each Sunday I would join them for a five-mile run on a course through the hills surrounding Sarajevo. It was a scenic run that afforded a panoramic view of the city and the surrounding countryside. We kept to main roads because some of the secondary roads were still mined. The French seemed to run the hills effortlessly and at first it was difficult for me to keep up. Our security measures dictated we run in pairs, so one of them stayed behind with me until I caught up with the group. In my defense, everyone else was several years younger, but after I ran the hills a few times my stamina improved and I was able to keep up. It became an enjoyable routine and kept me in good physical condition during my otherwise-sedentary duties.

I eventually met informally once a week with one of the French officers who offered to tutor me in French. He brought me a copy of *Le Figaro*, a French newspaper published in Paris, and with his help I tried to translate some of the articles into English. He later gave me a French/English dictionary, which further aided my study.

The French soldiers in Sarajevo were a relaxed, fun-loving group who liked to party. During the course of my work I found it would be helpful to have a calling card to hand out during my liaison duties. One of my French comrades introduced me to Sgt. Gwenaele Kerven, a French soldier who worked in the printing section at CJCMTF. I requested some standard NATO/SFOR-style business cards with my name, rank, and position on them, which she printed within a couple of days.

One night she and other French soldiers convinced me to go to an amusement park in Sarajevo to enjoy live music, food, and games. We each took turns dancing with Sgt. Kerven, the only woman in the group. The evening solidified my friendship with the French, for I had never enjoyed so much entertainment and recreation on a military deployment.

Departure from Bosnia

It was customary to present awards to people departing a unit after long assignments, so in our final weeks recommendations for awards were submitted through command channels to SFOR headquarters. We were instructed to write our own recommendations. I wasn't sure what award to recommend for myself and someone in personnel suggested I should go for the Defense Meritorious Service Medal. I had such a good time in Bosnia, I felt somewhat guilty when it was approved. The award recognized service with joint staffs in NATO and other joint activities of the Department of Defense.

August 12 was a milestone day. The arrival of our replacements in Sarajevo signaled the end of our duty in Bosnia and a trip home. We were eager to return to our civilian lives and families. The next several days found us occupied with necessary transition activities as we were paired with our replacements, attended meetings, and introduced our replacements to the contacts we'd developed during the past several months. They accompanied us to the regularly scheduled meetings and we started to turn in the equipment we signed for at the start of our tour. My replacement was Maj. Larry Howard, a fellow Headquarters, 354th CA Brigade member in Riverdale. Maj. Howard accompanied me to meetings, at which I introduced him to my contacts at OSCE, to the personnel at the Swiss logistical support base, and at SFOR headquarters. He said he appreciated the time I took with him, but it was to ensure he was set up for success and to be effective as the SFOR liaison to OSCE.

During my final weeks in Bosnia I was elated to receive word from Dave Long that I was selected for the battalion command position at Fort Drum. It meant I would have the credentials necessary for promotion to colonel – but it also meant a transfer out of civil affairs. The upside was, instead of a six-hour commute to Maryland for training drills each month, it was only 90 minutes from home to Fort Drum.

Our trip home from Bosnia started with a bus trip to Eagle Base, where I looked forward to enjoying American food again. From there we would fly to Germany, then to the States. We were scheduled to leave Sarajevo on August 24, and as we prepared to board the bus at our compound, almost everyone at CJCMTF came out to say goodbye. I bade farewell to my replacement, Maj. Howard, and wished him good luck. My Swedish roommate and I traded phone numbers and he gave me his address in Sweden if I ever wanted to visit. Sgt. Kerven, the French soldier, approached me and I said goodbye to her in French. She surprised me with a hug and as we parted, she wiped tears from her eyes.

Touched by her show of emotion, I managed another "Au revoir," before I boarded the bus. After we left the compound, I took comfort in the hug she gave me but felt sad to leave her in tears. It was a bittersweet feeling to think of all the people I met from so many different nations whom I would probably never see again.

The four-hour bus ride gave me plenty of time to contemplate my assignment with the NATO troops and the people in the international civilian organizations. I was just a cog in the wheel but I felt good about my part in implementing the Dayton Agreement. It was difficult to quantify my contributions but I hoped I helped win some hearts and minds along the way. My association with the French and the contributions made at OSCE, where I was given a farewell party, gave me great personal satisfaction.

The Trip Home

At Eagle Base we were given temporary quarters to await the first leg of our flight home. Our belongings had to be spread out in an open inspection area before being loaded onto the aircraft. A young military police officer with a dog walked up and down between rows of open bags as we stood next to our belongings to inspect for drugs and contraband. The inspection went smoothly until the MP picked up what he believed to be a suspicious-looking item among a female soldier's belongings. It was cylindrical, about eight inches long, and battery operated. One of our travel restrictions prohibited batteries on the aircraft (to prevent static electricity from igniting fires or causing explosions). He held up the object in view of everyone and asked his supervisor if it was permitted. It was obviously a personal vibrator. The supervisor told him to remove the batteries and return it to the soldier to put with her other belongings. Afterward Col. Joe Davis and I went to the provost marshal's office to object to the MP's handling of the matter. We told his supervisor it should have been handled more discreetly; there was no need to hold it up and wave it around. The MP was given a verbal reprimand for his lack of discretion.

Our flight, scheduled to leave August 26, was delayed due to brake trouble on the Air Force C-141 cargo jet. The next evening, with the brake problem resolved, we took off from Tuzla. We sat on the uncomfortable web seats that ran along the inside of the fuselage. A couple of hours later we landed in Ramstein, Germany, for an overnight stay before the final leg of our trip. We left August 28 for what should have been our last flight before reaching the States. But the plane developed landing-gear problems and we were forced to land at a U.S. Naval Air Station in Keflavik, in Southwest Iceland. We were advised we would have to stay overnight while the landing gear was repaired. In August the temperature there ranged from 50° F during the day to 40° at night, so we had to dig out our sleeping bags. During our time in Iceland, I walked around the base to recon the area. The soil was black and powdery, which I learned was ash from a volcanic eruption that formed Iceland out of the Atlantic Ocean.

Our C-141's landing-gear problem was so severe we had to transfer all our baggage to another C-141 for the remainder of our trip. The following day we boarded a new aircraft and flew to Fort Benning. We reported to the replacement center about 8 p.m. A few days later I flew home on a commercial jet. Nancy and the kids met me at the Syracuse airport.

Before we left Fort Benning we were given re-integration counseling to assist us in transitioning back to civilian and family life. At the counseling session we were advised if we returned to our usual roles in the family too soon, it could disrupt the order our spouses had created in our absence. Nancy had done a wonderful job of managing our household and caring for the children. An unfortunate by-product of my military deployments, she was becoming an expert as a single parent. I returned to my position with the courts in September and began my term as a battalion commander in October.

Col Joe Davis and myself at our headquarters, 1999

Chapter 13
Battalion Command (1999-2002)

In October 1999, I accepted command of the 2nd Battalion, 313th Regiment (Logistics Support), under the 2nd Brigade, 78th Division (Training Support) at Fort Drum. The battalion's mission was to provide supply and maintenance support to three training-support battalions in the brigade and to operate an equipment concentration site that included 174 tactical vehicles and vehicle-mounted radios. The training-support battalions provided Observer/Controller/Trainers (OCTs) who evaluated training at Army Reserve and National Guard units. They also provided Mobilization Assistance Teams (MATs), which guided units through the mobilization process and prepared them for overseas deployment. The chief of the MAT used input from the OCTs to determine whether a unit was ready for deployment.

This new assignment was the biggest responsibility of my career. The brigade's mission was training instead of operations. Training units taught tactics, techniques, and procedures; operational units executed them during deployments. The logistics-support battalion provided support services to the training battalions, so they could function properly. One of my first priorities was to hire a full-time unit administrator and become acquainted with the command sergeant major and the rest of my staff: an executive officer, a personnel officer, a training officer, and a supply officer. I also met with Brigade Commander Col. Michael Krejci, an active-duty officer, who would be my rater. We were a subordinate unit under the U.S. Army Forces Command (FORSCOM), the pre-eminent provider of expeditionary, campaign-capable land forces to Combatant Commanders. When I met Col. Krejci, he asked about my background and my family, and let me know about his style of leadership. He expressed confidence in my abilities, which made me more at ease about the assignment. I had developed the perception active-duty officers were skeptical of Reserve officers' qualifications because we served part time, but I felt differently after I met Col. Krejci. His style appeared laid back and he wasn't one to micromanage his subordinate commanders. He believed officers who reached the rank of lieutenant colonel and given a battalion command were mature, responsible, and had the judgment and experience to work independently.

In December we held an assumption-of-command ceremony, in which I formally accepted command of the unit. Although a written order had already given me legal authority as the commander, the Army had its traditions, and ceremonies were a prominent part of them. Nancy, Kevin and Scott attended the ceremony, along with at least 100 others, in addition to the unit members, including representatives from the 2nd Brigade and the 78th Division, based in Edison, New Jersey. The ceremony began with the battalion in formation and our executive officer posted at the head. I would be the first commander since the battalion was relocated from Pennsylvania to New York. The battalion flag was passed from the brigade sergeant major to me; I passed it to our battalion sergeant major. The senior NCO was charged with custody of the flag, and the commander's acceptance of the flag symbolized his/her acceptance of the responsibility of command.

The master of ceremonies then read the assumption-of-command orders and remarks were given by the 2nd Brigade Adjutant, followed by the 2nd Brigade Command sergeant major, the Battalion Command sergeant major, and finally me. The remarks consisted of general comments about the meaning of command, the importance of training, and the unit's mission. My mind was on my speech and I gave only superficial attention to the other officers' remarks, but I doubt anyone paid much attention to my remarks, either. I spoke about my responsibility to the people in the battalion, the unit's mission, and our duty to carry on its legacy, which dated back to World War I. In my remarks I also mentioned the new training paradigm, which involved working together with Regular Army soldiers to prepare Reserve and National Guard units for mobilization.

Nancy and I made the ceremonial cut into a large decorated cake with a sabre, the traditional symbol of command, then members of the unit gathered for a group photo with the battalion's regimental flag. I wanted Nancy at my side as I socialized, but she was busy keeping Kevin, age 13, and Scott, age 6, in line. My career in the Army Reserve had reached a peak I never imagined as a newly commissioned first lieutenant in January 1978, let alone as a private in 1969. My previous success as a company commander, along with Dave Long's recommendation, and my increased levels of responsibility during real-world operations in Vietnam, Somalia and Bosnia, laid the foundation for command at the battalion level.

The battalion was blessed with highly competent officers and NCOs. The executive officer was Maj. Doug Goodfellow, a quiet but bright and reliable officer who ironically was CA qualified and was also a master fitness trainer. Doug was from the Watertown, New York, area and I knew him from my previous assignment with the 3rd Battalion, 389th Regiment between 1986 and 1988. He would be among my closest advisers. It raised my comfort level to have a key staff member I was acquainted with and whose abilities I trusted from the start.

The operations and training officer was Maj. Miyako Schanely, a West Point graduate who taught part time at Jefferson County Community College in Watertown. She was the most professional and committed woman I ever met in military service. Besides which, she was married and the mother of two children. She was about 20 years removed from West Point and had never been deployed overseas, but her educational background intimidated me. For the first time in my career I outranked a West Point graduate and it was somewhat disconcerting to this ROTC dropout who came up through the ranks. Our association felt strained to me at first, but as we got to know each other better, we developed a mutual respect. I realized she respected my experience in real-world operations the day I overheard her explaining to a young soldier (who asked about the patch on my right shoulder) it was a combat patch and it meant I had been places. The tone of her voice told me she meant to assure the young soldier I was an experienced leader. About four years after I retired, we met again unexpectedly when she and her husband attended a holiday party for retirees. She went on to command the battalion and had recently been promoted to colonel. Four years after that, I felt a sense of pride (tinged with a bit of envy) when I received an invitation to attend her promotion ceremony to brigadier general.

As I settled into my new assignment, I emphasized the importance of effective communications among the staff and their sections, and I stressed to our maintenance section something I learned many years ago as supply technician for the 403rd Civil Affairs Company: "Maintenance is training." In other words, when we maintained the vehicles it should be a training opportunity to become better drivers and mechanics. Maintenance was one of our critical mission tasks, and I understood its importance to prevent equipment failure and injuries. I conveyed this philosophy to our maintenance section, but soon realized they lived by the same philosophy, as most of them were full-time mechanics in civilian life.

I went a step further and encouraged the officers and NCOs to become certified as observer/controllers and trainers

(OCTs) to enhance our value to the brigade, even though there was no requirement for it. Every staff member, including our key maintenance personnel and me, attended the training course; we became the only battalion in the 78th Division with every staff officer certified as an OCT, either for maintenance operations or to direct role players' activities as "civilians on the battlefield." The role-player certification was possible because we had three civil affairs-qualified staff members, which gave us the knowledge and skills to direct civilian role players during training exercises. Civilian role players added a measure of reality to tactical training scenarios because we could present soldiers with reality-based civilian issues needing to be resolved. As for the unit's performance, our maintenance personnel exceeded the standard to perform maintenance on 20% of our vehicles, and they reduced vehicle-operating costs to $300 below the minimum standard expected by the First U.S. Army. We were off to a good start and I enjoyed my role as battalion commander perhaps more than any position I ever had in the Army.

The Forgotten Uniform

In 2000, I was scheduled to attend my first division conference. Command Sgt. Maj. Wolanin picked me up at home and we began the 275-mile trip to Fort Dix. After we'd gone about 70 miles, I realized I left my uniform at home and had only packed my hat and boots. By then, we were past the point of turning back. We were scheduled to give an important presentation on our unit-readiness status the next day and it would reflect poorly on me – and perhaps the battalion – if I appeared out of uniform, or worse, dressed in only my hat and boots.

The only viable option was to hope we arrived at Fort Dix in time to purchase a new set of BDUs (Battle Dress Uniform) before the clothing store closed. I was able to buy the BDUs but the trickiest uniform item to obtain was a personalized name tape for the right pocket, which usually had to be special ordered. I went to the tailor shop to have the U.S. Army tape sewn on and asked how soon I could get a name tape made. The clerk said it could take at least two days. In desperation, I asked the clerk to check the name tapes he had available on the chance he had one already made for someone with the same last name. He checked in the back as I prayed someone else named Mitchell at Fort Dix had a name tape ready to be sewed on his/her uniform. It wasn't as common as Smith or Jones and I thought about using someone else's name, but I was identified as a presenter on the program and with my luck, someone would notice my name was wrong. The clerk returned a few minutes later and said they indeed had a name tape for Mitchell. I anxiously inquired if I could purchase it and have it sewn on my uniform by morning. The tailor agreed it could be done, but it wouldn't be ready until about 10 minutes after the conference began. I contacted the sergeant major and explained I would be a little late, but I should arrive before the presentations started. The next morning, I rushed to the tailor shop in my new uniform, minus the shirt. I examined the name tape on the shirt and breathed a sigh of relief. I put the shirt on, rushed to the conference, and found Command Sgt. Maj. Wolanin and the seat he saved for me. Smiling, I turned so he could see my name tape. He shook his head in wonder at my stroke of luck. After the conference the sergeant major remarked I had the best luck of anyone he'd ever met and predicted I would have a good command tenure. I thought, *I wouldn't have been so lucky if my name was still Gigliotti.* We returned home after the conference with my confidence and pride intact.

The Rich History of the 2/313th Regiment

One of my interests after I joined the unit was to learn about its history before it was reorganized as a logistics-support battalion. Command Sgt. Maj. Wolanin did some research and came up with an interesting history of the 2/313th Regiment.

According to the U.S. Army Center of Military History, the 313th Regiment was originally constituted in August 1917 at Camp Meade, Maryland, as the 313th Infantry Regiment and assigned to the 79th Infantry Division. During World War I it participated in the Meuse-Argonne and Lorraine campaigns in France. It was demobilized in June 1919 and reconstituted in the Organized Reserve in June 1921, again assigned to the 79th Infantry Division. The 313th Infantry Regiment was ordered to active military service in June 1942, participating in campaigns in Normandy, Northern France, the Rhineland, Ardennes-Alsace, and Central Europe. It was decorated with the French Croix de Guerre three times during World War II. In action with the 79th Infantry Division in the Rhineland between February and May 1945, the regiment participated in the Ninth Army's burst across the Rhine. According to a 1945 account by Division Commander Maj. Gen. I.T. Wyche, two regiments (the 315th and 313th) moved abreast across the Rhine, fanned out and took the high ground. His standing order was to "close with the enemy and exterminate him." The 79th Division was reported to be the first U.S. Division to reach the Rhine in December 1944. On April 10, the 313th and 314th regiments attacked and by early afternoon the 313th Regiment captured the town of Bochum. A captured German report said the 79th was "considered one of the best attack divisions in the United States Army." The account went on to say, "The honor of capturing the most important prisoner of the war by the 79th Division was bestowed on the *2nd Battalion of the 313th Regiment*, who took Alfred Krupp, the head of Germany's largest munitions industry" (emphasis added). With Essen and its famous Krupp armament works in the hands of the Allies, many military observers believed the German Army could not continue to wage war. Near the end of the war, the 313th Regiment was assigned to military-government duties in Essen, Germany, a duty which evolved into the civil affairs branch of the U.S. Army.

The lineage and honors of the 313th Regiment, and in particular of the 2nd Battalion, linked us with the battalion's combat history and, for me (and the two staff who were civil affairs officers), provided a connection to the military government duties it performed in World War II. I presented a brief version of the battalion history to the unit members and stressed although we were now a logistics battalion, we had a duty to carry on its honored past.

Turn of the Century Issues

The first major crisis our new battalion faced was the arrival of the year 2000 and the 21st century, nicknamed Y2K, and its potentially disruptive effect on technology. By 1999, we relied upon computers for time keeping, scheduling, record keeping, document production, and even the control of electrical grids. Plans had begun a few years earlier to adjust for the change because computers manufactured up to that time had not been programmed to recognize years that began with 20. Every facet of government, academia, business, and industry made contingency plans for the arrival of Y2K. It was feared our reliance on technology might bring everything to a halt. To complicate matters, 2000 was a leap year and there were concerns some systems might not recognize a 366th day at the end of the year. As a logistics unit, our assignment was to provide generator support to the brigade headquarters as a backup source of power to the electrical grid. Some unit members were placed on duty for the night of December 31, 1999, to operate the generators so the computers wouldn't crash in the event of a power outage. Computer technicians had made adjustments to accommodate the 2000 series of numbers, but they enacted contingency plans, just in case. After some anticipation, midnight came and went and the situation was normal, so everyone was sent home. The anxiety about a possible Y2K disaster, at least at Fort Drum, appeared to be over. Although there were some glitches around the country, for the most part the anticipated crisis never materialized.

During the summer of 2000, Col. Krejci's command tenure ended and he was reassigned. His replacement was Col. Kevin Connors. I would serve under his command for the remainder of my tenure as a battalion commander. Like Col. Krejci, Col. Connors was a Regular Army officer whom I found to be congenial and easily approachable. By the time he assumed command, my concerns about being rated by a Regular Army officer had vanished.

A Missed Promotion

That summer I had accumulated almost seven years in grade as a lieutenant colonel and would soon be considered for mandatory promotion to colonel. A letter confirming it included instructions and a deadline to submit a packet for consideration. My packet consisted of an application, an official photograph, my last three OERs, and my military biography. A specialist in the personnel section helped me assemble the packet and send it through channels in time to be considered by the next colonel promotion board. My command tenure was due to end in October 2001, when I would complete the two-year limit for command positions, unless I obtained a waiver. The time limit was imposed so a commander didn't become too entrenched in a unit or get stale professionally. Limits on tenure gave other officers the opportunity for command, so I began to make plans to move to another unit if promoted.

Several weeks after submitting my packet, I received a non-selection letter. It not only meant I would not be promoted, but it was a negative reflection on my potential. If passed over a second time, I would have to retire. The Army had an "up or out" policy in which officers were either promoted regularly, forced to resign, retire, or go to a Reserve control group in a non-pay status. The loss of income would have a serious impact on my family if I was forced to retire or get reassigned to a control group. I examined my record to determine what led to my non-selection and asked Col. Connors for his advice. I completed the Army Command and General Staff Officers Course in 1988 and I'd had good officer evaluation reports showing I successfully performed at ever-increasing levels of responsibility. Col. Connors' believed my non-selection was based on the absence of an evaluation as a battalion commander. The OERs I sent to the promotion board were very good and one was superior, but they didn't include one as a battalion commander, a vital measure of my potential for promotion. My rating from Col. Krejci had not made it through channels yet, so I didn't have a copy for the promotion board.

In July 2000, I finally received my OER from Col. Krejci, who gave me an excellent evaluation. It would be another year before I could include it for the next colonel promotion board.

Motivations for Self-Improvement

By the time I accepted battalion command I had formed my leadership style. I made it a point to participate in all the training and field exercises we conducted. However, one of my biggest shortcomings was that I was not well read, especially in the art of military leadership, which would broaden my knowledge and effectiveness as a military officer. It became more evident to me as I advanced in rank and responsibility. Maj. Schanely, the West Point graduate, influenced me to read more, as did my wife, herself a prolific reader. One day, as Maj. Schanley and I talked about battalion training issues, I noticed she was reading *The Seven Habits of Highly Effective People* by Stephen Covey. I mentioned if she was reading it, then it was something I should read. Although she likely had greater potential for advancement in the ranks, I reminded myself I had risen through the ranks, served two combat tours and had a major peacekeeping assignment under my belt. I got Covey's book to read and also decided to choose a book from the Army chief of staff's reading list, *The Challenge of Command*, by Roger H. Nye. He wrote it to help military officers form a vision of themselves as potential commanders. Nye stated although few men and women who entered the Army had the opportunity to command battalions and larger military units, all officers would perform better if they saw their work through the eyes of a commander, who must act as a generalist in an age of specialization to form a cohesive force. Leadership styles exhibited by famous commanders of the past were used as examples throughout the book. It was more natural for me to lead by example, so I became a visible presence in the battalion.

In the summer of 2000, the 2/313th Regiment participated in a major combined arms maneuver exercise at Fort Drum. We performed several missions, including maintenance and communication support, and we used our civil affairs and OCT knowledge to train, direct, and monitor a group of civilian role players for the exercise. It demonstrated the value-added assets we had in the 2/313th Regiment as civil affairs specialists. Thanks to Capt. Magnus, our computer guru in the personnel section, and

Master Sgt. Linda Belile, our unit administrator, we established a battalion website and published a monthly newsletter to improve communications with members of the battalion and our brigade headquarters. As a master fitness trainer, one of my goals was to schedule physical fitness training during our monthly training weekends. I asked Maj. Doug Goodfellow, also a master fitness trainer, to conduct a fitness program each month. He also administered our annual physical fitness test.

In November, three coworkers at the U.S. District Court and I applied for admission to a master's program in public administration at Marist College, in Poughkeepsie, New York, south of Albany. They had an off-campus cohort program in public administration which they planned to start in Syracuse. If they met their quota of students, classes would begin in the spring 2001 semester. I was admitted but not matriculated because of my marginal grade-point average in college. I had to complete six semester hours of courses with a grade of C or better to be officially admitted into the program. I harbored a desire to earn a master's degree for several years as my military career advanced and I compared my education to that of my peers. Thanks to a greater level of maturity and improved study habits, I met Marist's requirements and was matriculated into the master's program after my first semester.

The Battalion Cruises On

Between May and June 2001, the battalion operating tempo increased as we provided a wide range of logistics support to the 2nd Brigade. We held our annual training for 11 days at Fort Drum to coincide with a training exercise we'd been tasked to support for a visiting brigade. For our unit training we conducted a compass orienteering course and a vehicular-mounted team competition. Because compass orienteering was one of the most difficult soldier skills for me to master, I teamed up with Capt. Magnus, who was skilled in land navigation; thanks to him, we won the competition.

During June we sent a two-person maintenance team to Camp Blanding, Florida, to provide maintenance support to one of our sister training battalions for a major training exercise. It was customary for the commander and sergeant major to visit unit members who were on assignment away from the unit. So, on June 11, 2001, Command Sgt. Maj. Don Wolanin and I flew to Camp Blanding. About 25 miles southwest of Jacksonville, Camp Blanding served as the primary training base for the Florida Army National Guard. We spoke with members of the unit our maintenance team supported and asked for their candid opinion of the support they had received. They told us the maintenance support was excellent and they had nothing but rave reviews for Master Sgt. Rushlow and his assistant.

Our accommodations were in an unusual setting: a rustic one-story building among similar-looking buildings nestled among tall pine trees beside a placid, man-made lake. We stayed two nights. On our way back to the airport we visited historic St. Augustine, where we toured an old Spanish fort on the coast – a pleasant diversion before our flight back to Syracuse. I was approximately 20 months into my assignment as a battalion commander and the unit was in good shape. It met or exceeded every requirement, thanks to unit members' efforts and skills. But soon the world we knew would change forever.

September 11, 2001

Lee Greenwood's song, "God Bless the USA," enjoyed another revival following the attacks of September 11, 2001. Its patriotic message touched a generation not yet born when it was released in 1984.

At the end of the first week of September 2001, my annual-training orders sent me to Fort Dix, about 100 miles south of New York City, where in 1969 I completed boot camp. My assignment was to help prepare an Army National Guard unit for deployment to Bosnia. My higher headquarters at the 2nd Brigade had the mission to provide Mobilization Assistance Teams (MATs) to help guide units through the mobilization process and get them validated for deployment. The MAT chief originally assigned could not arrive for a few days, so Col. Connors asked me to fill in. As commander of the logistics battalion I was not the most likely candidate. MAT chiefs were typically selected from the commanders of the training-support battalions because their units had the mission to train Reserve and National Guard units during their normal training cycle. Col. Connors may have assigned me because I was the most experienced commander available. I had completed the mobilization planners' course, had previous duty as a mobilization officer, and had gone through two mobilizations for tours in Somalia and Bosnia.

On Saturday, September 8, I arrived at Fort Dix as the temporary MAT chief. As it happened, Command Sgt. Maj. Donald Wolanin was also there on a short tour of duty, so we took the opportunity to go on a fitness run, which we had often done together at Fort Drum on weekend drills. He left the next day and I assumed MAT chief duties. Ironically, the September 7 edition of *The Post*, the unofficial publication for the Fort Dix community, ran a front-page article titled, "Security Measures Tighten on Post." It stated the post had increased anti-terrorism measures to prevent unauthorized access and to minimize the possibility of a terrorist attack against the post. For the rest of the weekend I met with the observer/controllers who made up the team and familiarized myself with the status of the National Guard unit bound for Bosnia.

On Tuesday, September 11, I attended the morning briefing to get the status of the National Guard unit. Col. Connors had arrived the night before and sat next to me for the briefing. While we listened to the briefer, a sergeant who monitored the morning news in the next room told us a plane crashed into one of the towers at the World Trade Center. We thought it was an accident, but minutes later he announced a second plane had hit the other tower. We feared the worst; soon the news reported terrorists had apparently hijacked an unknown number of aircraft and the Federal Aviation Administration announced all flights in the United States were grounded. A short time later the news reported a third plane crashed into the Pentagon. It became clear this was some sort of coordinated terrorist attack on select high-value targets; but, we wondered, how many more were there? Stunned by the news, I wondered how something this horrible could happen on American soil. I hoped the Air Force could quickly scramble jet fighters to intercept any additional planes and force them to land or shoot them down before they caused more carnage.

Col. Connors was the designated military disaster-response officer for the Northeast region. He was responsible to provide military support to civil authorities. He immediately notified the 2nd Brigade soldiers who were designated as the response team to proceed to New York City. I volunteered to extend my assignment until a replacement could arrive. Within a few hours, Col. Conners left with a team for Ground Zero in New York City.

Later it was reported the passengers on Flight 93 prevented a fourth hijacked aircraft from hitting another target, presumed to be the Capitol building in Washington, D.C. Calls to loved ones from the passengers' cell phones indicated they overwhelmed the terrorists on board. They forced the plane to crash in a field in Western Pennsylvania, killing all 33 passengers, 7 crew members, and the terrorists. Their courage and sacrifice in the face of certain death must rank among the bravest acts of valor in our nation's history. They were ordinary citizens with extraordinary courage who thwarted the final objective of the terrorist plot.

After volunteering to extend my tour, I called home to tell Nancy, then notified Larry Baerman, who told me to stay as long as necessary, adding the courts were also under a security alert, in case of an attempted attack on our judicial system. At the time there was no way to know the extent of the terrorist plot. I was originally supposed to be away for three or four days. Soon Fort Dix was placed on a high-alert status. Armed guards were posted at the gates and inside the base at high-security areas including the weapons-storage building and the ammunition point. Snipers were placed at strategic rooftop locations, and no one was permitted to enter or leave the base.

I spent several more days at Fort Dix as MAT chief until I was relieved. I briefed the incoming MAT chief on the status of the National Guard unit and the security situation at Fort Dix. Sending a National Guard unit to Bosnia seemed secondary to what we needed to do in the United States. After eight days I was finally able to drive home. Within 18 months I would be directly involved in the Global War on Terrorism.

At the next battalion staff meeting before our regular weekend drill, I gave instructions for them to plan a family-support day to advise unit members and their families about a possible activation. They were instructed to present information about resources available to family members if the unit was ordered to active duty. Two months after the attacks of September 11, our battalion conducted the meeting with unit members and their families. I gave the staff guidance on what information our unit members and their families would need to prepare them for a possible mobilization. It was unlikely we would be deployed as a unit because we were part of a training-support brigade, but individuals might be mobilized on a by-name basis if their skills were needed. A more likely scenario was the whole unit might be activated at Fort Drum to support Reserve units designated to mobilized there. At the family-support day, we gave presentations on the mobilization process, financial considerations, and medical benefits entitled for personnel serving on active duty. A JAG officer (military attorney) at Fort Drum gave a presentation on wills and powers of attorney. It was essential to prepare members of the battalion and their families for that contingency.

Another Promotion Board

During the summer of 2001 I had prepared a packet for an upcoming promotion board. This time I included my OER from Col. Krejci, which rated my performance as a battalion commander. However, any thought of promotion was pushed into the back of my mind amid response to the 9/11 attacks.

I eventually received a letter from the U.S. Total Army Personnel Command in St. Louis, Missouri, dated December 4, 2001, congratulating me on my selection for promotion to colonel resulting from a promotion board convened on July 10. The letter stated, "To be promoted, you must remain in an active status, be medically qualified for retention and meet the standards of the Army Body Composition Program… If you are assigned to a troop program unit, you must be assigned to a duty position authorized at a grade equal to or higher than the grade in which selected." The next sentence contained language I'd not seen in my previous promotion letters: "Your selection for promotion to the grade of colonel requires that you be confirmed by the United

States Senate before issuance of your promotion memorandum." I already understood the usual conditions of promotion. The most troubling part to me was the absence of an effective date for my promotion. Every promotion letter I received from captain through lieutenant colonel gave an effective date for the promotion to be official.

After I digested the contents of the letter, I began my search for a position at the grade of colonel. A colonel typically commanded a brigade or acted as a chief of staff at a division headquarters, or maybe as a staff officer at some higher echelon. Command of the training brigades was reserved for regular Army colonels, so it was not an option. Given my primary branch qualification, the best chance for me to get billeted as a colonel was at a civil affairs brigade or higher. I still had contacts at Headquarters, 354th Civil Affairs Brigade, from serving with them in Bosnia during 1999, so I called the full-time administrator, Maj. Beatrice Maxey, and said I was on the colonel-selection list. When I asked about a colonel vacancy, she said there were none at the time but she would mention me to the commander, Col. William McCoy, in case a vacancy occurred.

Fortunately, I knew Col. McCoy from two previous assignments. As a lieutenant colonel with the 354th CA Brigade at Riverdale in 1998, I conducted an investigation into a report of survey regarding missing government property at a subordinate unit. Col. McCoy initiated it as the commander of the 414th CA Battalion in Utica, and I worked with him during the course of the investigation. The next time we interacted was in 1999, when he succeeded Col. Joe Davis as commander of the Combined Joint Civil Military Task Force in Sarajevo. Despite our acquaintance, I worried there might be other promotable lieutenant colonels in the brigade, or someone who already lived in the Maryland/D.C. area who wanted an available colonel slot.

Maj. Maxey's offer to mention my name didn't give me much encouragement, so I expanded my search to other civil affairs units. My time as a battalion commander might give me an advantage when compared to someone without a battalion command on their resume. Meanwhile, my tenure as a commander officially ended in October 2001, but the powers that be must have overlooked me in the chaos following 9/11. I asked Col. Connors for a waiver and was granted a six-month extension, which bought me some time to find a new position before I was transferred to a control group.

In the spring of 2002, Col. Connors selected me for a rotation, this time as the chief, rather than a fill-in, of a mobilization assistance team. It involved operations Noble Eagle and Enduring Freedom, the two major operations that resulted from the September 11 attacks. Noble Eagle was the code name identifying the domestic mission against further attacks. It involved National Guard troops assigned to guard critical infrastructures such as airports, subways, and nuclear power plants, and to prevent looting in the area around Ground Zero. Operation Enduring Freedom was the code name for the military response which sent U.S. troops into Afghanistan and Iraq as part of the war on terrorism. I eagerly accepted the chance to prepare troops for deployment after the September 11 attacks.

I believed my best chance for assignment to a colonel position remained with the 354th CA Brigade so I followed up with Maj. Maxey, to remind her I was still interested in a position there. She transferred me to Col. McCoy who, to my surprise, said he would have a colonel vacancy in June and offered it to me on the phone. With a sigh of relief, I thanked him for the opportunity. I later learned Col. Joe Davis, who appointed me as his executive officer in Bosnia, was consulted and he recommended me for the position. It also helped that he and Col.

McCoy had known each other for many years. Once again, I benefitted from someone who remembered me from a previous assignment.

Challenge Coins

In May 2002 I prepared for reassignment to the 354th CA Brigade and promotion to colonel. Maj. Goodfellow, my executive officer, acted as commander until a selection board met to appoint a new commander. I cleared my unit hand receipt, which relieved me of responsibility for one million dollars' worth of equipment. At the end of my last weekend as battalion commander, I met with the battalion staff and thanked them for their support which established the battalion as an efficient, value added unit of the 2nd Brigade, 78th Division (TS). As a token of my appreciation, I gave each staff member a challenge coin that memorialized the September 11 attacks on our nation as the most significant event in my time as battalion commander.

Challenge coins had a long tradition in the military. The most commonly held belief was they originated during World War I. When the Army created flying squadrons, they were staffed by volunteer pilots from every walk of life. Some were wealthy college students who withdrew from classes midyear for the adventure and romance of the new form of warfare. One such student, a wealthy lieutenant, ordered small, solid-bronze medallions (or coins) struck, which he presented to the other pilots in his squadron as mementos of their service together. The gold-plated coin bore the squadron's insignia. The tradition of giving out coins evolved through the years. They were eventually presented to members of a unit to recognize dedicated service or a job well done which may not qualify for a medal. The coins normally depicted the unit's insignia and slogan.

Those who received a coin from a unit sometimes carried it as a souvenir of the time they served together. At social gatherings, a coin holder "challenged" another by placing a coin on a table or on a bar. If the person challenged couldn't produce the same coin, he/she had to buy a drink for anyone in the bar who held the same coin. Conversely, if the person challenged produced the same coin, the challenger had to buy the drinks.

I received my first coin at Fort Bragg in 1993, from the U.S. Army Civil Affairs and Psychological Operations Command (USACAPOC), prior to my deployment to Somalia. Maj. Gen. Montgomery presented me with my second coin at the end of that tour. In subsequent years I received coins to commemorate deployments, and as mementos of major training exercises. The Anheuser-Busch Brewing Company even distributed coins to the troops in Iraq to show their support with the inscription, "Saluting Those Who Proudly Served, Thank You from Anheuser-Busch."

Farewell to Command

On May 4, 2002, a change-of-command/farewell ceremony was held for me at Fort Drum. Invitations were sent and some of my family members made the 150-mile trip from Penn Yan. They included my brother Gene and his wife Trudy, my great uncle and great aunt, Frank and Shirley Condella, and my sister Rosemary. Nancy was there with Stephen, Kevin, Scott and Catherine. Our eldest, Greg, was serving in the Air Force. Col. Connors and other members of the 2nd Brigade attended, as well as members of the battalion. Nancy was presented with the traditional bouquet of red roses, which symbolized the unit's thanks as a farewell to the outgoing commander's spouse; Doug Goodfellow's wife received a bouquet of yellow roses, symbolizing the unit's hope for a successful future and to welcome her as the incoming commander's spouse.

Later that day Nancy and I were honored at a farewell party in Watertown, during which Col. Connors presented me with the Meritorious Service Medal. According to the *Army Officer's Guide*, the Meritorious Service Medal is "awarded to a member of the Armed Forces who, after 16 January 1969, has distinguished himself by outstanding meritorious achievement or service in a non-combat situation." The battalion members then presented me with a wooden plaque that contained the unit crests of the 2/313th Regiment and the 2nd Brigade, 78th Division. The plaque also displayed the division shoulder patch and two 2nd Brigade coins, one showing the obverse, the other showing the reverse. The center of the plaque had a photo of the whole battalion in front of our headquarters building. Across the top, wooden letters read, "2/313 Regt, LSB"; under the photograph at the bottom was an engraved plate that read, *LTC Terry J. Mitchell, 1 Oct 99-4 May 02. Thank you for your outstanding leadership. You will be missed. Your 2/313th Regt Family.*

The surprise presentations overwhelmed me with emotion. I could only summon a few words in my remarks that followed. I commented there were only a few times in life when someone was honored by those they worked with, and for me this evening was one of those times. I thanked everyone for their support and complimented them on the teamwork we developed during the past two and half years, then sat down to everyone's applause, a little embarrassed by the accolades. My military career had entered a new and promising phase with my promotion and assignment to the 354th CA Brigade, so I didn't want to sound like my career was finished. As I reflected on my time with the battalion, I thought about what an honor and privilege it was to serve with such a dedicated and talented group of soldiers and to be entrusted with the responsibility of command.

In June, I reported for my first drill with the brigade headquarters company and once again had to make the long monthly commute from New York to Maryland. Many of the same people remained in the unit from my previous assignment from 1996 and 1999. I was initially assigned as economics team chief but was soon reassigned as government team chief, a position I would retain until retirement.

In August, Nancy, Kevin, and Scott accompanied me to Virginia while I attended a training exercise at Fort A.P. Hill. They stayed at a motel near Fredericksburg, about 30 minutes away, while I was billeted on base with the unit. On our second day of training, Maj. Maxey received my promotion order. It indicated my promotion to colonel was retroactive to June 18, 2002. The next day a promotion ceremony was held in the field, with Nancy and the boys present. Brigade Commander Col. David Blackledge, pinned on my new rank, depicted by a spread-winged silver eagle, and congratulated me. When I returned to work at the court the following week, I couldn't contain my excitement and told my co-workers about the promotion.

I knew my promotion was official, but my mind kept going back to the selection letter which stated it had to be approved by the U.S. Senate. I had to see my name in the Congressional Record to satisfy the court clerk side of me. I did some research and found the Senate Record (S12060) dated November 27, 2001, which listed the executive nominations received by the Senate. It is reproduced below:

IN THE ARMY

THE FOLLOWING NAMED OFFICERS FOR APPOINTMENT TO THE GRADE INDICATED IN THE RESERVE OF THE ARMY UNDER TITLE 10 U.S.C. SECTION 12203 (I was one of 655 nominations):

To be colonel

TERRY J MITCHELL, (SSN redacted)

Legislative Actions

November 27, 2001 – Received in the Senate and referred to the Committee on Armed Services
December 06, 2001 – Reported by Senator Levin, Committee on Armed Services
December 06, 2001 – Placed on Senate Executive Calendar
December 08, 2001 – Confirmed by the Senate by Voice Vote

My promotion was confirmed by the Senate on December 8, 2001, four days after the date on the letter which announced my selection for promotion, but it only became effective June 18, 2002, the date I was assigned to a colonel position in the brigade.

Battalion Staff Photo, 2001
Standing L-R: MAJ Kamide, CW2 Runge, CSM Wolanin, CW4 Wilson
Seated L-R: CPT Maclaren, MAJ Goodfellow, Me, CPT Jenkinson, MSG Belile

Chapter 14
Operation Enduring Freedom/Iraqi Freedom (2003)

As the government team chief, my civilian and military careers were more aligned than ever. By 2003, I accumulated 22 years of experience as a deputy clerk with the federal courts and, as an enlisted soldier and reserve officer, I participated in several military operations that included counterintelligence and civil-military operations. Both required discretion, fairness, and good communication skills. My work in the courts was a major influence on my work as a civil affairs officer. I worked with federal judges and attorneys for many years and witnessed their mediation and critical-thinking skills firsthand. The lessons I learned had been helpful when interacting with people in other countries and foreign military personnel, but my biggest challenge was yet to come.

The position description for my first OER as head of the government team stated it was "one of the most important functional teams in the brigade." Ideally, someone well connected at the government level would hold the position. Headquarters, 354th Civil Affairs Brigade, was inside the Washington Beltway, which led me to believe there might be political considerations involved. As a Washington outsider, and new to the unit, my initial thought was the position would be given an officer already in the unit, or to an officer who worked in the Washington bureaucracy. I rationalized they would have better political connections, and therefore be more a more likely choice to lead the government team. Privately, I doubted I would keep the position very long.

I decided the best thing to do was act like the position was mine to keep. Being deployed was a real possibility in the Special

Operations Command and I needed to have the team ready, whether I was replaced or not. I introduced myself to the team members and became familiar with the team's equipment, its mission, and its functions. I was most familiar with the public-administration and public-safety functions from past experience in government and law enforcement, but I eventually became familiar with all the government functions contained in the civil affairs field manual. They included public administration, public education, public safety, and public health.

Operation Enduring Freedom

In May 2003, we received a warning order notifying us the entire brigade would be ordered to active duty in support of Operation Enduring Freedom.

Prior to our scheduled training drill in February 2003, we were instructed to arrive at the Reserve center in Riverdale, with everything necessary to deploy overseas. During the weekend training we were put on orders for active-duty training for an extra 10 days to prepare for mobilization. Ten days passed, and no mobilization order came, so we were sent home, told an order would follow soon. We waited three weeks until a written order arrived on March 6, directing us to report for duty the next day.

I wasn't happy about a one-day notice and called the brigade headquarters to request deferment of the report date. In addition to the need to identify a sudden replacement for me at work, I explained I was matriculated in a master's program and should be allowed to finish it. Col. Joe Davis, who recommended me for the position at the 354th, called back to say those were not valid reasons for deferment and I had to report for duty as ordered.

When I informed Marist College, they suspended me from the master's program, but assured me I would be reinstated when I returned. It worried me to take a break from the program because an extended absence might sabotage my incentive to finish.

The court gave me a great deal of support. Clerk of Court Larry Baerman was aware I could be deployed and assured me of my re-employment when I returned. Nancy was also prepared for my absence and gave her unwavering support. She understood my only other choice was to resign my commission; something neither of us wanted after I'd served so many years.

As I prepared to leave home again for an extended absence, I mentally reviewed my previous overseas deployments and how they differed. In Vietnam I arrived late in 1970, when the United States began to withdraw troops and we were protecting our bases to cut our losses. In Somalia I arrived 30 days after the battle of Mogadishu as part of the reinforcements sent to conduct stability operations. In Bosnia I arrived after the Dayton Peace Accords ended the interethnic fighting, as part of the NATO Stabilization Force. In Iraq, for the first time I would arrive near the beginning, just as major hostilities ended but where an active combat environment still existed.

Mobilization at Fort Bragg

On March 9, we assembled at the Army Reserve Center in Riverdale, and boarded three chartered buses for our trip to Fort Bragg, to undergo our final training and administrative processing before we deployed to the Middle East. My family was unable to travel to Maryland, so we said our goodbyes at home. At the reserve center I felt awkward and alone as family members bade farewell to their soldiers. My spirits rose somewhat when several former officers of the 354th CA Brigade approached to wish me a safe and successful tour of duty. It was a great show of camaraderie from the previous generation of soldiers. The sad thing was, at 56 I wasn't much younger than they were.

At Fort Bragg we were billeted in a large gymnasium. We slept on Army-issue cots arranged in rows on the gym floor. We stored our gear next to or under the cots, wherever we found room. We were within walking distance of a convenience store and the PX, where we could purchase comfort items and snacks during breaks in training. Several of us took advantage of the exercise rooms equipped with free weights, resistance machines, treadmills, and stair steppers. Prior to an active-duty tour, I ramped up my exercise routine. Because this would be a combat deployment, I was highly motivated to stay in shape to increase my chances of surviving. The scene at the gym resembled an emergency shelter for displaced persons. There were more than 100 of us crammed onto the gym floor with all our gear piled between the cots. We wouldn't be there long enough to be issued regular quarters.

The day after we arrived we were issued desert-camouflage uniforms and boots. The OCTs from the mobilization assistance team guided us through the required training and administrative requirements. It felt good to be on the operational side of the Army again. As our pre-deployment training progressed, we qualified with our assigned weapons, which for me was the M9, 9mm Beretta semi-automatic pistol. I became quite familiar with it after it replaced the .45-caliber M1911A1 semi-automatic in 1985.

The 9mm Beretta magazine held 15 rounds; the M1911A1 magazine only held seven. Although the Beretta had more muzzle velocity, it did not match the stopping power of the M1911A1. Aside from my personal bias for the Beretta (because it was an Italian-designed weapon), I preferred it because it was safer to use. It was less prone to malfunctions, easier to disassemble and clean, and it was more accurate. My qualification scores were always better with the Beretta than the M1911A1.

Our training included tactical convoy procedures, chemical self-defense measures, counterterrorism measures, and classes in the Arabic language and culture. We underwent medical and dental exams and reviews of our financial records. At a legal briefing, we signed powers of attorney and executed wills. We also visited the ID section, and had photos taken for our active-duty ID cards.

At the medical station we were given a smallpox vaccination and our third dose of the anthrax vaccination. According to the Department of Defense Armed Forces Epidemiological Board, anthrax vaccinations were initiated for military personnel in 1996. The vaccination program was implemented in part due to the increased threat of biological warfare during the Gulf War in 1991. The program was discontinued for a time for further study prior to the 9/11 attacks, and because there was an inadequate supply of the vaccine. In 2002, after the anthrax deaths following the 9/11 attacks, the program was resumed with FDA approval. In the year before we were mobilized, I received two doses of the anthrax vaccine. The 354th CA Brigade was identified as one of the units likely to be sent to an area where there was a credible risk of exposure. The anthrax vaccine was considered presumptively effective after three doses, but the full series consisted of six doses administered over an 18-month period. Prior to each anthrax vaccination, medical personnel briefed us on the agent and the possible side effects of the vaccine. Mild side effects included tenderness, redness, itching, a lump or bruise at the injection site, muscular aches, headaches, and fatigue. A rare side effect involved a serious allergic reaction. According to the Department of Health and Human Services' Centers for Disease Control and

Prevention, there was no evidence of long-term health problems. Independent civilian committees had also not found anthrax vaccinations to be a factor in unexplained illnesses among Gulf War veterans. In addition to the anthrax, smallpox, and myriad other vaccinations for duty in the Middle East, we were issued a prophylaxis medication to prevent malaria. All the vaccinations led us to joke that our bodies might undergo some kind of genetic mutation.

In many ways the mobilization process reminded me of basic training. Our days were regimented and involved long hours. During the training events we were all treated alike, regardless of rank. We were allowed to leave the base at certain times but had to sign out. Reveille was at 0500 hours and lights out came with the sound of Taps at 2200 hours. We stood in formation for roll call in the morning and each time we arrived or departed a training area. When we didn't march to our training area, we were transported in "cattle cars," 40-foot trailers pulled by 2½-ton trucks. Inside each trailer were long wooden benches on each side and hand rails for standing-room-only troops who were last to board. There were four small windows on each side of the trailer and doors on the rear and right side. We were packed in like cattle to fit the maximum number of troops in each trailer. We ate meals together in a cafeteria-style dining facility with the same kind of flatware, plastic trays and cups I used in basic training 34 years earlier.

Part of our validation process involved extensive training in chemical-biological-defense measures. One phase involved the dreaded gas chamber. We donned protective masks within nine seconds and walked into the gas-chamber building, where CS (tear) gas was released. We had to move our heads side to side and up and down to ensure our masks were sealed properly. Then we did 20 jumping jacks, dropped to the ground and low crawled toward the center of the room, then backward toward the wall to test our ability to function with the protective mask. Finally, we paired up and held our breath while we unscrewed our filters and reattached them on our partner's mask.

Another phase of our chemical-biological-defense training included how to decontaminate our skin. The Decon Kit contained a pad filled with carbon powder. We rubbed the pad on our faces while holding our breath to simulate being de-masked in a chemical environment. We were also taught the proper way to excrete bodily wastes when wearing the chemical-protective suit. A buddy would have to stand guard and help us dress afterward so we wouldn't contaminate ourselves, which punctuated the fact there was little privacy on the battlefield. Finally, we learned how to inject ourselves with atropine, a drug used to counteract nerve agents.

Many of us with several years of service had all this training at various times in our careers but this was the first time I remember training for it because we might have to use it. Saddam was known to have used chemical weapons on his own people, so it was a contingency we had to prepare for.

Another day we received urban-combat training to teach us how to defend a building and react to an ambush. It was a sober reminder that even civil affairs troops might get involved in combat situations. We would be ineffective if we couldn't interact with civilian populations. We typically entered a town after the combat troops cleared it, but once we were there, we usually provided our own security.

At age 56 I had some anxiety about being medically fit for active duty. I was in good physical condition, but an unsatisfactory blood test or eye exam could disqualify me. After my hearing test, the technician said I had very good hearing for someone my age. After a thorough medical exam, I was cleared for deployment. Although disappointed about the interruption of my graduate studies and another prolonged absence from work and family, it would have been a blow to my ego if I were rejected for active military service.

I still had my cell phone at Fort Bragg, so I could call home to speak with Nancy and the kids each day, but I would need to send it home when we left. Catherine lived only three hours away, where she taught second grade in the Charlotte-Mecklenburg School District. I called her, and we arranged to meet at a local mall before I deployed. A fellow unit member, Lt. Col. Joe Wunderlich, who lived in the Fayetteville area and had his car on base, dropped me off at the shopping mall. Cathy and I had lunch and went out for ice cream like we sometimes did before she left home. Before we parted, she gave me an Incredible Hulk T-shirt and a card with a handwritten message calling me a "lean, green fighting machine."

There's a special place in a father's heart for a daughter, and I cherished her card and gift–and was grateful we could spend some time together before I went to war.

At Fort Bragg we listened intently to daily news for word about the much-heralded "shock and awe" attack on Baghdad. In response to Saddam Hussein's defiance of U.N. sanctions, President Bush issued an ultimatum that Saddam and his sons, Uday and Qusay, leave Iraq within 48 hours. When no word came of their departure, the liberation of Iraq began on March 20. We watched as video feeds of the shock-and-awe attack on Baghdad were broadcast on television. There were some "Hooah!" yells in reaction to some of the explosions, but some said the shock and awe appeared to fall short of the hype. We knew it was only a matter of time before we would get the order to move out.

Our Going-Away Show

Joe Wunderlich, who took me to meet Cathy, was active in community affairs in the Fayetteville area. He was initially assigned to the government team. Joe had many contacts in the area and found out Art Garfunkel (of Simon and Garfunkel) was scheduled to perform in Fayetteville while we were at Fort Bragg. A woman Joe knew in Fayetteville was involved in the arrangements for Garfunkel's visit, so he told her his unit would soon deploy to Iraq and asked if we could attend the show. Our whole unit was invited to attend the concert, free, on March 27 at the Cumberland County Civic Center. At least two dozen members of the brigade headquarters enjoyed a great show by Art Garfunkel, his wife and son. It proved a welcome diversion from our mobilization preparations.

One day during our preparation for deployment, Sgt. 1st Class Doug McLaughlin of the 403rd CA Battalion showed up at the gym. I'd served with Doug for years and he was on an active-duty tour to help with the deployment of troops during mobilization for Enduring Freedom and Iraqi Freedom. It amazed me how frequently chance meetings occurred when I considered how large the Army was and how widely dispersed its personnel were. Doug noticed the 354th CA Brigade had been activated and so he paid us a visit. He invited Col. Joe Davis and me to join him for dinner at a local American Legion club. We enjoyed a couple of beers together and had a great visit. Doug was an upbeat guy who always raised my spirits with his storytelling and offbeat humor.

When our validation process ended, we awaited our departure for the Middle East. We would first go to Kuwait and convoy into Iraq. As a civil affairs unit, we would be part of the support troops to arrive after the air bombardment softened up the Iraqi defenses and combat units neutralized any remaining opposition. A massive buildup of troops was needed to establish the logistics, medical, and communication bases throughout the country. Civil affairs troops would coordinate rebuilding critical infrastructure, government institutions, the education system, the economy, civil administration, and attempt to win over the Iraqi people.

On April 1 we received our flight manifest and boarded a flight to Kuwait. Most of us flew on commercial aircraft, but some were designated as security escorts for our vehicles, equipment, and baggage on an Air Force C-5A cargo jet. For those of us on the commercial aircraft, the trip felt like the start of a vacation. We were served meals and snacks by several attractive flight attendants. One of the attendants singled me out, either because I looked older than most or she recognized my rank as a senior officer. She presented me with a 3'x5' American flag to carry into Iraq on behalf of the unit. The other flight attendants joined in for a photo opportunity with the flag draped behind us. I retained custody of the flag for our whole tour and displayed it while in Kuwait, then later at my quarters in Baghdad.

At the end of my tour, I presented it to the U.S. District Court as a token of thanks for their support and the huge welcome-home party they gave me upon my return to work. The message I wrote along the border of the flag read, "Flown in Baghdad, Iraq, in the name of liberty and justice." Larry Baerman had the flag framed in a glass case with an engraved plaque affixed at the bottom. The plaque commemorated my service in Iraq as a member of the U.S. District Court. It was displayed in the lobby of the clerk's office in Syracuse.

During our flight to Kuwait we had an overnight refueling stop in Rome. A new set of flight attendants and pilots came on board and I struck up a conversation with one of the Italian flight attendants. I spoke very little Italian but fortunately she was fluent in English. It was the closest I would get to Italy, because we weren't permitted to leave the aircraft.

Staging in Kuwait

We landed in Kuwait the next day with temperatures in the upper 90s and hardly a cloud in the sky. Our baggage and equipment arrived about an hour later, then we gathered our personal baggage and boarded buses to Camp Arifjan, a U.S. base south of Kuwait City. When we arrived, we were assigned to a large warehouse-like building about half the size of a football field, filled with dozens of bunk beds. Several similar looking buildings housed the troops awaiting transportation to the front. During our stay we had access to amenities like those at any Stateside Army base: flush toilets, showers, a PX, telephones, internet-equipped computers, fast-food stands, a chapel, an air-conditioned gymnasium and recreation center, and a dining hall. Despite the availability of toilets, the ever-present portable toilets were scattered throughout the base to accommodate the huge influx of troops. Lines for the PX were so long, it took about two hours to get inside the building. The dining facility was huge and could accommodate about 2,000 troops at a time, with four serving lines. The wait to get into the dining facility was easily a half hour but the food was well prepared and there was a good variety. One entrée served daily included a choice of meat or vegetable lasagna. Men and women were billeted together to maintain unit integrity, but for privacy we draped blankets over the sides of the bunkbeds. The warehouse building had no air conditioning, so its large sliding doors were left open to provide ventilation, as daily temperatures reached 103°. It took about three minutes to walk through the sand to reach the showers and latrines and we usually had to wait in line for a shower.

The memory of desert living had faded during the ten years since my deployment to Somalia, but it quickly came back to me. Walking in the sand was an effort; it somehow seeped into everything, especially when it was windy. Sweat rolled off me with the slightest effort and after freshening up with a shower, I broke a new sweat within seconds.

After settling into our warehouse accommodations, we began planning for our mission in Iraq. We grew accustomed to living out of duffel bags and footlockers, something we would do for the remainder of our deployment. Our assignment would be in Baghdad, the Iraqi capital, arguably the most dangerous place in the country. It was exciting to be chosen to operate in the most-vital city in the country, but we felt some natural anticipation about the dangers we'd face. We conducted collective training as a unit, but most of it was at the team level since each team would operate independently. Training focused on convoy organization and security, reaction to ambush, and communication procedures. In the evenings I worked on our mission statement and operations plan, which gave the members in each functional area of our team their detailed planning guidance.

The final version of my mission statement read: "On order, the Government Team of the 354th Civil Affairs Brigade Headquarters conducts civil affairs operations in the vicinity of Baghdad, Iraq, to support the civil-administration objectives of the Organization for Reconstruction and Humanitarian Assistance (ORHA) in coordination with the area military commander and to assist with the restoration of order, governmental functions, and public-health conditions." (Soon after our arrival in Baghdad, ORHA would be reorganized as the Coalition Provisional Authority (CPA), headed by Ambassador L. Paul Bremer). ORHA, later CPA, was the civilian organization charged with rebuilding Iraq after major hostilities ended. I felt confident about the people assigned to the government team and was eager to get started. Initially the team had 20 people assigned to it, including a doctor, a veterinarian, two lawyers, a police officer, an environmental-health specialist, and a medic. Their occupations illustrated the uniqueness of the civil affairs branch. They were professionals in their civilian careers and became a force multiplier when on active duty.

At Camp Arifjan we were introduced to a former Iraqi colonel called Bahkteer. He was a member of the Free Iraqi Forces (FIF) who volunteered to assist the coalition in the liberation of Iraq. The FIF were members of the Iraqi military who defected because they opposed Saddam Hussein's regime. They underwent a security screening and given a four-week basic training course that included civil-military operations.

Bahkteer gave us his perspective on the situation in Iraq. He told us more than 200,000 Iraqi citizens were murdered by Saddam Hussein's regime through the years. He emphasized Iraq was an advanced society compared to Afghanistan, and we should not underestimate the education level of the Iraqi people, almost 60% of whom were literate, but most of the educated people who remained in the country were members of the Baathist Party loyal to Saddam. Many professionals who opposed Saddam's regime left the country after the Gulf War ended in 1991. He said we would find most people in the country receptive to the American presence. Those who supported our presence most likely belonged to the Shiite Muslim majority, whom Saddam severely punished for trying to overthrow him after the Gulf War ended.

About two weeks after we arrived at Camp Arifjan, we no longer had to carry our chemical-protective masks but must be able to retrieve them and our chemical suits within 10 minutes of a siren-blast warning. As time went on the need for chemical protection disappeared. After we arrived in Iraq, we stored our chemical-protective apparatus in our bags and, thankfully, never had occasion to use it.

As we waited and planned for our entry into Iraq, we were glued to the news of the war on CNN. Reports indicated Saddam Hussein's Baath Party and his prized military had been virtually demolished. The fury of the United States and its coalition partners was finally unleashed on a regime known to brutalize its people, use weapons of mass destruction on them, and sponsor international terrorism. It appeared Saddam's loyalists paid the price for mass murder, torture, and other human-rights violations. In my opinion, the eventual objection of many Americans to our involvement in Iraq was sorely misplaced. We were there for good and just reasons. I maintain those Iraqi soldiers who died with the belief that Allah promised them 72 virgins would be surprised to discover there were no virgins to greet them, because there were no virgins in hell.

On April 13, the Sunday before Easter, the government team traveled in convoy to the airport near Kuwait City to pick up some late-arriving unit members. It was our first venture outside Camp Arifjan since our arrival. The trip also afforded us the opportunity to exercise convoy procedures on a public highway. I viewed it as a rehearsal for our eventual trek into Iraq. We performed a communications check and I gave a standard mission brief that included the procedure for reaction to an ambush, and safety and first-aid measures. We carried loaded weapons because intelligence reports indicated an active terrorist threat in Kuwait City, even though the Kuwaiti government and most of its citizens were supportive of our presence. When we arrived at the airport the movement officer asked us to provide a security escort back to Camp Arifjan for a Kuwaiti flatbed truck loaded with supply pallets, and for a small bus. Suddenly we were on a security mission for two civilian vehicles. We returned safely to Camp Arifjan with an unintended training benefit, which demonstrated the versatility of civil affairs troops.

Crossing "The Berm" into Iraq

With news the 3rd Infantry Division had captured Baghdad and formal military resistance was eliminated in the major cities, we were given orders in late April to enter Iraq. For our final preparation, we conducted operator maintenance on our Humvees and cargo trucks, filled our gas tanks, practiced radio checks, repacked our bags, loaded the vehicles, cleaned our weapons (a daily task), received our basic load of ammunition, and were briefed about the convoy-movement plan. I prepared myself for a significant decrease in our quality of life after we left Kuwait. Baghdad was a large international city with modern facilities and infrastructure, but it suffered extensive damage from the "shock and awe," so we prepared for the most austere conditions.

On the morning of April 23, we lined up 22 tactical vehicles to begin our journey across "the berm" into Iraq with approximately 60 troops. An advance detachment of 10 troops left with another unit's convoy a few days earlier to locate the area we would occupy in Baghdad. The command initially named me to lead the advance detachment but decided to leave me with the government team. The berm was a 10-kilometer (6.2-mile) wide, 10-foot-high mound of sand with electrified fencing, concertina wire, trenches, and guard posts. Erected after the first Gulf War, it served as an obstacle belt between Kuwait and Iraq to defend the Kuwaiti border and delay an attack by Iraqi troops.

During the first four days of ground operations (March 20-23), the Army's 3rd Infantry Division spearheaded the drive into Iraq from Kuwait. They completed a difficult night breach of the berm that required rapid action to deny the Iraqis the opportunity to attack vulnerable coalition units while they advanced slowly, single file, through lanes opened in the berm. The 3rd Infantry Division had to execute the breach to accommodate not only its own troops but other coalition forces, as well. The 354th CA Brigade was attached to the 3rd Infantry Division to provide civil affairs support.

Our convoy crossed into Iraq on the afternoon of April 23. Baghdad was about 360 miles and 2½ days away. I felt a mix of adventure and anticipation as we moved into Iraq. Although the roads were cleared for travel, the possibility of hostile action remained as we went farther north. We didn't possess the firepower of a combat unit, but with our M16s, a few M249 light machine guns and grenade launchers, we had enough weaponry to defend ourselves until we drove out of any fire zone or until help arrived. Given the size of our convoy, I thought only a large force would dare attack us. I rode in a tactical radio-equipped Humvee toward the middle of the convoy with my driver, 2nd Lt. Christopher Lynge. We proceeded quickly up Highway One, taking occasional breaks. Whenever we stopped, a security detail was posted along the road to watch our flanks. Highway One passed through a remote section of desert in southern Iraq that provided little or no cover, either to us or to the enemy. Much of the road was a paved four-lane highway, but some stretches of hard-packed sand kicked up clouds of dust and hindered our visibility.

We made it to a refueling point by dusk, but with so many vehicles from other convoys in line, it took more than three hours to refuel. By then darkness and increased risk of ambush prohibited further travel, so we set up a defensive perimeter in a barren piece of desert on the other side of the road. We posted security guards and ate our MREs in shifts. Members of the brigade staff and the team chiefs met for a situation update and to plan the next day's movement. When we called it a night, some of us slept on vehicle hoods, some found space in truck beds on top of the baggage; others slept on the desert floor. I found space in the cargo bed of a truck on top of some duffel bags. The desert air at night was cold, and it was difficult to get comfortable on the lumpy duffel bags. I was lucky to get two hours of sleep.

About an hour into our second day of travel, one of our Humvees broke down. It was hooked to a truck and towed to the next logistics base for repairs. We arrived at the Talil Air Base, a logistics support area (LSA) established after the 3rd Infantry captured the base March 23. In Southern Iraq, Talil lay about 190 miles southeast of Baghdad. It had been in coalition hands for a month, time enough to establish some basic support services. A field dining facility was available that served "tray" meals. These pre-prepared bulk meals, heated in large trays, were a step above MREs. Our accommodations were slightly better than the previous night's. We slept on folding cots in a large tent. At least we were off the sand and not sleeping on a lump of bags or a vehicle hood.

The Ancient City of Ur

While we waited for the Humvee to be repaired, Maj. Vince Cooper, the headquarters company commander, discovered we were near a historical landmark, where the ancient Sumerian city of Ur once existed. He convinced the brigade commander we should stay an extra night to visit the site, because it was a chance to see one of the most culturally significant places in the world. As a civil affairs unit, it would be relevant to our mission to understand the culture and history of the area in which we operated. As a more practical matter, the maintenance shop reported our vehicle wouldn't be repaired until late afternoon, too late for us to travel before dark. While Maj. Cooper arranged a tour, most of us waited in our vehicles. My small thermometer indicated the temperature was 97°. We were hot, bored, and impatient about the delay. Several people complained we needed to get to Baghdad to begin our mission and shouldn't go "touring" while in a combat zone. An hour later we were told to prepare for an overnight stay. That afternoon we drove a short distance to Ur, just outside the Talil LSA, accompanied by an Iraqi interpreter who acted as a tour guide.

We were told Ur was Iraq's most-famous archeological site and the world's earliest-known urban area. It was identified as the birthplace of the biblical patriarch Abraham. Ur's dominant feature was the remains of a ziggurat, or temple tower, the best-preserved one in Iraq. The ziggurat was built around 2000 B.C. by the Sumerians. The massive step pyramid was about 210 feet long, 150 feet wide, and estimated to be more than 100 feet high. It stood as a temple to a moon god, the patron of Ur. Much of the ziggurat had crumbled through the centuries and only the original foundation remained. It was restored at one time, but it suffered some damage during the first Gulf War. A couple of shell craters were in the ground next to it, and the structure itself was pockmarked with hundreds of bullet holes. At the time of our visit, the steps were roped off; we were not permitted to climb it, to avoid further damage to the structure. Nearby we saw remains of a house that allegedly belonged to Abraham. Much of the area had been excavated, but we were able to walk inside Abraham's residence, an open-air structure surrounded by walls with several rooms inside. At one entrance was an arch; our Iraqi guide stated it was one of the oldest-known examples of an arch in the world. We spent about two hours in the area, then returned to our vehicles and drove back to the Talil

LSA for the night. It turned out to be one of the most culturally enriching experiences I had in Iraq.

The Convoy Continues

Early on the morning of April 25, we continued toward Baghdad with our repaired Humvee. The length of our trip felt more like an odyssey than a convoy movement. The next area we passed through was near An Nasiriyah, known as "ambush alley" because of the number of suicide and sniper attacks which occurred there.

The ambush of the 507th Maintenance Company at An Nasiriyah a month earlier was still fresh in our minds. The 507th was a unit based at Fort Bliss. They took a wrong turn and became separated from the main convoy. The attack resulted in 11 soldiers killed, nine wounded and seven others captured. The incident stood as a stark reminder: Support units were not immune from attack.

Several hours later we finally approached the outskirts of Baghdad. Along the road lay several pieces of Iraqi armor, destroyed when the 3rd Infantry Division pushed through to the city. Some still sat alongside the road and some were partially hidden among the palm groves along the highway. As we entered the city, people were lined up along the street, cheering. Everyone seemed happy to see us, but we remained guarded. It felt like a victory parade, and some even waved American flags. Our reception in Baghdad reminded me of what our troops during World War II might have experienced upon liberating Paris. We arrived about three weeks after the 3rd Infantry Division fought their way into the city. It was a nice welcome, but it didn't seem fair for us to receive the accolades when the 3rd Infantry had done the work.

Republican Guard Compound

Our convoy entered a walled compound on the south side of the Tigris River at 2:45 p.m. on April 25. The general area would become known as the "Green Zone," which was cleared of the enemy before our arrival. We were advised the compound had formerly been occupied by Saddam's Special Republican Guard. There was no indication the troops had left in a hurry. The streets were clean, and the grounds were well manicured. The buildings were virtually undamaged, but there was no electricity or running water. I walked around the area after we unloaded our gear to do a personal recon and found dozens of leaflets scattered on the ground, apparently dropped as part of our psychological operations. They warned of the impending American invasion, that Saddam's regime would be toppled, and people no longer needed to fear his brutality. The leaflets also encouraged people to listen to their radios and televisions to keep informed. I collected a handful of them for souvenirs.

I was initially assigned a billet in a concrete building with seven other colonels. The well-constructed building stood next to the Tigris River. Its walls and floors were made of marble; a deck in the back offered a view of the river. The building was furnished with beds made of wood slabs topped with thin mattresses having very little cushioning, but they were better than anything we'd slept on since we left Kuwait. Exploring the area, I discovered a park-like grassy area and a water canal that wound through the compound, as well as what appeared to be an outdoor theater with a large white concrete screen next to a small pond where the Republican Guard soldiers could view outdoor movies with sound piped in through speakers. There was also a 20-foot-high wall with a cascading waterfall next to the pond. Beautiful palm trees were scattered throughout the area. At a nearby building I found some exercise equipment (which I would use often while there). It appeared the Republican Guard was treated well. The side of our building facing the river was at the top of a steep hill covered with vegetation, which caused me some security concerns.

The main entrance to the compound was framed by a tall, arched-concrete structure with an enclosed stairway leading to the top; this might have served as an observation post. Two large iron gates secured the entrance, giving it the look of an upscale gated community. Initially we had no generator power, so the lights and the water pumps were inoperable. We used portable toilets and hauled drinking water from a water trailer. At least we had a roof over our heads and solid walls around us.

Down the street from the compound was Saddam's presidential palace, where I was eventually assigned office space. It was a huge structure, the length of two football fields. On the roof at equal intervals stood four giant bronze cast sculptures of Saddam's head wearing a medieval-style helmet. Supposedly they symbolized his connection to Iraq's past grandeur and his watch over its sovereignty. The inside of the palace appeared to be made entirely of marble, including the stairs and rails. Huge ornamental chandeliers hung from the ceilings. It was the most ostentatious building I ever saw and must have cost several million dollars to build. The furniture was ornate but poorly constructed, with thin cushioning. The palace became the coalition headquarters, to include international civilian organizations working to rebuild Iraq. It looked like a private resort. Behind the palace was a picturesque in-ground swimming pool surrounded by a grassy area adorned with flowering bushes and tall palm trees to provide shade. A white stone bathhouse was set back from the pool. In front of it was a wet bar with umbrella tables and chairs. In the center of the pool was an island with a large fountain. High and low diving boards completed the pool accessories.

Across the street was another palace extensively damaged in the bombing. Belonging to Saddam's son Uday; it was where his storied gold-plated AK-47 was found. About a mile from our compound was the parade ground where Saddam displayed an iconic symbol of his military power. Two giant swords rising 50 feet in the air spanned the width of the parade grounds. They were anchored at each end by replicas of Saddam's hand grasping each sword at its base. Piled at the base of each hand were hundreds of helmets said to belong to Iranian soldiers killed in the Iran-Iraq War from 1980 to 1988. The whole Green Zone encompassed an area of 10 square miles. After we occupied the area it became an American fortress, ringed with strands of concertina wire, guard towers, and concrete blast walls.

Initial Fears

After settling into our new surroundings, my team members convinced me we should recon the area around the inside the perimeter for any Iraqi soldiers who might be hiding out. When I thought they were going too far away, I motioned them to come back. I appreciated them being proactive, but I was afraid we might get ambushed by a lone shooter hiding in the brush.

At the residence I shared with my fellow colonels, we walked out to the deck overlooking the Tigris River to admire the view. We were cautious not to expose ourselves too much because we didn't know if snipers might be on the other side of the river. The river was only about 500 yards wide, well within the range of a good sniper. My primary concern, however, was the heavily wooded hillside obstructing our view of the shoreline below. For the first few nights I slept on the floor next to my bed with one hand on my 9mm Beretta. It seemed nothing could prevent a group of insurgents from crossing the river in a small boat, climbing under cover of the heavily wooded slope to our building, and ambushing us in our sleep. I devised a personal-protection plan, which I shared with my roommates. If anyone entered the house, I would be hidden on the floor on the far side of my bed, out of their line of fire, and would kill them before they saw me. Each night, I tried to keep one eye open; but that turned out to be fruitless, as I soon dozed off. Maybe I was paranoid, but after two previous combat tours, this one seemed more dangerous; although my roommates apparently weren't concerned. At the end of our first week we learned the area across the river was secured, so I put my fears to rest.

Observations of Baghdad

During our first few weeks in Baghdad I saw much of the city during our patrols as we visited various government buildings, hospitals, and schools. About the size of Chicago, Baghdad had a population of about 7.2 million people. It appeared to be a blend of cultures. Modern, high-rise buildings and four-lane highways offered a sharp contrast to the narrow dirt streets lined with clay buildings whose thatched roofs were reminiscent of biblical times. Like many large cities, Baghdad featured upscale sections and poor sections. The better neighborhoods, in the southwestern and eastern parts of the city, boasted paved streets lined with shade trees, street lights, and well-constructed concrete homes with slate roofs. Baath Party members and Sunni Muslims typically occupied them.

Shiite Muslims lived in Northern Baghdad. Their streets were primarily hard-packed sand or poorly paved, and the houses looked shoddy. The streets in the Shiite sections were often strewn with garbage, much like what I'd observed in Mogadishu.

Most of the coalition efforts to improve the infrastructure and restore electricity focused on the poorest sections of the city and essential government services.

Ziggurat of Ur in Southern Iraq

Chapter 15
The Baghdad Brigade (2003-2004)

One of the Brigade's first tasks in Baghdad was to operate a Humanitarian Assistance Coordination Center (HACC). The HACC was not a new concept for civil affairs, but its scale and scope took the 354th CA Brigade into unchartered territory. The chief of operations for the HACC was Lt. Col. Daniel L. Robey, who trained with the government team before being selected to run the HACC. He was featured in an article from the Winter 2005 edition of *Veritas*, the Journal of Army Special Operations History. The article stated, "The work was demanding, the pace relentless, and guidance often nonexistent; but, if the job was difficult, Robey's tireless diligence seemed equal to the challenge."

Humanitarian Assistance Coordination Center

The HACC operated from a nondescript one-story building down the street from the presidential palace, co-located with Headquarters of the 354th CA Brigade. When we arrived, the building was filled with ornate furniture, some of which was retained to furnish the HACC. The rest was stored within the building or taken to other sites for use by soldiers. The HACC was modeled after a Civil Military Operations Center (CMOC), but on a larger scale. Its purpose was to foster relationships between the international aid organizations and the Iraqi people. They ranged from empowering local leaders to run a new government, to persuading an international organization to fix a broken sewer system. To better serve the city, the brigade's subordinate battalions set up CMOCs in each of the city's nine political districts. Lt. Col. Robey credited the rapid rate of the

HACC's success to the solid foundation laid by his predecessors at the battalion level.

The 422nd Civil Affairs Battalion, based in Greensboro, North Carolina, conducted daily meetings with international and nongovernmental organizations three weeks before our arrival. They met at a Civil Military Assistance Center (CMAC). The HACC team expanded on their operation and borrowed procedures learned in Kuwait City when they visited the Humanitarian Operations Center (HOC). They attended the Kuwaiti-run HOC for three days and gathered pointers on its daily operations, which provided a working model for our HACC operations.

Gen. Ricardo Sanchez, commander of U.S. forces in Iraq, visited the HAAC and the 354th CA Brigade headquarters early in our tour. He met individually with each team chief to get familiar with the civil affairs mission in Baghdad. In my meeting, I explained the government team's mission and organization. A career soldier, Gen. Sanchez mentioned the maturity level of many of us in the CA branch. He commented about the value our age and years of experience brought to the mission. He knew the average age in a Reserve unit was older than in a regular Army unit, but it didn't make us less effective in the performance of our mission.

Despite President Bush's announcement on May 1 of the end of major combat operations, many civilians in the international relief organizations had safety concerns about entering Baghdad. There was widespread looting and pockets of Sadaam loyalists still existed who refused to concede defeat. To dispel their fears, Lt. Col. Robey's team implemented an "Adopt a Neighborhood" program to match nongovernmental organizations (NGOs) with civil affairs units in the city, encouraging them to move into some areas of Baghdad. In a series of presentations at the HACC, unit members provided aid workers with a virtual tour of Baghdad neighborhoods and some of their rehabilitation projects using digital images. It introduced a human dimension for the NGOs to the jobs of repair and construction. Lt. Col. Robey also enlisted the help of maneuver commanders with civil affairs missions, which yielded important info on local leaders who were eager to participate in the rebuilding process. When one commander thought he recognized a unifying political ally in a person known as Mr. Mustafa, he told the HACC. Lt. Col. Robey contacted the CPA and within a week Mr. Mustafa met with CPA officials to discuss the rehabilitation of his neighborhood. Dialogue with community leaders was a key component of the HACC effort because it accelerated the return of power to the residents of Baghdad. Lt. Col. Robey's ability to realize the effects of small actions on the big picture led the HACC's success.

His goal was to no longer be needed in Baghdad and joked, "Our measure of success is putting ourselves out of business."

Larger governmental agencies such as the U.S. Agency for International Development stepped in with money to award contracts for rehabilitation projects, and the HACC experienced a decline in business. It acted as the hub for the complex civil-military relationships in Baghdad and was one of the 354th CA Brigade's key accomplishments. Our shared office space enabled us to coordinate team activities with NGOs in the area.

At times local vendors were invited into the HACC to sell their goods, which made it convenient for us to purchase souvenirs. I purchased a hand-painted oil canvas of a Baghdad street scene featuring minarets and the gold domes of one of Baghdad's main mosques. I also purchased three 21kt gold cartouche pendants. I had each one personalized with the Arabic names for Nancy, Catherine, and Rosemary. According to the vendor, the ancient Egyptians believed the person whose name was on the pendant would be protected.

Coordination with Justice Officials

One of the government team's first initiatives in Baghdad was to contact the coalition[1] justice representative. We arranged a meeting with the representative at the HACC. It included Col. Joe Davis, who was assigned to the HACC as a JAG officer, JAG officers from the 3rd Infantry Division, two Iraqi judges, and me, to discuss re-establishment of the court system in Baghdad. Because of the meeting, on April 28 we made a trip to the Ministry of Justice. We met with the president of the Iraqi High Court, and several Iraqi judges and administrators to identify courthouses to be restored. Coalition officials arranged to make a $20 emergency payment to each court employee as an incentive to keep the courts in operation. Afterward we visited a courthouse to assess the damage and applied for funds to make necessary repairs.

Thereafter, I was only marginally involved with the justice system for much of my tour. As chief of the government team, my responsibilities were too broad to put my entire focus on the courts. Col. Davis and an attorney from the government team, Capt. Bruce Fein, would have primary involvement with the Iraqi justice system.

During my second month in Baghdad my civilian job led to an unexpected meeting with a group of court officers from the States. A JAG officer visited me from coalition headquarters to say a federal judge and a court clerk from Louisiana had arrived

---

[1] For purposes of brevity, ORHA (Organization for Reconstruction and Humanitarian Assistance) and its successor, CPA (Coalition Provisional Authority) will be referred to interchangeably as "the coalition".

to meet me. He introduced me to U.S. District Judge Donald Walter from the Western District of Louisiana. Judge Walter had just arrived in Baghdad with two other judges and Clerk of Court Dan Thomas from that district, to work with the Iraqi court system. When my boss, Larry Baerman, became aware a contingent from the Western District of Louisiana would be in Baghdad, he told them I was there serving with a civil affairs unit and suggested we meet.

After our visit, I introduced the judges and the court clerk to Col. Davis, who in civilian life was an attorney with the U.S. Department of Labor, so they could work together on a more strategic mission for the court system in the entire country.

In 2008, I would renew my acquaintance with Judge Walter at the U.S. Courthouse in Syracuse, when he sat as a visiting judge. I went to see him after his court session ended and re-introduced myself. He remembered our meeting in Baghdad and suggested we get together for dinner to talk about our time in Iraq. We discussed our mutual belief that the security situation had to improve before significant progress could be made. Judge Walter questioned whether democracy could survive in a country where religion was so intertwined with politics and there was no separation of church and State.

Force Protection

One of the coalition's first initiatives was to establish a city advisory council as a step toward a transparent, democratic government for the citizens of Baghdad. Members of the government team would play a key role in that effort. I assigned Lt. Col. Jerry Wilson as the liaison officer to the coalition and we began to travel outside the Green Zone to visit with local leaders. When I was approached by a colonel on the headquarters staff who questioned what my team was doing, I reminded him we couldn't stand up government institutions in an unsecure environment.

We soon received a stark reminder the city was still a dangerous place. Four soldiers from the 352nd CA Command were ambushed by an insurgent when they left a meeting. A short gun battle ensued, during which the attacker was killed by a colonel among the group.

By mid-May, I had led my team on several missions into the city to meet with local officials, visit schools, court buildings, and to coordinate with the 3rd Infantry Division headquarters. The air in Baghdad was permeated with the stench of burnt trash and garbage strewn along many of the streets. It was partially covered by the smell of exhaust fumes from small pickup trucks rumbling through the streets. People often gave us thumbs-up signs and shouted, "America good!" as we passed them. During our meetings, I spoke with the Iraqis through an interpreter. They were unanimous in their gratitude for liberation from Saddam; most were Shiite Muslims. Children would approach us on the street to ask for water, food, and "chocolata." Women were more reserved about our presence than men because of cultural/religious taboos against speaking with unrelated males without a male relative present. We were constantly on alert for ambushes, and employed security measures to minimize our exposure, although generally when children were present we considered the area to be safe.

All travel consisted of at least two Humvees, each carrying at least two soldiers aside from the driver, and the front passenger armed with an M16. We drove fast through traffic, banging on our horns to warn other vehicles to move out of our way. We kept tight intervals between vehicles and stayed in the left lane when possible, to force vehicles to pass on the right (so the driver would be protected by the M16 if we were fired upon).

I usually drove because it was easier to fire a 9mm Beretta from the driver's seat. I rested the Beretta in my right hand on my lap while I steered with my left. The M16 was awkward to fire from inside a Humvee; its length made it difficult to swing around and engage a target, so it was always pointed to the outside. It had to be fired from the hip because it was hard to aim it in a moving vehicle. The Army had issued the smaller, lighter M4 assault rifle to combat troops for several years, but CA troops during our tour still carried the M16.

We also didn't have armored Humvees like the combat units and military police, even though our mission required us to operate outside the wire. We felt vulnerable to attack and floated around ideas about how we could improve on the sandbags piled on the floor of each Humvee. Fortunately, a resourceful engineer officer at brigade headquarters solved the problem (one of many instances when individual soldiers came up with their own solutions rather than wait for the Army to provide it through official channels). He contacted some local welders through the Iraqi civilians hired to do maintenance and cleaning and contracted with them to procure and cut steel plates to retrofit the doors, roof, and cargo area of each Humvee. These were bolted onto our Humvees during the next few weeks and the modifications provided some protection from small-arms fire.

Most of us felt confident with the added protection, but one officer decided to test it just to make sure. One night, Col. Bill Kern parked one of the retrofitted Humvees on a dead-end street inside our compound, near a building occupied by members of our brigade headquarters. He pulled out his 9mm Beretta and fired several rounds into the Humvee's side at close range. The startled soldiers inside the building rushed out with their weapons to investigate. We were used to gunfire, but not inside our compound. After everyone rushed outside, Col. Kern told everyone it was nothing to worry about; he was just testing the armor. News of the incident quickly reached the brigade commander, who relayed it to the division commander. An investigation discovered the first round narrowly missed the gas tank, which came as no surprise to those who knew Col. Kern. Bill's eyesight was marginal at best. He wore thick eyeglasses for distance and had to hold written material inches from his face to read it. Following the investigation, Col. Kern was given a written reprimand and his mental state was questioned. A psychologist determined he wasn't crazy, just foolish.

The Nomadic Colonels

About six weeks after we moved into our "home" on the banks of the Tigris River we got evicted. A member of the family who owned the house before Saddam's government confiscated it had become an American citizen and filed a claim for return of the property. There wasn't enough rank among the eight of us to overturn the State Department's decision and we were forced to move into another building. Within a few days we were evicted again, this time by the commanding officer of another unit who wanted the building for his quarters. It became a grind to move all our bags and footlockers from place to place. We were eventually split up and I moved into another building with colonels Joe Davis, William "Solly" Sollenberger, and Bill Kern, where we remained for the rest of our tour. Just to be clear, I was not assigned to room with Bill to keep an eye on him, as I was with John Whidden in Somalia, but I wondered how he ever passed his deployment physical at Fort Bragg with such lousy eyesight.

In June our living conditions in the Green Zone improved with the arrival of generators. We finally had power for lights and were able to enjoy air conditioning to relieve the oppressive heat, which made it easier to sleep at night. With the water pumps repaired, we could shower and flush the toilets; but toilet paper had to be thrown in the trash. Thanks to the generators we enjoyed electricity about 75% of the time. When they ran out of fuel we had to wait up to 24 hours for fuel trucks to come along.

Our new building was smaller but situated next to a large duck pond surrounded by tall palm trees and flowering bushes. At one end of the pond I discovered a small red flat-bottom sheet-metal rowboat overturned beneath a giant shade tree. I found a pair of oars underneath, so I put it in the water to make sure it didn't leak, then rowed it around the pond. I retreated there whenever I had a chance. It gave me some exercise and had a calming effect. I looked up at the sky and imagined I was back on Keuka Lake.

Valor Award

In May I received a large envelope from Nancy. The papers inside announced I received an award for valor from the Central New York Federal Executive Association. Included was a personalized certificate signed by Sen. Hillary Rodham Clinton, along with congratulatory letters from Sen. Charles Schumer and U.S. Rep. James Walsh. Also enclosed were photos of the awards event which showed some of my coworkers and my family in attendance. Nancy's enclosed letter said I received an engraved trophy signifying the award.

Each year the Association held an awards luncheon to honor federal employees in the Central New York area for a variety of achievements. Unknown to me, Judge McCurn and his judicial assistant, Judy West, had nominated me for the award. Nancy and our sons Stephen, Kevin, and Scott attended the luncheon and accepted the award on my behalf. The award surprised me because I didn't feel I'd done anything to deserve it. The valor apparently referred to my willingness to serve in the Global War on Terrorism and put myself in harm's way.

A short time later I wrote a lengthy email message to my co-workers at the court in which I stated how proud I was to serve our country, but I had given all I could and had reached a point in my career when I could give no more. I anticipated Iraq would be my last deployment before I retired from military service and I looked forward to rejoining them upon my return to the court.

Hotel California

There was a large hotel at the airport south of Baghdad named the California Hotel. It was a popular place for tourists during more peaceful times. The exterior was a pastel yellow and blue and was only slightly damaged; inside, the rooms had been ransacked. The hotel's name reminded me of the Eagles song, "Hotel California," about materialism and excesses in America, but I thought some of the lyrics had an uncanny similarity to Baghdad's California Hotel. The hotel certainly represented the excessive materialism for which Saddam was known and the opulence he wanted to present to the world. Like the lyrics from the Eagles' song, the hotel was off a desert highway. On the surface it looked like a piece of heaven but inside it looked like hell.

Reassignment to the 1st Armored Division

The 354th CA Brigade was reassigned to the 1st Armored Division in June when they succeeded the 3rd Infantry Division in providing security for Baghdad. I viewed the change as the next phase in the Army's doctrine of taking and occupying a city. Replacing infantry with armor indicated to me the end of street-to-street urban fighting to capture the city and the start of occupation by fortifying it.

The new division commander was Maj. Gen. Martin Dempsey, who believed civil affairs troops should be moved from the Green Zone to the airport; it meant we would live in tents. Spoiled by the Green Zone's park-like surroundings and its elaborate buildings, we claimed if we were moved it would degrade our ability to provide civil affairs support. We explained in the city we could interact with people more effectively and remain near the coalition headquarters to better coordinate civil-military operations with them. At the same time, however, it was becoming more dangerous to work in the city because of increased attacks by the Fedayeen and other insurgent groups against coalition forces. It was more dangerous to travel between the city and the airport, which we would have to do more often if we were based at the airport, near division headquarters. The use of roadside bombs, or improvised explosive devices (IEDs), had increased significantly by the summer of 2003.

We ultimately arrived at a compromise and sent two members from our headquarters company to live at the airport. We would keep a civil affairs representative at division headquarters who had communication with the CA teams in the Green Zone to present daily situation reports to the division staff. As a result, our CA teams remained in the city to conduct operations. Because we were able to keep our base of operations in the city, we called ourselves the Baghdad Brigade.

The other team chiefs and I eventually presented weekly briefings to Gen. Dempsey at division headquarters for our situation reports or sitreps. We didn't know we were briefing someone who would later become the highest-ranking military officer in the United States. In 2011 Gen. Dempsey became the

18th Chairman of the Joint Chiefs of Staff, the second time in my career I would encounter a future JCS Chairman.

The Most Dangerous Road in Baghdad

The airport became the major support base for troops in Baghdad, so we often had to send a convoy from the Green Zone to the airport to pick up mail and rations. The four-lane, six-mile paved highway from central Baghdad to the airport was one of the most dangerous stretches of highway in Iraq during 2003 and 2004. It was a critical supply line for units in Baghdad, traveled daily by military convoys, as well as Iraqi officials, the media, and civilian aid workers. Every CA team took turns providing a security escort for the supply section to pick up rations at the airport, so they had more fire support. The vital stretch of highway was difficult to protect because insurgents knew it was a key supply route, and despite numerous U.S. military checkpoints, they tried to circumvent every security measure we devised. Several incidents on the road left soldiers dead... by snipers, IEDs, and by decapitation wire stretched across the road. We made field-expedient modifications to our Humvees and used evasive tactics whenever we traveled to and from the airport. One modification was a vertical steel pole attached to the front of our Humvees. A notch cut in it just above the roof height would cut any decapitation wires meant to kill troops standing watch in the cargo bed. We also shifted lanes under overpasses to avoid snipers who might be perched on the other side. Roadside terrain was flat and lined with palm trees and scrub brush, so Army engineers cleared the median to eliminate any cover. Car bombers cruising the highway for potential targets also posed a threat. Each time I traveled the airport road, my "pucker factor" was elevated. I felt relieved after every trip, thankful to be inside the Green Zone.

After one meeting with division personnel, traffic leaving the airport drew to a standstill. We typically encountered traffic jams upon *entering* the airport because of how long it took the MPs to conduct security checks on each vehicle. After a few minutes, we heard an explosion and watched a cloud of smoke rise into the sky ahead of us. The MPs at the checkpoint told us an explosive device had been discovered near the road and it had to be detonated by an explosive ordnance-disposal unit.

<u>My Reluctance to Obey an Order</u>
One evening I received a call from our operations officer at headquarters just as we settled in for the night. He said the division chief of staff, a brigadier general, wanted Lt. Col. Jerry Wilson, whom I'd assigned as a liaison with the coalition, to personally brief him at the airport on the status of the city advisory councils being formed. This was prior to Jerry's move to the airport as the CA representative at division headquarters. Knowing the danger lurking on the airport road, I didn't want Lt. Col. Wilson to make an unnecessary trip at night. I asked why the general couldn't do it on the phone or wait until morning. The operations officer replied only that the general wanted the meeting in person ASAP. I felt the trip was too dangerous to make at night and told him we wouldn't be going.

Without further information, I couldn't put Lt. Col. Wilson and the troops needed for a convoy in needless danger just for a briefing; but, if he had to go, I would go with him.

A few minutes after the call ended my brigade commander, Col. Dave Blackledge, called and calmly said, "Terry, you have to go."

I reluctantly informed my roommates. We canvassed members of the headquarters company for volunteers and soon had more than enough troops to navigate Ambush Alley. Our convoy consisted of three Humvees: Lt. Col. Wilson and me in the lead vehicle, several other officers, and enlisted soldiers in the other two.

Soldiers do what needs to be done and when necessary they adapt and overcome when faced with obstacles and challenges. They never questioned the mission, just stepped up to do it. I was humbled by their courage and the trust they placed in me. I was also prepared to confront the chief of staff about the necessity for the trip. My fellow officers prevailed upon me to remain calm, lest I embarrass myself and say something I would regret. Thankfully our trip was uneventful. It turned out the general would be briefing incoming Secretary of the Army Les Brownlee in the morning and he wanted a face-to-face meeting with Lt. Col. Wilson to obtain the information he needed. Nothing was easy in Iraq.

Demonstration in the Streets

On a trip back to the Green Zone one afternoon in July, our convoy encountered a large crowd of demonstrators. Thousands of Iraqi army veterans and supporters protested a recent announcement by the coalition that dissolved the Iraqi army. They were peaceful enough, but they had traffic backed up for nearly a half mile. We drove slowly alongside the crowd and finally made it to the safety of an M1 Abrams tank positioned at the edge of the Green Zone. Although we were armed, we could have easily been overwhelmed by the large crowd. Despite the apparent risk we faced, I viewed the demonstration as a positive sign in the Iraqis' progress toward democracy. Under Saddam's regime a crowd of protesters would have found themselves forcibly dispersed.

At the entrance to the Green Zone there appeared to be a verbal altercation between some demonstrators and the U.S.

troops guarding the entrance. Against the advice of one of the officers on our team, I approached them to offer my assistance, followed by some of my team members. Given my experience with unruly crowds in Mogadishu, and the knowledge I gained from working with the alternative dispute resolution program at the court, I felt I could help negotiate an end to the altercation. I viewed it largely as a matter of adapting to the culture. Like Somalia, Iraq was a clan-based society and people often gathered together, not to be violent, but to use the strength of numbers to voice their opinion. When I arrived at the gate I discovered an Arabic-speaking civil affairs officer had already identified the leaders of the demonstrators. I offered my assistance and he approached me accompanied by the demonstration leaders, who identified themselves as high-ranking army officers. They spoke good English, and I listened to their concerns about pay they were owed and questions they had about dissolution of the Iraqi army. I offered to facilitate a meeting between them and a coalition representative from the Ministry of Defense. They agreed so I walked to the nearby presidential palace and advised someone in the defense ministry of the situation. An officer accompanied me back to meet with the Iraqi officers, spoke with them at length about their complaints, then scheduled a meeting with them for the next day at the Ministry of Defense.

  I accompanied the Iraqis back to the gate, where they agreed to disperse the crowd. Before they left, the Iraqis asked if two demonstrators who had been detained could be released. The Iraqi officers explained the detainees were merely caught up in the emotion of the demonstration and were not a threat to anyone. I spoke with the MP captain at the gate to find out the reason for their detention. As they weren't guilty of anything more than disorderly conduct, I asked whether they could be released as a goodwill gesture. The captain agreed but before the detainees left

I warned them not to abuse their right to demonstrate. I advised them their names were on a list, so if they were arrested again they would not receive their promised severance pay. It was an empty threat, but it was the best I could come up with. The Iraqi officers thanked me for my assistance and the release of the detainees.

Measures of Success

As time went on, efforts on behalf of the CA teams in Baghdad started to yield noticeable results. The public facilities team aided the restoration of power, water, sewage treatment, and garbage collection with civilian contractors. The economics team made site assessments of banks, coordinated salary payments to city departments, helped re-establish the chamber of commerce, and assisted with conversion of the Iraqi Dinar featuring Saddam Hussein's likeness with a new Dinar more nationalistic in nature. The special functions team helped get the Baghdad Zoo re-opened and rescued some escaped zoo animals. They also re-opened the national museum and coordinated the distribution of food with international aid organizations. The public health team assessed the capabilities of several hospitals and inspected food warehouses. The government team provided needed school supplies to several schools and assisted the justice ministry with re-opening local courts. We were instrumental in the creation of the city's first representative government in the form of interim advisory councils at the neighborhood, district, and city levels.

Metrics were established to quantify results for each of the city's 9 districts, and measures of success were color coded on a PowerPoint presentation. Red meant it was non-functional, amber meant it had limited functionality, and green meant it was fully functional. The measures pertained, for example, to hours of electrical power supplied to the city each day, or the number of neighborhood and district advisory councils in operation. The division commander tracked a total of 13 measures of success. In June, most were either amber or red; but by December the status of the city sewers and police force were the only measures primarily in red. Problems with upgrading the police force would continue well beyond my tour of duty due to internal corruption and inadequate vetting of new officers. The team chiefs briefed Col. Blackledge, our brigade commander, daily and we briefed Gen. Dempsey at division headquarters once a week. The team chiefs became obsessed with the metrics because they were indicators of our success or failure.

 I met with an Iraqi judge through an interpreter and was advised, for the first time since Saddam took power, defendants were entitled to an attorney at their initial appearance. It was the due process we took for granted in the United States, but it was denied to Iraqi citizens under Saddam's regime. The Iraqi justice system utilized an investigative judge who interviewed the defendant in the presence of his attorney and took the initial appearance, then decided whether probable cause existed to hold the defendant for trial, much like a preliminary hearing in the United States. However, the right to bail was suspended until the Iraqi police could enforce it. There was no pretrial discovery because that was included in the trial proceeding. I also worked with a legal specialist from another unit for a few days to assist with management of court dockets.

 In July, we delivered school supplies to a disadvantaged school on the Northeast side of Baghdad after an assessment identified the assistance they needed. The supplies included pencils, pens, crayons, writing tablets, chalk, pencil sharpeners, and rulers, and were donated by people in the United States, some of it from North Syracuse where Nancy helped coordinate the effort. Shiite Muslims attended the school, against whom

Saddam discriminated in favor of Sunni Muslims. It was built from mud bricks and straw by residents for their children, ranging from six to 10 years old. I met with the headmaster, or principal, who expressed gratitude for the school supplies through an interpreter. He assembled all the children in the school yard and under his direction, they sang the Iraqi national anthem for us, after which we mingled with them. It was an emotional scene to witness their smiles and enthusiasm for ordinary things we take for granted. We routinely had security troops posted around the area during visits. We may have won the hearts and minds of the school children, but we had to constantly watch our backs for anyone still loyal to Saddam Hussein.

During one courthouse visit, the government team acted as good Samaritans for a sick Iraqi prisoner. One of the MP prisoner escorts was qualified as a combat lifesaver (a qualification short of being a medic) and noticed a prisoner was quite ill. He suggested the prisoner might have tuberculosis and should be evacuated. Our team was the only group available, so we placed him in the cargo bed of one of our Humvees with the MP to watch him. We drove to the nearest coalition medical clinic, where we left him with the MP to be evacuated to a hospital.

By July one of our major successes included establishment of an interim city council made up of members from the 88 neighborhoods and nine districts that comprised the city. Lt. Col. Wilson took the lead in that effort with our battalion CA teams. Elections were held at the neighborhood level; local leaders were elected to represent their respective areas. It was an important step toward a democratically elected government in Baghdad. The council consisted of members from each ethnic group and included several women, a policy in line with coalition directives for a representative, transparent government in the capital.

Danger in the Streets

Baghdad was still a dangerous place. As of July, there were 11 casualties among the 440 civil affairs soldiers there. One soldier was shot in the neck by someone in a crowd. Bullets shattered another's upper arm. A senior NCO I knew was killed in a noncombat-related vehicle accident that injured two others. To my knowledge civil affairs soldiers suffered more casualties in Iraq than during any previous conflict.

Trips outside the Green Zone were physically exhausting and mentally challenging. The oppressive heat, combined with the protective vests, long-sleeved uniforms to guard against sunburn, and our helmets and web gear, required us to keep copiously hydrated; we often flavored our water with powdered drink mixes from our MREs. There was an unspoken sense of fear and anxiety each time we embarked on a mission, masked by talk about home, family, and bits of humor that usually included comments about our living conditions or observations about Iraqi personalities we encountered. Our senses were heightened as we visually surveyed buildings, overpasses, and crowds which might harbor an ambush.

In the streets we had to strike a delicate balance with Iraqi civilians between presenting ourselves as helpful and friendly and being armed and ready to kill if necessary. Two examples came to mind. One was reported on July 14, when a civil affairs team from one of our battalions was conducting an assistance visit. An explosive device thrown at their vehicle wounded two soldiers. One lost his leg in the attack; another suffered superficial shrapnel wounds. A female soldier, using the squad's automatic weapon, returned fire, killing one attacker. The incident demonstrated women might be involved in combat even though they weren't in a combat unit. The second, in another effort to win hearts and minds, involved a young soldier I knew, assigned to the 422nd Civil Affairs Battalion, from Greensboro. Mark Bibby was killed on July 21, when his vehicle was hit by an IED while in a convoy to survey a water treatment facility in Baghdad. We had just spoken the day before the ambush. He had an infectious smile and each time I saw him, it lifted my spirits. I learned his studies at North Carolina A&T University were interrupted when his unit was mobilized but he seemed upbeat about his situation. It made my objection about interrupting my studies seem trivial. He unknowingly re-instilled in me the value of a good attitude, something I'd forgotten through the years. I attended his memorial service at the chapel and was shaken more by his death than anything else I experienced in Iraq. That young soldier sacrificed his life. I merely had a short interruption of mine.

Heat Wave

By August the daily temperatures in Baghdad often reached 120° F. I was careful to keep hydrated and either drank from the tube in my hydration backpack or carried a bottle of water. We had no refrigeration, so we kept cases of water in our air-conditioned building. Pallets filled with water bottles were set in shaded areas around the compound. When we started out for the day, the water was cool, but after an hour in the sun it became warm.

The Baghdad Five Kilometer Race

We occasionally had morale and welfare activities to divert attention from the daily rigors of our mission. On October 3, I ran in the first Baghdad 5k race (3.1 miles), organized to support a local charity. For an entry fee of $7, I received a commemorative T-shirt. The waiver each runner signed read in part, "I verify that I have full knowledge of the rigors of this race, and the risks involved in movement in and around a hostile environment." The race was run within the Green Zone to minimize danger. The course took us along the perimeter, shielded by concrete blast walls. I ran on a regular basis as part of a personal fitness program and wanted to get an idea how I placed among other soldiers, both regular and reserve. My time of 24 minutes, 4 seconds put me sixth in my 50-59 age group – and 19th of 34 runners in the 19-29 age group. It gave me some consolation to know I ran faster than 15 soldiers who were at least 25 years younger than me.

R&R Breaks

In September, we received amended orders extending our tour of duty to 12 months. We were previously led to believe we'd be home in time for Christmas, so the extension was a morale breaker. I relied on information received at the start of our deployment and even told one officer it was safe to tell his family he'd be home for Christmas. I felt worse about giving him wrong information than having to stay longer.

After receipt of the news, many of us took advantage of the leave we'd accumulated and scheduled a trip home for 15 days to break up the length of our tour. I decided to forgo my leave; after going home midway in my deployment to Bosnia, I realized it was worse to go home for a short time and then leave. I opted for a couple of short in-theater R&Rs instead. I left another officer in charge of the team and took a weekend off in October to stay at a morale and welfare center inside the Green Zone. I had a private room and access to a swimming pool, a television lounge, recreation room, snack bar, and a restaurant with table service. It provided me with a needed break from the frequent armed convoys into the city, the preparation of daily PowerPoint slides, and the collection of statistics to meet the benchmarks toward the rebuilding process.

A few days before Christmas I took a second break to Qatar. I flew out of Baghdad on an Air Force C-130 for a three-day R&R, authorized for all soldiers who served in Iraq. Due to the threat of enemy rocket fire, the aircraft used avoidance tactics on takeoff from the renamed Baghdad International Airport. It made a wide circular path as it climbed into the sky and it fired flares to evade any heat-seeking missiles. On our return, it did the same thing prior to landing. It was a nauseating experience for me, like a bad roller coaster ride.

Qatar is a small, American-friendly peninsular nation that extends into the Persian Gulf and shares a border with Saudi Arabia. Our destination in Qatar was Camp As Sayliyah, forward headquarters of Central Command (CENTCOM), whose home base was MacDill Air Force Base near Tampa, Florida. CENTCOM was the unified command of the United States Armed Forces responsible for U.S. security interests in the Middle East. Camp As Sayliyah was a resort area for those on R&R. It had all the amenities: a fitness center, internet café, massage parlor, movie theatre, bowling alley, outdoor swimming pool, medical clinic, and a large dining facility. Restaurants at the camp included a Burger King, Subway, Pizza Inn, a coffee shop, and a Chili's.

Soldiers on R&R could choose from three different field trips: a shopping trip to a mall in Doha City, a watersports excursion, or a guided desert safari. I preferred a low-key activity, so I chose the shopping trip. The mall was a modern, multilevel, air-conditioned shopping center. It rivaled anything I ever saw in the United States. It included many familiar

American-brand stores, a food court, and an indoor ice rink, where I watched some children play ice hockey.

Another amenity at Camp As Sayliyah was a beer tent, where we could get snacks, drinks, and listen to American music. Alcohol was prohibited in Iraq, but in Qatar we could have beer, limited to three drinks a day. Our ID card was swiped each time we bought a beer to ensure we didn't exceed the limit.

For exercise, I ran around the camp and visited the fitness center and swimming pool. I enjoyed a meal at Chili's, which was next to an Olympic-sized pool. The temperature averaged about 80° each day, about 10° warmer than Baghdad in December. I felt considerably lighter without 30 pounds of equipment weighing me down. By the time I returned to Baghdad, I was refreshed and ready to finish the rest of my tour.

Green Zone Attacks

It became clear to me that it didn't matter how experienced or how well trained we were, survival in combat was largely a matter of luck. To illustrate, an hour after our convoy returned to the Green Zone, another convoy was attacked on the same street. On October 26, I woke up to the sound of booming noises in the distance. I was still half asleep and initially thought it sounded like thunder. After I woke from my initial daze, I realized loud noise in Baghdad was more likely to be explosions than a thunderstorm. Insurgents reportedly launched about seven rockets against the Al Rashid Hotel, about a half mile from our living quarters, within the Green Zone. Several people were wounded, and an American lieutenant colonel was killed. The news was reported back home, prompting a text message from my brother Dale, himself a combat veteran in Vietnam, to be sure I was okay. Deputy Secretary of Defense Paul Wolfowitz was in one of the rooms on the upper level but wasn't injured. The Al

Rashid Hotel was a popular place for civilians to enjoy food, music, and dancing. Soldiers were permitted there but were barred from the restaurant after 7:30 p.m. Intelligence reports from the past several weeks indicated the Al Rashid was a "Kobar Towers waiting to happen." Kobar Towers was a U.S. compound in Saudi Arabia bombed in 2002, killing several U.S. military personnel. The attack on the Al Rashid resulted in the first casualties inside the Green Zone since we occupied it the previous April.

At the beginning of November, rocket and mortar attacks increased in frequency. On November 3, as we relaxed in our quarters after another tense day in the streets, a mortar round landed inside the Green Zone and damaged a shower trailer down the street from our building. There were no injuries, but it was the closest impact yet to our building. The next night the impact from several mortar rounds shook our windows. Sporadic rocket and mortar attacks continued throughout November. Our building would shake from some of the explosions; others were far enough away to sound like distant thunder. The people who tried to kill us ranged from the skilled to the incompetent. One insurgent blew himself up as he tried to arm an explosive device along a roadside in the city.

One of my closest brushes occurred on January 18, while at breakfast in the dining facility, some 500 feet inside the Green Zone. Our convoys often passed by there when we returned from the city. Each morning separate lines for pedestrians and vehicles passed through slowly as security checks were conducted for contractors and civilian employees. In the line of vehicles that day, a man waited in a pickup truck. As his vehicle inched closer to the gate he detonated a bomb. The force of the explosion shook our dining facility; debris from the blast hit the roof. Everyone in the dining facility jumped from our seats to seek cover. I ran to my quarters to await instructions from our internal-defense team. The blast reportedly killed more than 20 people, including one of our Iraqi interpreters; more than 60 others were injured. Thankfully, blast walls at the gate prevented an even greater loss of life.

During the next few nights our area was hit with more mortar rounds close enough to shake our building. Insurgents or Saddam loyalists finally figured out how to zero in their mortars and rocket launchers on the Green Zone. More attacks followed. At the start of the Muslim holy month of Ramadan in late October, several attacks against coalition and Iraqi targets were launched. It was not a good beginning to the holy month. A lockdown order was issued; no travel was permitted outside the Green Zone until further notice.

Because of the attacks most of us in the brigade headquarters were awarded the Combat Action Badge at the end of our tour. The badge had recently been authorized for support troops either targeted by enemy fire or who had engaged the enemy in combat while not assigned to a combat unit. In Iraq, support troops were increasingly involved in firefights and other kinds of enemy contact. They were being killed and wounded just like combat troops, but had no equivalent recognition, hence the Combat Action Badge. Many of us, me included, were never in direct contact with the enemy, so I felt some embarrassment to get the award. I jokingly referred to it as the "indirect fire" badge.

In response to the increase in attacks on the Green Zone, the 1st Armored Division launched Operation Iron Hammer, a combined air and ground operation to conduct pre-emptive strikes on insurgents, intended to degrade their ability to launch attacks. A video demonstrating our superior technology went viral. Taken during a night aerial patrol from a AC-130 Spectre gunship, (a heavily armed, modified version of the iconic C-130

Hercules transport), it showed a small group of insurgents attempting to set up a mortar under cover of darkness. As they got out of a truck to set up a mortar emplacement, they were wiped out by aircraft-fired tracer rounds. They never knew what hit them. That video really boosted our morale!

Capacity Building

In October we began a new capacity-building effort to strengthen city government. We mentored city council committee members through the democratic process by teaching them the use of parliamentary procedure, to ensure issues were brought to closure through committee discussion and then prepared for a vote by the general council. The intent was to keep them focused and to become effective legislators. Iraqis tended to go off on tangents into unrelated matters. In their culture, things happened "Inshallah" (God willing), so there never seemed any urgency to finish anything.

On October 31, several of us were invited to the re-opening ceremony of the Al Rashid District Advisory Council building, in Southeast Baghdad, made possible through funds provided by the 325th Airborne Infantry Regimental Combat Team. Tribal sheiks and coalition officials attended, to mark the official occupancy of the newly refurbished building. Inspirational speeches referred to the courage, sacrifice, and unity shown by the Iraqi people to build a free society. The new Baghdad city government continued to improve, despite increased attacks by Saddam loyalists and insurgents imported from neighboring Iran, which supported the installation of a Shiite-dominated government based on Islam. However, the momentum for a democratic, inclusive Baghdad government was building, and it appeared nothing would stop its citizens from achieving it.

Tragedy Strikes Japanese Goodwill Effort

In November Japan sent two diplomats – Katsuhiko Oku and Masamori Inoue – to Baghdad with the authority to commit $1.5 billion for humanitarian projects. Col. Joe Davis and I met with the diplomats at CPA headquarters to discuss the possibility of funding some projects. They spoke good English and described the details of the Japanese donor program. Eligible projects included primary healthcare, education, poverty relief, public welfare, and the environment. They were authorized to pay up to $100,000 for each project. The intent of the Japanese donor program was to provide grassroots development assistance. Members of Iraqi advisory councils were to complete and submit applications for the funds as an exercise in self-help and to familiarize them with the democratic process. I coordinated the implementation of the Japanese donor program in Baghdad and scheduled a meeting for members of our direct-support teams at the CA battalions to explain the application process. They were to use the information to teach and mentor members of the Iraqi advisory councils in their districts. On November 26, 2003, I announced details of the program at the HAAC to about 20 battalion representatives. An application had to be completed for each project, including photos of the proposed site, two estimates from contractors, and a final site examination conducted by Japanese representatives prior to approval. According to Mr. Oku and Mr. Inoue, funds had to be obligated by March 31, 2004, so we acted quickly to get the word out. I was eager to work with them in what was a major commitment to rebuild the city and we established a good rapport.

Tragically, in December Mr. Oku and Mr. Inoue were both killed when their vehicle was ambushed north of Baghdad. The diplomats' deaths put a temporary halt to the donor program, but the Japanese Embassy vowed the program would continue in their memory. At a memorial service for them in a large tent used as a chapel on the grounds of the coalition headquarters, I introduced myself to the Japanese embassy officials and expressed my sympathy for their loss. It was another stark reminder of the difficulties we faced. Despite the two diplomats' deaths, the donor program continued to grow in the ensuing months–and it resulted in many worthwhile projects throughout Iraq.

New Responsibility

In November, my title changed from government team chief to deputy chief of the 1st Armored Division's governance support team. It was an expansion of my original role and reflected a shift in priorities by Gen. Dempsey, commander of the 1st Armored Division and the U.S. forces in Baghdad. The remaining civil affairs teams in the brigade headquarters were consolidated under it. As part of my new duties, I selected several brigade soldiers as committee advisers to the city advisory council. They were to assist each committee to develop a mission statement and guide them through the parliamentary process. It was a significant step in the eventual transfer of responsibility for self-governance to the Iraqi people. I was assigned a desk at coalition headquarters and became fully embedded in the civilian effort. When I wasn't at city hall assisting with the committees or attending city-council meetings, I commuted a quarter mile in my Humvee from my residence to my office at coalition headquarters. By November I was enjoying freshly cooked meals and baked goods at the dining facility and had the luxury of virtually continuous air conditioning and hot showers in my quarters. Living conditions improved greatly from our first weeks in Baghdad when we ate heated tray meals or MREs, and had no lights, plumbing, hot water, or air conditioning.

On November 17, at a general meeting of all military and coalition partners, Paul Bremer, chief civilian administrator for the coalition, outlined a new U.S. agreement with Iraq accelerating the handover of authority to the Iraqi government. The coalition and the Iraqi Governing Council would agree on a "fundamental law" by February 28, 2004. It would act as an interim constitution and include a bill of rights, declare the independence of the judiciary, acknowledge civilian control of security forces, and set a timetable to form a permanent constitution. It also set a date for the first national elections to choose delegates for a constitutional convention who would draft a new, permanent constitution. A final draft of the constitution would be ratified through a popular referendum. Once it was ratified, elections for a new permanent Iraqi government would take place.

The Abu Ghraib Scandal

In November prisoner-abuse reports surfaced at Abu Ghraib Prison, about 20 miles west of Baghdad. Situated on 280 acres, it housed as many as 3,800 prisoners and was operated by the military police. Most of the abuses were committed during night shifts by the 372nd MP Company, an Army Reserve unit from Maryland. That terrible scandal cast a dark cloud over the Army's conduct in Iraq. Several people, including officers, were charged with crimes, and punished; the highest ranking was Brig. Gen. Janis Karpinski of the 800th MP Brigade. In charge of all 12 Iraqi detention facilities, she was demoted to colonel and considered by some to be a scapegoat for what occurred.

The abuses occurred partly because of a policy change from General Sanchez's headquarters, which directed a change in interrogation techniques to a more violent treatment of Iraqi prisoners. It was motivated by a rise in American casualties to get more information about insurgent plans and attacks. The prison was also overcrowded because of hundreds of raids conducted around the country. The ratio of guards to prisoners rose from 1 for every 11 prisoners to 1 for every 20 prisoners. I believe the abuses would not have occurred if a civil affairs public safety team had been available at the prison to support the MPs. A prison wasn't the ideal place to win hearts and minds, but I felt confident civil affairs soldiers would have counterbalanced the culture of torture. They would have reset the guards' moral compass and brought a sense of civility to the prison. We were more mature and better educated than the average reservist but, that aside, I found it incomprehensible that no one in charge with any conscience was present on the night shift to monitor soldiers' behavior and prevent abuse. It stung me personally that the acts of a few corrupt and immoral Army reservists tainted the good deeds of thousands of reservists who served honorably in Iraq.

Preparation for Redeployment

A redeployment briefing in early December 2003, gave us a definite timeline for our return home. Our replacements were due to arrive in mid-February 2004, and we would begin our mission handoff. Our convoy was due to leave for Kuwait around March 1. While in Kuwait we would go through the RSOI (Reconstitution, Staging, Onward Movement, and Integration) redeployment process. In plain language, reconstitution meant maintaining and repairing equipment, decompressing, and getting needed medical treatment. Staging meant readying equipment/supplies for shipment and positioning it for airlift. Onward movement meant getting the hell out of there (in an orderly fashion, of course) and return to the United States. Integration meant rejoining our unit to resume training and return to our families and civilian life.

As Christmas approached, the dining facility and many offices at coalition headquarters took on a traditional holiday appearance. Decorative lights and posters heralded the season. Some offices had artificial trees decorated with lights and ornaments. We had a small artificial tree in our living quarters with lights and ornaments. Some offices even held secret-Santa gift exchanges. We took every opportunity to give our surroundings the look and feel of home.

Saddam Is Captured

On Saturday, December 13, several team members and I, along with representatives of the coalition, attended a city advisory council meeting at the Amanat, or city hall, on the north side of the Tigris River. While a member of the Iraqi Governing Council addressed the city council about the transition to Iraqi sovereignty that was agreed upon for June 2004, an aide approached him and whispered in his ear.

The council member joyously announced Saddam had been captured. The meeting came to an abrupt halt as council members burst into spontaneous celebration. Iraqi women shed tears of joy; Iraqi men hugged. Soon we heard celebratory gunfire outside, our signal it might be a good time to leave. We donned our Kevlar helmets and body armor and walked down seven floors (the elevators rarely worked) to our Humvees and our security escort waiting outside. We ran toward our vehicles amid continuous gunfire in the streets. Our security detail advised us to keep our weapons at a low profile, in a non-threatening manner, but to shoot anyone who pointed a weapon at us, as if we needed to be told. I stood in the back of a Humvee with other CA soldiers. As we drove through the city to the Green Zone, we scanned the streets for possible threats, but most people seemed focused on the news of Saddam's capture. Back at the Green

Zone I listened to Paul Bremer's speech on television as he proclaimed, "We got him."

Everyone in the coalition could take pride in Saddam's capture because our presence forced him into hiding after the Iraqi military's defeat, and most of his support disappeared into the population. When defeat seemed imminent, most of his inner circle abandoned him. His capture completed the elimination of the three most-wanted people in Iraq. Saddam's sons, Uday and Qusay, had been killed in July during a raid on a house they used as a hideout in the northern city of Mosul.

Saddam Hussein was captured by soldiers from the U.S. Army 4th Infantry Division. He was found at a walled compound on a farm in Ad Dwar, 10 miles from his hometown of Tikrit, not far from one of his former palaces. Maj. Gen. Ray Odierno, commander of the 4th Infantry Division, reported to *The Stars and Stripes* newspaper that Saddam was found hiding in an underground crawlspace at the compound, armed with a pistol. It appeared he was not involved in the direct leadership of any resistance movement, as no communication devices were found in his hiding place; this led Lt. Gen. Ricardo Sanchez, commander of U.S. forces in Iraq, to say he did not expect Saddam's capture would result in the elimination of attacks on coalition forces. He was right. Despite the news of Saddam's capture, hostile activity continued each day and sporadic gunfire continued throughout the city.

On returning to the Green Zone from city hall, we were advised to wear our Kevlar helmets and body armor when outside to protect against spent rounds falling from the sky amid the celebration. One report indicated a soldier near the airport was killed by a falling bullet. The Iraqis seemed oblivious to the fact bullets fired into the air also fell back to the ground. Stray bullets from celebratory fire or even friendly and hostile fire were a constant threat. I worried more about stray bullets than one aimed directly at me.

In January 2004, the end of our tour was on the horizon, but we did our best to remain focused. No one wanted to become a casualty in the last weeks of deployment. On January 6, we held a change-of-command ceremony for our new brigade commander who recently arrived from the United States. The ceremony was held in our compound, in front of the building that housed the HAAC and brigade headquarters.

I was chosen to act as the Commander of Troops for the ceremony, which meant I stood at the head of the formation to bark out orders on cue. I needed several rehearsals to get it right. After the ceremony a reception inside the HAAC featured cake, coffee, and soft drinks. Our new commander was Col. Jeff Jacobs, a West Point graduate, who coincidentally was the MAT chief during our mobilization at Fort Bragg the previous March. I'd submitted a packet for the command vacancy and was encouraged by some of my fellow colonels, but realistically I had no chance against a candidate commissioned out of West Point. It was my last attempt at a command position before I retired.

By January I was the only one of five original civil affairs team chiefs still in place. The others were reassigned to staff duties and redeployment planning because their team missions were completed. Governance became the First Armored Division's main civil-military priority, because much of the effort at coalition headquarters focused on government functions.

To prepare for the transition to Iraqi sovereignty, several town-hall meetings were conducted to promote discussion of the Transitional Administrative Law among the populace. A key step toward the first national election was to select a constitutional delegation and draft a permanent constitution. The intent of these town-hall meetings was to attract diverse groups and get as much input as possible.

In February, our replacements arrived, and I began handing off to another CA officer my governance mission. At city hall, I introduced him to the Baghdad Advisory Council's committee members. During our meeting, we discussed our transition and the benchmarks established for return to a sovereign and secure Iraq.

As we sat around the U-shaped conference table, one of the sheiks said, "Colonel Mitchell, you were usually quiet and had little to say in our meetings, but when you spoke it was important."

I smiled and thanked him for the compliment. I explained my purpose was mainly to listen, to guide the conversation and keep it focused. I emphasized the importance for council members to work together and discuss solutions to the issues.

My replacement and I visited coalition headquarters to meet with the civilians in the governance office. I later turned in the equipment issued to me which was assigned to the government team. At our departure ceremony I was presented a certificate of appreciation from coalition officials for my assistance in the restoration of democracy in Baghdad.

Final Thoughts About Iraq

As we prepared to leave Iraq, I hoped for a government which allowed all its citizens opportunities for individual growth and economic prosperity, regardless of race, gender, religion, or political affiliation. The United States had to stay the course and keep faith with those who paid for the liberation of the Iraqi people with their lives.

Our brigade headquarters and its battalions suffered 23 wounded and two killed during our deployment. We lived on the edge each time our convoys left the Green Zone as we watched for roadside explosives and potential ambushes. Occasional nighttime rocket and mortar attacks shook our buildings and kept us awake as we wondered if the next one would hit us. We repeatedly trained in force-protection measures to avoid the complacency threatening to cloud our focus toward the end of the deployment. Much of my sense that we were ill-prepared for the kind of environment we faced was supported by the results of an investigation by the Center for Public Integrity released in 2011. It found although civil affairs soldiers made up only five percent of the Army Reserve, they suffered 23 percent of combat fatalities among reservists in Iraq and Afghanistan. The report indicated they "lacked protective combat gear and training."

I believe we were underequipped and unprepared to deal with the types of hostilities we encountered. Despite the disadvantages we faced, our civil affairs teams achieved several notable accomplishments: We surveyed several schools and secured funds for their repair or improvement; we helped to form the first democratically elected government in Baghdad in more than 30 years; we taught parliamentary procedure to city officials and reopened several courts. We assisted with conversion of the currency system, distributed food, supplies, and assessed the status of banks and medical facilities. We established a business center to bring people and prospective employers together and helped to protect artifacts at the national museum. We even saved several animals at the zoo. The Baghdad Brigade had performed its mission well.

It has since been reported the terrorist group ISIS grew out of the power vacuum created when Saddam Hussein was overthrown. ISIS consists mostly of Sunni Muslims; the same sect of which Saddam was a member and favored during his regime. It was wrong to: 1. disband the entire Iraqi army and 2.

purge the Baath Party (Sunnis) of its most-knowledgeable and skilled people. Some vetting took place to let select members participate in the political process but it's unclear how effective it was.

I believe those two actions by the coalition made our mission more difficult. First, by disbanding an established and experienced army generally accepted by the Iraqi people, it made us look like occupiers instead of liberators, and it resulted in hundreds of thousands of people suddenly unemployed. Second, by purging the dominant political organization of its most-experienced and knowledgeable members, we effectively excluded them from eligibility to participate as candidates in a democratically elected government.

After I returned home in March, I monitored the news as the timeline for the first constitutional election began to unfold. The first national election to choose constitutional delegates was held on January 30, 2005, ahead of the March 15 deadline set in the agreement. In October, the Iraqi constitution was ratified by popular vote with a 63% voter turnout. After the draft constitution was ratified, a new parliament was elected on December 15, with a high Sunni turnout and a low level of violence–two important measures of success, since Sunni Muslims were in the minority and generally supported Saddam's government. The low level of violence indicated the security situation had improved. I felt like our efforts were successful on several levels, unlike when I left Vietnam and Somalia.

Destroyed Ministry of Information building, taken from Baghdad City Council building

With interpreter, greeting school headmaster

Protest march by disbanded Iraqi military

Gen. Blackledge, Gen. Dempsey, Me, Col. Jacobs

Chapter 16
The Road to Retirement (2004-2008)

The Journey Home

On March 1, 2004, our main convoy was assembled for the trip to Kuwait, where we would begin preparations for our redeployment. Four of us were designated as the rear detachment to remain in Baghdad to tie up any loose ends with our replacements. We'd have the luxury of flying out of Baghdad, but we felt a hint of jealousy when the ground convoy left, because we couldn't go with them.

We remained in Baghdad two more days before we received orders to move out. On March 3 we gathered our bags and boarded a convoy organized by our replacements for our last trip to the airport. After we passed the iconic California Hotel one last time, we checked into the flight-control tent to await our trip to Kuwait. The area around the tent looked like a refugee camp. There were no support services or shelters. Troops were spread out around the tent on cots with their baggage. That evening I slept under the stars on a folding cot. On March 4, we boarded a C-130. Our flight from Iraq was faster and more pleasant than the vehicle convoy, which had traveled more than 300 miles through the desert in Southern Iraq.

After we landed in Kuwait, we were taken to Camp Doha, where we remained until cleared for our return home. We slept on folding cots in a warehouse, and lived out of our duffle bags, but we had access to many amenities, including a movie theater, gym, telephones, PX, and a barber shop. Our first task was to clean our weapons and vehicles and turned in our ammunition. I was happy to be relieved of daily PowerPoint presentations and briefings on measures of effectiveness. Our duty day usually ended around noon, then we changed into our physical-fitness T-shirts, shorts, and sneakers for the remainder of the day. I called home to speak with Nancy each day to talk about life at home and keep her updated on our schedule.

We had to attend a multiday presentation designed to prepare us for reunion with our families. As a veteran of two previous mobilizations, I was familiar with much of the material, but it was mandatory. Our homes, marriages, children, and jobs had changed since we left. We were cautioned about resuming our family responsibilities too quickly.

For recreation, I entered a 5k road race on St. Patrick's Day. I finished it 52 seconds faster than the Baghdad 5k I ran the previous October, which convinced me I was getting better, not older. By the time I reached 57 years of age, I didn't run against others so much. I ran against myself and the passage of time.

On March 21, our gear was inspected, packed, placed on pallets, and loaded on an Air Force C-5A cargo jet. For our trip home, we were told to pack two bags to be shipped in sealed containers, which we wouldn't see again until after we arrived in the States. We were permitted two additional bags and a carryon that would accompany us to Fort Bragg. We boarded the aircraft for our flight to the United States the next morning. After a refueling stop in Budapest, we landed at Fort Bragg at 0430 hours the next day. We were tired, but we received a warm welcome from family members and friends. Gen. Autschuler, commander of the U.S. Army Civil Affairs and Psychological Operations Command, was there to greet us with a crowd of family members and supporters.

I didn't expect to see anyone from my family; but to my surprise, my daughter Cathy took a day off from teaching and drove three hours from Charlotte to meet me. She was the last family member I saw before I left and the first one I saw when I returned. Did I mention daughters had a special place in their fathers' hearts? We stood in formation and listened to welcome remarks by Gen. Autschuler, during which he paid tribute to our sacrifices and those of our families and commended us on the progress we made while in Iraq. We were then dismissed to mingle with friends and family. There were snacks available, but I was tired from the trip and had no appetite. It was rare for me to pass up a snack. A member of the family-support group taking pictures photographed Cathy and me together. Cathy brought along a new cell phone Nancy had mailed her, so I could call home and let her know I was back safely. Cathy and I spent the rest of the morning together. We had lunch at Fort Bragg and shopped at the PX, where I purchased matching Army hooded sweatshirts for us. Cathy returned home later that day.

Father/Daughter Reunion at Ft. Bragg, March 22, 2004

It took us 10 days at Fort Bragg to complete the demobilization process. Unit members who lived in the

Maryland/D.C./Northern Virginia area were flown to Baltimore, then bused to the Reserve Center in Riverdale to turn in unit equipment before being released home. Those of us from other states were permitted to fly directly home, so I booked a flight to Syracuse and arrived on the evening of April 1. A whole contingent greeted me at the Syracuse Airport: Nancy, Kevin and Scott, Rosemary, Dale and his wife Stacey (Dale lost his first wife, Susan, to cancer in 1982), and Gene and his wife Trudy, who held a large handmade sign that read, "Welcome Home Colonel Mitchell." The local news media asked me for an interview, but I declined, referring them to a young soldier on the flight who belonged to the 403rd CA Battalion.

When Trudy said Nancy had a "honey-do" list for me, I replied it was a good thing I'd been taking my vitamins. Nancy greeted me with a long hug; then I hugged Kevin and Scott, realizing I would never have to leave my family again. My mandatory retirement was approaching, and I had been, as an Army recruiting slogan suggested, 'all I could be'.

After our reunion at the airport, Nancy drove me home. I stared out the car window along the way and looked at everything as if seeing it for the first time. The same buildings, stores, and restaurants were there, but I felt like a visitor. The temperature that year in early April was about 40°-nearly 50° colder than Kuwait when we left. As we turned onto our street and approached our house, I wondered how much it changed in 13 months. Nancy had been my support system while I was away, and my spirits rose every time I received a letter or care package from her. And thanks to the internet, we were able to keep in touch several times a week from Iraq. When our home came into view, it seemed like it was frozen in time. The only thing that changed was Nancy had converted an upstairs bedroom into a laundry room, which made doing laundry more convenient by eliminating two flights of stairs to get from the bedrooms to the basement. Everything else was the same as the day I left.

Welcome Home Tributes

I paid a visit to the courthouse before my official return to work, to say hello to my coworkers. They greeted me warmly and expressed relief for my safe return. I used the rest of the leave I'd accumulated in Iraq to get settled into life at home and officially returned to work June 1st. Upon my return I was given a surprise welcome-home party in the jury assembly room. There were at least 75 people there–from the U.S. District Court, the U.S. Attorney's office, and U.S. Marshals Service. A contingent from the Syracuse Armed Forces Examining and Processing Station was present with a member from each branch of the Armed Forces. A large poster with my picture on it greeted guests at the entrance, which they were invited to autograph as they entered. Nancy was tipped off to the party in advance and arrived after me.

A large cake sat on a table, decorated in red, white, and blue, inscribed, *Welcome Home Colonel Terry Mitchell.* Several federal judges attended, and Judge Neal McCurn presented me a scrapbook containing many of the emails and pictures I sent to the court, along with written notes from coworkers who expressed their gratitude for my service. Laminated newspaper articles featured me in interviews about my deployment. The scrapbook, compiled by his law clerk, Carrie Lynn Richardson, and his judicial assistant, Judy West, contained articles and pictures from my 1999 tour in Bosnia, too. Carrie Lynn suggested it was something I could build on for a more complete record of my years of service.

The highlight of the day was the presentation of an American flag accompanied by a certificate signed by U.S. Rep.

James Walsh, which attested the flag was flown over the U.S. Capitol Building. The certificate read in part, "...for his sacrifice and service in Operation Iraqi Freedom." It was presented by the armed forces contingent through a traditional military ritual in which a folded American flag was passed from the lowest-ranking service member to the next in rank until it reached the highest-ranking member–the commander of the Military Entrance Processing Station–who handed it to me with a salute.

I thanked everyone for their support while I was away, then faced the American flag in the corner of the room. Overcome by emotion, I said I was proud to serve the flag and what it stood for. Later, I reflected on the day and my homecoming reception. Many other veterans, who deserved it more, never received a formal coming-home party complete with accolades. Maybe in some way I represented the sacrifices made by all veterans who went voluntarily into harm's way.

Almost a year later, in January 2005 the NBC affiliate in Syracuse searched for a local veteran who served in Iraq for their coverage of the four-year anniversary of the Iraq War. My name was provided to them by Sacred Heart Parish in Cicero, where I was a parishioner. When contacted by the television station, I agreed to appear on their *Weekend Today* show with news anchor Lisa Spitz. She interviewed me on January 29 about my experiences and my opinion of the upcoming elections in Iraq. Coincidentally, she went to Penn Yan a few weeks later to interview Gene, who was the chief of police, about an incident that occurred there. It must have been a million-to-one chance two brothers would be featured in different news stories by the same reporter, 75 miles apart.

While in Iraq I was "adopted" by St. Thomas Aquinas Elementary School in Binghamton, thanks to a referral by Father Charles Vavonese, who taught one of my graduate courses at

Marist College. Father Vavonese formerly served as a parish priest in Binghamton and was well known there. The school sent me a letter and a couple of care packages while I was in Iraq, to which I responded with my gratitude. The summer after I returned home, they invited me to attend a welcome-home ceremony during which they presented me with a framed plaque containing the names of all the children and faculty at St. Thomas Aquinas, and a message of thanks for my service. The event was covered by *The Catholic Sun*, official newspaper for the Diocese of Syracuse. The Knights of Columbus council I belonged to in Cicero, NY presented me with a certificate from the Supreme Assembly in New Haven, Connecticut "for selfless and patriotic service in the United States Armed Forces in Afghanistan and Iraq". The recognition seemed endless and in stark contrast to the public attitude toward soldiers returning from Vietnam.

The Role of Movies

Movies played a significant role in how the public viewed veterans after Vietnam. *First Blood* and *Born on the Fourth of July* depicted the plight of returning veterans who weren't appreciated for their service and sacrifice and who never received a proper transition to civilian life. They demonstrated a lack of care by our government for post-traumatic stress and Agent Orange exposure. More recently, movies like *Home of the Brave* showed the trials of National Guard soldiers returning to civilian life. *The Messenger* showed the human toll of war on families who lost loved ones. With the release of these movies, the American public began to appreciate the sacrifices made by our volunteer military and their families. It became commonplace in public for soldiers in uniform–and even veterans–to be greeted with, "Thank you for your service." Television spots, billboards and signs honor our troops, and many businesses offer discounts to active-duty troops and veterans. I was fortunate to have served in the armed forces long enough to witness the shift in attitude and benefit from expressions of gratitude from the public.

Parallel Careers

At the district court my military background and familiarity with Fort Drum led to my assignment as courtroom clerk for every judge who heard cases at Fort Drum between 1994 and 2008. It was a convenient arrangement, because I was familiar with the post, the various duty descriptions, and the many acronyms used in the Army. I easily established rapport with the JAG officers assigned to prosecute cases, which facilitated management of the court docket.

When I returned from Iraq I began a new phase of my career at the U.S. District Court. I was reassigned as the courtroom deputy to U.S. Magistrate Judge George H. Lowe, who was appointed in February 2004. I first met Judge Lowe 20 years earlier, when he was the U.S. Attorney for the Northern District of New York. When his term as U.S. Attorney ended, he returned to private practice with a Syracuse law firm. I occasionally saw him when he brought papers to the clerk's office for filing, or when he argued a case in court. Judge Lowe became the fifth judge I served for as a courtroom deputy clerk.

In 1981, when I was first employed by the court, I was assigned to U.S. Magistrate Judge Edward M. Conan, until his death in 1987. There were two memorable cases before Judge Conan in which I was involved.

The first case involved a draft protester named Andrew Mager. In 1983 he was prosecuted for an unrelated petty offense. At his court appearance he stated to Judge Conan he did not register for Selective Service as required by law. I was present in court and operated the tape recorder that preserved the official record of the proceedings. Mager was eventually prosecuted for the offense and his case went to trial before Judge Howard G. Munson in January 1985. Assistant U.S. Attorney Joseph A. Pavone asked me to testify on behalf of the United States. I was called as the final government witness and testified about the validity of Mr. Mager's signature on various court documents and identified Mr. Mager's voice on the official court tape recording. Mr. Mager acted *pro se* (as his own attorney) and cross-examined me. The jury returned a guilty verdict based in part on my testimony. By then I was a captain in the U.S. Army Reserve; I was especially pleased to help convict a draft evader.

The second case involved former Syracuse Mayor Lee Alexander, who came before Judge Conan in 1987 to answer charges of racketeering and tax evasion. Alexander had gained national stature as president of the United States Conference of Mayors. At the initial appearance, Judge Conan granted him pretrial release, so I prepared the appropriate papers for the judge. When I presented them to the mayor for his signature, he extended his hand and, always the politician, introduced himself as if he were running for office. Alexander eventually pleaded guilty before a U.S. district judge and served nearly six years in prison.

In 1990 I was assigned as the courtroom clerk to Judge Thomas J. McAvoy in Binghamton. During that assignment, I volunteered to serve in Somalia. In 1994, I was reassigned as alternative dispute-resolution clerk for the district. That year Larry Baerman assigned me to a fact-finding mission at the U.S. District Court in Scranton, Pennsylvania, to gather information about the policies and procedures for naturalization ceremonies in federal court. I traveled to Scranton, in the Middle District of Pennsylvania, to observe a naturalization ceremony and consult with members of the clerk's office who administered the program for their district. The information I gathered was eventually used as a basis for the naturalization program in the Northern District of New York. Nancy and I were later asked to provide music for several such ceremonies, during which I accompanied her on the piano while she sang patriotic songs such as *The Star Spangled Banner, America the Beautiful,* and *God Bless America.*

In 1994, after returning from Somalia, I was reassigned to U.S. Magistrate Judge Daniel J. Scanlon, Jr., in Watertown. As his courtroom clerk, I traveled to Watertown once a month when he held court. Part of his court work involved adjudication of petty-offense and misdemeanor cases involving soldiers at Fort Drum.

When I was reassigned to Syracuse clerk's office in 1996, I worked as an intake clerk and continued as Judge Scanlon's courtroom deputy until he passed away in 1998. I was then assigned as the district court's restitution clerk. My responsibility was to process payments made by convicted persons who were ordered to pay restitution to their victims.

As Judge Lowe's courtroom clerk, I resumed responsibility for management of petty-offense and misdemeanor cases at Fort Drum, in addition to the caseload he carried in Syracuse. I retired from the courts on September 30, 2008, after 27½ years of service.

Final Days of Military Service

In August 2006, I participated in what would be my final training exercise before I retired. Retirement for officers was mandatory at age 60 or after completion of 28 years of commissioned service, whichever came first. I reached 28 years of commissioned service on January 31, 2006 and turned 60 in October of that year. To retain my current rank at retirement, I needed to hold it for at least three years, a milestone I'd reached in June 2005.

My final training exercise took place at Fort Indiantown Gap, Pennsylvania. I relished every moment of the week. I enjoyed field exercises best, because they added a touch of realism to our training – and they got us out of the reserve center.

At Indiantown Gap we stayed in the familiar World War II-era two-story wooden barracks still found on Army bases. Part of our training consisted of a land-navigation class, the bane of my existence during my Army career. It included classroom instruction on the use of a compass and a practical exercise with a topographical map used to navigate point to point over a designated area of terrain. I had received the same instruction many times, but land navigation remained one of my weaker skills. Land-navigation exercises usually involved providing an individual or team with a list of magnetic azimuths. Each was to be followed on a compass for a given distance to a reference point, identified by a code posted at each point. We recorded each code we found to verify the location. This continued until each reference point had been identified in its correct order. Distances were measured by a pace count, determined by the number of steps required to walk 100 yards. Pace count was not an exact measurement because various obstacles (such as fallen trees, brush, or swamp land) would vary the length of one's steps. At the end of the course the list of codes found at the various reference points was given to a controller to verify each point was identified in the correct order.

We had two hours to complete the exercise. A search party was sent out to locate anyone who had not returned within the designated time. I had trouble whenever an azimuth I shot led me through hilly, swampy, or wooded terrain, because the distance became hard to estimate. After the first two points I was usually off course. We did the course individually, each with a different list of azimuth points to follow. I trudged through the wooded and hilly terrain and tried my best to stay on course but had to wear eyeglasses for distance and repeatedly took them off to read the compass and the topographical map. I often carried the eyeglasses in my hand, along with my map and compass, and put them on to see the reference point I aimed at in the distance. At some point I dropped my eyeglasses but didn't realize it until I had already walked several more yards. I retraced my steps, to no avail. They probably got buried in the thick blanket of leaves covering the forest floor. I could read, but for distance I had to pick reference points close enough to see, which meant I had to re-aim my compass more often. That may have had the unintended benefit of keeping me on course. When I finished and gave my list to the controller, I had identified each reference point in the correct order. I finally succeeded at the one military task that frustrated me through the years. I remarked that I lost my glasses somewhere in the woods and a lieutenant asked if I needed them to drive. I said yes, but I kept an extra pair in my car. As I walked away I turned to the lieutenant and said, "Remember that: Always have a backup plan." It was a simple reminder of an important element in planning.

After the field exercise we packed up and prepared to convoy back to our barracks. I wanted one last ride in a Humvee, but safety rules dictated the driver and passengers in a tactical vehicle must wear Kevlar helmets. I had worn my camouflage baseball cap to the training area. Nonetheless, I asked another lieutenant who drove one of the Humvees if I could ride shotgun.

He said, "Well, sir, you don't have a Kevlar helmet, but you're a colonel, so I guess you can do whatever you want."

That wasn't true, of course, but I thanked him and said I'd take the responsibility if I got injured.

A female soldier in the back seat who was aware I was about to retire suggested I'd be a good candidate for a new volunteer program of Army ambassadors. I asked what it was about, and she said it was a way for veterans to promote the Army in their local communities. Several months after my retirement, I looked into it and discovered it was called the Army Freedom Team Salute Ambassador Program. I signed up and volunteered to act as a local ambassador to submit the names of honorably discharged Army veterans for a commemorative certificate digitally signed by the secretary of the Army and the Army chief of staff, thanking them for their service. Unfortunately, due to funding cuts and the existence of duplicate programs, the ambassador program was discontinued in 2010, but it was gratifying to present Army veterans who did not serve long enough to retire, with a recognition of their service. During that time, I even linked up with an officer I served with at the 403rd CA Battalion, Col. (Ret.) Ed Magdziak, who also acted as an ambassador for the Freedom Team Salute Program.

During the 15-minute ride back to our barracks, I reflected on the 33-plus years I spent in the Army and the realization it was about to end. I witnessed many changes in U.S. Army clothing, equipment, tactics and doctrine. I'd seen the transition from typewriters to computers, from landline telephones to cell phones, from C-Rations to Meals, Ready to Eat; from Jeeps to Humvees, from the M113 Armored Personnel Carrier to the M2 Bradley Infantry Fighting Vehicle, and from the M60 Patton to the M1 Abrams main battle tank. I flew in the UH-1 Iroquois "Huey" helicopter in Vietnam and the UH-60 Black Hawk in Somalia. Several field-uniform changes took place, from olive-green fatigues to the universal-camouflage pattern. Patches were no longer sewn on; they were attached with Velcro. I wore black combat boots during basic training, jungle boots in Vietnam, and desert boots during Somalia and Iraq. The shirt for the Class-A dress uniform changed from brown to green and eventually was replaced by dress blues with a white shirt as the standard dress uniform. Hats changed from the baseball style to berets. The baseball cap was still approved for work details and the saucer hat was still authorized for dress uniforms.

During my last weekend drill, I joined several officers for lunch at a dining hall on the University of Maryland campus, a couple of miles north of our Reserve Center. The brigade staff officers often met for lunch there during drill weekends but this time it was intended as an informal retirement luncheon. Our brigade commander, Col. John Murphy, asked me to say a few words as we finished eating. I've never been good at impromptu speeches, but for some reason I passed on thoughts about my late Grandfather, John Orsino. I mentioned he was too young to serve during World War I and too old for World War II, then I repeated the words he said to me before I left for Vietnam as he lay in bed recuperating from a stroke. He told me, "Be a good soldier." I said I believed I had done that and was proud to have served.

At my last formation later in the day, the command sergeant major called for new soldiers and anyone leaving the unit to be recognized. Another soldier who recently arrived at the unit and I went to the front of the formation. After the new soldier introduced himself, I was asked to say something. I tried to make a statement, to say I would miss the camaraderie and the formations, when a swell of emotion overcame me. I would never again stand in uniform, shoulder to shoulder with other soldiers.

Teamwork, sacrifice, and a sense of duty to my fellow soldiers and our nation defined military service for me. My life changed gradually during my years of service in the Army. It wasn't one event or one person that affected me, but the many experiences and the people with whom I served in Vietnam,

Somalia, Bosnia, and Iraq, in addition to countless training exercises.

Perhaps the biggest change in my life was becoming more aware and appreciative of the sacrifices my family made while I was away. I always took care to talk with Nancy about our benefits and financial matters prior to each deployment or extended active-duty training, but I often took for granted what she and our children endured while I was gone. I missed many precious family moments during my absences that will never be replaced.

After retirement I wanted to stay connected with other veterans and give back to those who suffered and sacrificed much more than I did, so I became a volunteer at the VA Medical Center in Syracuse. The veterans there suffered from a variety of ailments, both physical and mental, which were often service connected. The eighth-floor community-living center housed veterans suffering from long-term illnesses who were either bedridden or confined to wheelchairs. Some ambulatory veterans suffered from other illnesses. I reminded myself they were once young men and women. Many served during World War II and Korea and endured hardships that made my service pale in comparison. I was reminded of my own mortality when I saw Vietnam veterans becoming more-frequent patrons of the VA Medical Center. I wanted to provide them with whatever support I could. They deserved excellent medical care because they bore the burden of our nation's wars and conflicts, whether it was to secure our freedom at home or bring it to those who were denied it in foreign lands. A sign posted outside the medical center summed it up succinctly: *The price of freedom can be seen here.*

Most of my volunteer time at the VA Medical Center involved escorting patients to and from their treatment and entertaining them on the piano. I learned music was therapeutic for the patients and it was gratifying to see them respond to a familiar song. I owe a debt of gratitude to Suzanne Hawes, the lead recreational therapist, for encouraging me to enter piano solos in the annual VA Creative Arts Competition. It raised my confidence and I was awarded several medals during the next three years at the national level.

EPILOGUE

I served in some of the most dangerous places on earth and was blessed to come home unscathed, at least in a physical sense. I've been asked more than once how I coped with the danger I faced during my deployments. My response was I became emotionally numb to it. I couldn't let fear interfere with my duties. Although I had some close calls, timing, location–and the grace of God–often saved me from injury or death.

The personal-security measures I practiced during deployments became routine. I still practice some of them out of an abundance of caution. Closing the blinds at night and taking a seat facing the door in a restaurant or public place are just two measures I continue to practice.

The primary purpose of civil affairs is not to close with and kill the enemy, but to interact with civilians, coordinate assistance and promote goodwill on behalf of the United States. Every soldier represents the United States when overseas, but civil affairs soldiers are more; they are ad hoc ambassadors.

Prior to the deployment of civil affairs soldiers in large numbers during Operation Desert Storm, it was a largely misunderstood, complex branch of the Army. Considered by some as the "stepchild" of the massive military campaigns in Afghanistan and Iraq, civil affairs soldiers nevertheless performed an essential mission in those countries. We worked under difficult and often hostile conditions to gain the trust and support of people in countries where U.S. forces operated. We were there to preserve the victory. The paradox inherent in our operations was to act friendly but be ready to shoot and kill, if necessary. In mid- and high-intensity conflicts we coordinated humanitarian assistance and organized camps for refugees and displaced persons. During low-intensity conflicts, we engaged in civil administration, institution building, and the repair of infrastructure.

The eventual reassignment and reorganization of the branch under the U.S. Army Special Operations Command put us in the forefront of operations during Desert Storm, Iraqi Freedom, and the Global War on Terror. I enjoyed a unique opportunity to work with people in foreign countries and immerse myself in their culture.

Civil Affairs Lessons Learned

At the end of my final deployment and prior to retirement, I wrote remedial action reports and lessons learned for our brigade headquarters. I discussed two main areas of concern to me: team operations and force protection.

In my opinion, civil affairs units in Iraq were not properly trained, equipped, and armed to operate in the rising insurgent environment we encountered. I discussed the absence of armored Humvees, crew-served weapons operated by qualified individuals, and reliable tactical communications. Those items, and the lack of other force-protection measures, I believed, resulted in the highest casualty rate ever suffered by civil affairs units.

We were initially issued protective flak vests, as opposed to ballistic vests with plates, which would protect against bullets rather than just shrapnel. We finally received ballistic vests only after making a special request through channels. We often had to combine teams to meet the personnel protection requirement for convoys, leaving teams short of sufficient personnel to perform assigned duties. This often resulted in field-grade officers (major and above) performing security details because we were so rank heavy.

Civil affairs units cannot function effectively "behind the wire." They must be able to access the population, civil authorities, institutions, and infrastructure facilities to accomplish their mission. Civil affairs units at the battalion and brigade levels should be equipped with armored Humvees and squad automatic weapons (SAW). They should be issued M4 assault weapons in place of the M16A1 because they are more maneuverable inside vehicles. Tactical training should extend beyond mere familiarization; or, if time does not permit thorough training, teams should receive priority of effort from their supported combat command after major combat operations have ceased, so adequate firepower and security are available to them.

I also commented on the role of civilian organizations in nation-building efforts. If a civilian organization like the Coalition Provisional Authority is given primary responsibility for nation building, civil affairs teams should stay long enough to fix issues existing during stability and support operations, then sent home when the environment becomes less hostile and more permissive for civilian organizations to operate. Keeping civil affairs units, primarily comprised of reservists, on active duty longer than necessary wastes money, further endangers personnel, and increases the hardships suffered by families and civilian employers at home.

Comparing Vietnam to Iraq

As someone who served in both conflicts, it was inevitable I would compare our involvement in Vietnam to Iraq. During my readings on the subject, I concluded there are more differences than similarities. First, it's nearly impossible to compare two wars that occurred 40 years apart in different parts of the world. The technology existing during Iraq was not available during Vietnam and the political, social, and economic environments were very different.

We entered Vietnam because of North Vietnamese aggression and a concern if South Vietnam fell, it would encourage a global advance of Communism. We also had to protect the credibility of the United States by honoring our treaty to protect South Vietnam. In Iraq, we conducted a preemptive invasion of the country resulting from the political mood of the United States after the 9/11 attacks. It was fueled by misinformation about Saddam Hussein's stockpiling of weapons of mass destruction and his real use of chemical weapons on his own people.

North Vietnam had the backing of military powers like the Soviet Union and China, whereas Iraq was virtually isolated in the Arab world, with no one to come to their aid. Vietnam was an outgrowth of the Cold War with the Soviet Union while Iraq could be viewed as a continuation of the 1990 invasion by Iraq which resulted in Operation Desert Storm that drove Iraq out of Kuwait, followed by years of containment, followed by Operation Iraqi Freedom to depose Saddam Hussein and liberate the Iraqi people.

The South Vietnamese government was corrupt and alienated its people, whereas the North Vietnamese people were committed to Ho Chi Minh's ideology to unify the country. In a contrast of the two cultures, most people in South Vietnam lived in an agrarian society and were poorly educated, while the people of Iraq lived in a clan-based society that was industrialized and better educated. The South Vietnamese government was secular-based while Iraq's government was religious-based although Saddam, who was a Sunni Muslim, attempted to make it appear more secular.

Any similarities between the two are mainly related to attempts at nation building, and the military tactics and strategy employed by the United States. In both wars we employed the right tactics, but we had no clear strategy for attaining an end state. We sent enough troops to Vietnam to obtain tactical success, but an insurgency led by the Viet Cong (National Liberation Front) was already in progress when we arrived. We eventually crushed the Viet Cong insurgency primarily through the Phoenix Program, which was designed to destroy its political infrastructure and capture or kill its operatives. Other methods included pacification efforts to win over the people, and the Chieu Hoi (Open Arms) program, which encouraged members of the Viet Cong to return to the South Vietnamese government. Initially, we did not pour enough troops in Iraq to prevent the insurgency that resulted after a power gap was created when the government was overthrown. In Iraq, the insurgency started after the end of major combat operations, led by Sunnis loyal to Saddam. The counterinsurgency effort eventually became effective due to a surge in troops and a reset of our priority of effort from capture and kill to working with the civilian population to gain their support. The role of civil affairs was an important factor, but we weren't there in numbers great enough to diminish the insurgency.

History shows the United States leaves a lasting impact in every country it becomes involved. People wear American-style clothing provided by relief organizations. I've seen children wear T-shirts and hats emblazoned with logos of iconic American products and sports teams and it seemed as if every child spoke some English.

Although Vietnam is still a communist country, we have normalized diplomatic relations. We have a cooperation agreement with the government to search for and recover the remains of missing American military personnel, and we hold regular dialogue with government representatives on human rights. We import several goods from Vietnam, including food and clothing. The dreaded Domino Effect of neighboring countries falling to communism never materialized.

Somalia remains a dangerous country, but we continue to have a presence there assisting African Union forces in fighting the terrorist group Al Shabab, which has lost much of its foothold in Somalia after being forced out of Mogadishu by Ethiopian forces. In 2012, Somalia held limited, indirect elections of a new federal parliament and president. With the adoption of a provisional constitution, the United States formally recognized the new Federal Government of Somalia (FGS) on January 17, 2013. In February 2017, the FGS completed its first national electoral process since the 2012 transition, selecting a new federal parliament and a new president.

Bosnia is a relative success story, thanks to NATO involvement and ratification of the Dayton Peace Accords. As a result, the country was divided into two entities: the Bosnian Federation and the Republic of Serbia. Dayton brokered a peace that still stands today, but the wounds of war still exist. In a December 13, 2015 article by Morgan Meaker, it was reported there are still nationalistic feelings that separate Bosnians and Serbs. There still exist community and group divisions because of the war. The negative legacy of the war was transferred to the next generation, but today it is not ethnic based, it is political.

In Iraq, we left a fragile, but democratic government in place, and we rid the country of a tyrannical ruler. The insurgency, although not eliminated, has been greatly suppressed. Although the Sunni-dominated terrorist organization ISIS came into existence and established a caliphate in Mosul, a second campaign led by Iraqi forces and assisted by the United States, eliminated the caliphate and virtually drove them out of Iraq. Iraqi leaders have pledged to run an all-inclusive, more transparent government. The sacrifices we made there must not be in vain.

My duties in Baghdad permitted me to work with many city leaders and influence the formation of city government. Although we won the support of many people, I held out the most hope for the future of Iraq with the children, that they will grow up with a thirst for peace, democracy, and freedom.

During naturalization ceremonies at the U.S. District Court, and later when Nancy and I provided the music, I witnessed people from Vietnam, Somalia, Bosnia, Iraq, and many other countries, take the oath of citizenship for the United States. Their desire to become American citizens validated to some degree the efforts and sacrifices made by civil affairs soldiers, and all U.S. military personnel, during operations in those countries ... and just maybe we succeeded in winning some hearts and minds.

Private Mitchell, 1969

Colonel Mitchell, 2006
(Photo Courtesy Cahill Photography)

BIBLIOGRAPHY

Books
Holbrook, Richard; To End A War, Random House, 1998
McNamara, Robert S.; In Retrospect, The Tragedy and Lessons of Vietnam, Random House, 1995
Mitchell, Charles R.; Images of America, Penn Yan and Keuka Lake, Arcadia Publishing, 1997
Ricks, Thomas E.; Fiasco, The American Military Adventure in Iraq, The Penguin Press, 2006
Stewart, Richard W. PhD; The United States Army in Somalia, 1992-1994, U.S. Army Center for Military History

Field Manuals
FM 21-20, Physical Fitness Training, Headquarters, Department of the Army, 1992
FM 41-10, Civil Affairs Operations, Hqs., Department of the Army, February 2000

Articles
Herek, Gregory; Lesbians and Gay Men in the U.S. Military: Historical Background of "Don't Ask, Don't Tell Revisited" 1997
Stearman, William, The American Legion magazine, July 2016
The Army Times, October 1996

Internet
medical-dictionary.thefreedictionary.com
www.en.wikipedia.org/wiki/Bosnian_war
www.state.gov; U.S. Relations with Somalia and State Department Fact Sheet on Vietnam
http://ssi.armywarcollege.edu; Iraq and Vietnam: Differences,

Similarities, and Insights; Jeffrey Record and W. Andrew Terrill, May 2004

www.ingramcontent.com/pod-product-compliance
Lightning Source LLC
Chambersburg PA
CBHW051934290426
44110CB00015B/1971

"This engaging book draws the reader in to the world of psalm interpretation that reflects the experience of Christians in Late Antiquity, when the reception of Scripture, and especially of the Psalms, was conditioned by oral tradition, liturgical performance, and prayer. The commentator comes alive in Olsen's account, which folds the salient details of translation, symbolism, historical context, and transmission into a seamless narrative. His analysis of Cassiodorus's contributions is enriching for specialists and informative for less expert readers."

—Susan Leslie Boynton
Professor of Music, Historic Musicology
Columbia University

"Derek Olsen's conversational approach belies a serious scholarly study of one of the great figures of Western monasticism. He introduces us to Cassiodorus's seminal commentary on the Psalter by narrating the earlier influences on his thinking, his strategies for interpreting the psalms, and his legacy in art, music, and glossed psalters. By presenting history as story, Olsen enables his readers, whether familiar with Cassiodorus or not, to encounter this great scholar in fresh and memorable ways."

—Sue Gillingham
Professor of the Hebrew Bible
University of Oxford

"This authoritative study of Cassiodorus's *Explanation of the Psalms* is an engaging and scholarly guide to one of the most influential works in the medieval church. As well as being a thorough and very readable exploration of Cassiodorus's important book, *The Honey of Souls* takes the reader on a captivating journey through the intellectual world of late antiquity and the early Middle Ages, tracing the transmission of knowledge and learning and demonstrating with great skill the centrality of the Psalms to the life and worship of the early medieval church. In this book, Derek Olsen provides a fascinating insight into a rich, profound, and now largely unfamiliar way of reading the Psalms, one that reveals the unexpected layers of meaning upon meaning to be found within these well-loved texts."

—Eleanor Parker
Brasenose College
University of Oxford